Atomic Anxiety

Atomic Anxiety

Deterrence, Taboo and the Non-Use of U.S. Nuclear Weapons

Frank Sauer
Senior Research Fellow and Lecturer,
Bundeswehr University Munich, Germany

palgrave
macmillan

First published 2016 by
PALGRAVE MACMILLAN

Palgrave Macmillan in the UK is an imprint of Macmillan Publishers Limited, registered in England, company number 785998, of Houndmills, Basingstoke, Hampshire RG21 6XS.

Palgrave Macmillan in the US is a division of St Martin's Press LLC, 175 Fifth Avenue, New York, NY 10010.

Palgrave Macmillan is the global academic imprint of the above companies and has companies and representatives throughout the world.

Palgrave® and Macmillan® are registered trademarks in the United States, the United Kingdom, Europe and other countries.

ISBN: 978–1–137–53373–9

This book is printed on paper suitable for recycling and made from fully managed and sustained forest sources. Logging, pulping and manufacturing processes are expected to conform to the environmental regulations of the country of origin.

A catalogue record for this book is available from the British Library.

Library of Congress Cataloging-in-Publication Data

Sauer, Frank.

Atomic anxiety : deterrence, taboo and the non-use of U.S. nuclear weapons / Frank Sauer (senior research fellow and lecturer, Universität der Bundeswehr München, Germany).

pages cm

ISBN 978–1–137–53373–9 (hardback)

1. Nuclear weapons – Government policy – United States. 2. Nuclear weapons – Social aspects – United States. 3. Nuclear weapons – United States – Psychological aspects. 4. No first use (Nuclear strategy) 5. Deterrence (Strategy) 6. Anxiety – Political aspects – United States. 7. Taboo – Political aspects – United States. 8. United States – Military policy. 9. United States – Military policy – Decision making. I. Title.

UA23.S28 2015
355.02'170973—dc23 2015018872

Contents

Acknowledgments

I have benefited from numerous people who have provided me with inspiration, valuable insights and intellectual guidance over the past couple of years. They have done so either in person or through their writings, both with regard to this particular book project as well as above and beyond that. First and foremost, I would like to thank Carlo Masala and Gunther Hellmann for their continued support. In addition to that, I am grateful to (in alphabetical order) Benjamin Herborth, Gert Krell, Richard Ned Lebow, Harald Müller, Niklas Schörnig, Stephan Stetter, Nina Tannenwald and William Walker.

I would also like to thank Eleanor Davey Corrigan and Hannah Kašpar at Palgrave Macmillan for their support as well as the two anonymous reviewers for their valuable comments and suggestions on the manuscript.

Thanks to Munich's Westpark, I had a beautiful place to run while writing this book – which is what kept me sane, especially while coding the material for the empirical chapters.

Sebastian Enskat deserves special thanks. Not only is he a very good friend but he is as brilliant a sounding board and conversation partner as can be.

I am deeply grateful to my parents for the opportunities they have given me. Lastly and most importantly, I would like to thank my wife Eva Herschinger. She not only read the manuscript twice and provided countless suggestions for improvements but gave me constant support in a long research process with many ups and downs. I hope that our daughter, Marie, who is ten weeks old as of this writing, may grow up to live in a world free from atomic anxiety.

1
Introduction

Atomic bombs destroyed Hiroshima and Nagasaki in 1945. 'Wouldn't it be an odd thing if these were the only two atomic bombs ever dropped?', General Carl A. Spaatz (quoted in Life, 1945, p. 25) wondered back then. As it happens, nuclear weapons *were* never used again. This book is about this oddity.

Looking back at seven decades of nuclear non-use, some might find this not so extraordinary. After all, most of us probably take for granted that nuclear weapons are not to be detonated in war. But even while we may have gotten accustomed to this, questions arise as soon as one takes a step back and recalls history. What about the Cold War, the nuclear arms race? Why did the superpower confrontation never go nuclear? What about other wars such as the one in Vietnam? Why did the U.S. fight a protracted and bloody conventional war there, instead of simply ending things with one or two atomic blows?

The remarkable fact that decision-makers in (warring) nuclear states continuously *abstained* from using their 'super weapon' ever since 1945 becomes even more puzzling when the pace of technical development is factored in. After all, not only did the hydrogen bomb quickly join its atomic predecessor, dwarfing the explosive force of the fission bombs by the awe-inspiring power of thermonuclear fusion. Smaller, tactical nuclear weapons were also soon at hand, tailored to suit the military's every need in the decades laden with conflict after 1945. Pausing and thinking for a moment about the non-use of nuclear weapons against this backdrop, one cannot help but wonder.

Hence I pose the following question: *what can explain the persistent non-use of nuclear weapons after 1945, and how can we better understand (the causes of) this nuclear abstinence?* This two-part question will be pursued with the help of three specific queries, namely: What explains nuclear non-use and how do the existing explanatory concepts approach the phenomenon? Do the factors invoked by existing explanations as causes of nuclear non-use interact in decision-making practice, and if so, how? Lastly, are there other facets of nuclear abstinence that have so far not been analyzed systematically?

Regarding the first half of my two-part question, the bit asking for what can explain nuclear non-use, there seems to be a simple answer: luck. Robert McNamara and James G. Blight, for instance, reached the following conclusion in their assessment of the Cuban Missile Crisis, arguably one of the closest calls in regards to nuclear war erupting: '[W]hile the missile crisis was well-managed, under very trying circumstances, the escape from it without a major war, even a nuclear war, seems nothing short of miraculous. In the end we lucked out' (McNamara/ Blight, 2002, p. 2).

Luck may have been more involved with humankind's survival of the nuclear age so far than we would like to admit to ourselves. But this is not only an unsettling notion. It is also hard to believe. A lucky streak persisting for seven decades seems extremely unlikely. And as a matter of fact, there are two more plausible explanations for nuclear non-use.

The first and most widely known explanation is *nuclear deterrence*. In this line of thought, the mutual threat of retaliation with equal means kept – and keeps – nuclear weapons from being used by making the costs involved unbearably high (see e.g. Morgan, 2003; Freedman, 2004). Enter Nina Tannenwald. She argues that the deterrence account is 'inadequate', 'insufficient' and 'incomplete' (Tannenwald, 2007, pp. 2, 30–38, 55, 71), which is why she advocates 'a normative element [to] be taken into account' (Tannenwald, 1999, p. 433) – a prohibitive norm against nuclear use for which she coined the term *nuclear taboo*. Nuclear deterrence and the nuclear taboo provide two well-developed explanations for why nuclear weapons have not been used since Hiroshima and Nagasaki (and an additional perspective, the *tradition of non-use,* will be discussed later). That seems plenty. So why even bother with nuclear non-use again?

I argue that the current state of research is not entirely satisfying. Both explanations share similar blind spots resulting from the way they approach the phenomenon; hence, serious difficulties and question marks remain. Also, as I will argue as this study dives more deeply into the issue of nuclear non-use, there are important facets of the phenomenon that literature in the field has not yet systematically accounted for – most importantly, the importance of human emotion. In that sense, this book not only offers an opportunity to rethink the non-use of nuclear weapons and what we already know, but it also demonstrates that there remain new things to learn.

Scope and plan of the book

This study contributes to the body of literature in International Relations (IR) devoted to studying nuclear non-use. The idea is to take the comparably old and extensively researched question about the origins of nuclear non-use and expose it to a change of perspective. My overall goal is to both deepen and widen our knowledge about the phenomenon. In addition to that, the book also aims at a contribution to the field of methodologically reflected and methodically sophisticated qualitative studies in IR. Lastly, the results in this study hold some implications worth considering for policymaking.

Furthermore, I need to explain why this study focuses on the United States of America in studying nuclear abstinence. This is not only because the U.S. is the only country to ever actually use nuclear weapons. More importantly, the existing explanations of non-use draw on this example. The special provenance of deterrence as both theory and strategy makes it virtually synonymous with significant parts of U.S. foreign policy after World War II. Furthermore, to make its contending case, the taboo literature also deals with that same era. Since my study heavily draws on and at the same time dissociates itself from both these two lines of thought, a focus on the U.S. is required. In addition to that, only in the U.S. case is some of the empirical source material available on which my analysis relies.

Another characteristic of this book needs to be clarified upfront. Rather than presenting a theoretical framework, bringing it in touch with empirical sources in some methodical way and evaluating the results in conclusion (typically as an argument for the chosen framework's merits), this study strings together a comparably long chain of arguments. It touches upon different theoretical and methodological frameworks in Chapters 2 and 3, and it alternates between empirical analysis and conceptual reflections in Chapter 4. To unpack this argumentative concatenation process and provide the reader with a clearer guideline for what to expect, it helps to think of this study as progressing in three steps.

As a first step, Chapter 2 – Explaining nuclear non-use – reflects on the current state of the art. This brief review of existing literature will critically examine the two existing mainstream lines of thought that try to *explain* the long-standing abstinence from using nuclear weapons. I will deal with nuclear deterrence as both a theory and a strategy in the first half of Chapter 2. Then I turn to the nuclear taboo as well as the differences and similarities of the nuclear taboo and the tradition of non-use in the second half. Critically recapitulating the existing research not only yields important insights to hold on to and work with but also serves to identify the problems that I take as the starting point for developing my alternative perspective in the subsequent chapter.

Chapter 3 – Understanding nuclear non-use – fleshes out in a second step what I consider to be the genesis of the current unsatisfactory state of research. It does so by reviewing the existing explanations a second time, this time focusing solely on their theoretical background and methodology. This serves to show that the attempt to 'explain' nuclear non-use directs the focus to 'effects' and 'causes', but with nothing palpable *caused* in a *non*-event, existing explanations admittedly find themselves in a bit of a pickle. In answer to that, they amass empirical cases as plausible proxies to try to uphold the logic of causal chains. In taking this approach, however, hitherto research on nuclear non-use developed blind spots. Specifically, it lost track of how the non-event of interest actually 'comes about' in practice. This is the major research gap I address by 'understanding nuclear non-use'.

To that end, I present a novel, fine-grained way of inquiring into the phenomenon. It acknowledges contingency and focuses squarely on agency and choice, and is thus tailored to better suit the peculiar characteristics of the subject matter, a *non*-event. Because this study offers some criticism of existing explanations, it bears repeating that this alternative approach would be impossible without the intimate knowledge about them. In other words, my goal is not to dismiss existing knowledge, to wipe the slate clean and start over, but rather to retain and utilize key elements of it. So despite the blind spots of existing explanations, I propose a way to preserve and integrate the knowledge they hold, while at the same time inspecting the phenomenon from a different perspective to open up new avenues of insight.

Chapter 3 introduces the methodology of this alternative approach, the gist of which I sum up as 'making sense of abstinence'. It is characterized by two features: one, it puts heavy emphasis on a reconstructive way of inquiry without sacrificing the possibility of using, in a subsumptive manner, concepts that carry over from existing knowledge. Two, it relies on a software-aided qualitative analysis and proceeds in a comparably open research process.

This methodology yields two distinct advantages. One, while it allows me to hold on to established concepts derived from existing literature about the causes of nuclear non-use and to deploy these for my empirical research, I remain unencumbered by the need to either verify or falsify them in their general explanatory fidelity. This permits a comparably more open-minded analysis of how these concepts present themselves in the empirical material. In other words, existing literature relies on preformed hypotheses such as 'deterrence causes non-use' to explain nuclear non-use by subduing and sifting empirical material under this hypothesis. The goal is to find and present the necessary 'evidence' for the supposed existence of a specific cause-and-effect-pattern to be 'rigorously tested', 'verified' and 'proven'. I deliberately leave aside this research logic that relies on causality as well as the notion of conducting empirical work in a purely subsumptive fashion. Instead, by putting a much stronger emphasis on reconstructing insights from within empirical sources, I probe the *meaning* nuclear non-use holds for decision-makers, aiming at a more detailed picture of the beliefs and convictions involved. This yields the desired *understanding* of the process in which the non-event comes about, including crucial insights into how the key drivers emphasized by existing explanations – the causes of non-use – actually play out and interact in decision-making praxis. In this way, I am able to shine some light into the aforementioned blind spots. Consequently, my research not only profits from existing explanatory research by utilizing it but it might also cross-fertilize and inform its further development in turn. So holding on to the existing knowledge about nuclear non-use and combining key concepts derived from existing top-down approaches with the bottom-up perspective of my reconstructive approach is crucial for arriving at this study's first main contribution, a better understanding of how the causes of non-use established in literature play out in practice and from a decision-makers' perspective.

Two, an open research process facilitates insights into the phenomenon that go over and above the already existing conceptual notions about nuclear non-use. After all, reducing the fixation on pre-formed notions and beaten paths means that the empirical material can be viewed in a less 'filtered' manner. Hence there is a greater chance of recognizing so far overlooked or underexposed aspects of nuclear non-use. Conducting such an exploratory analysis yields the second main contribution this study offers, namely a better understanding of nuclear abstinence by way of focusing on a largely neglected facet of the phenomenon: human emotion.

Chapter 3, after having set up the methodology of my approach with all its assumptions, also explicates the research method applied. These passages introduce and explain the mix of deductive and inductive software-aided coding that allows for coupling subsumptive concepts with a reconstructive inquiry as well as for providing an overall systematic and transparent qualitative analysis of the source material.

As a third and final step, Chapter 4 – Revisiting nuclear non-use – presents the results of my empirical analysis. By inquiring into empirical sources as well as by intermittently reflecting further at the conceptual level, it sheds some new light on the non-use of U.S. nuclear weapons. After having discussed the source selection criteria for the first empirical analysis, Chapter 4 presents the analytic narrative resulting from an in-depth empirical inquiry conducted at the micro level of presidential decision-making practices during the crises in Berlin and Cuba. Revisiting the phenomenon of nuclear non-use with the pertinent existing knowledge in mind, but from a new methodological angle, this empirical section of Chapter 4 produces some first results regarding how nuclear abstinence comes about in practice.

First, analyzing nuclear deterrence and the nuclear taboo, and their role as beliefs that rule action in practice, my analysis demonstrates that the requirements of a deterrence posture and the moral obligations associated with the nuclear taboo work at cross-purposes. This is my study's first *main argument*. Second, a specific conjecture about a so far understudied facet of nuclear abstinence is arrived at: the importance of fear. This trail is followed, at the conceptual level, by first reviewing the existing non-use literature yet another time, but also by expanding the horizon via the inclusion of literature from historic, cultural and critical security studies, as well as the recently burgeoning body of 'emotional turn' literature in IR.

Against this background, I propose that the corporeal-emotional embeddedness of nuclear decision-making must not be ignored, and I develop the concept of 'atomic anxiety' (while borrowing the term from Paul Boyer, 1994 [1985], p. 21). I show that while atomic anxiety as a sociocultural state has subliminally been present in reflections on nuclear non-use, its impact remained conceptually underdeveloped and empirically understudied until now.

Chapter 4 thus progresses by fleshing out atomic anxiety conceptually and analyzing its role regarding nuclear abstinence in a subsequent, second empirical inquiry. This inquiry puts even more emphasis on analyzing the subject matter reconstructively, that is, on generating substantial insights from within source material.

As a result of that inquiry, I develop an argument about how we can better understand (the causes of) nuclear abstinence by studying the phenomenon through the lens of atomic anxiety. I argue that two distinct types of reactions for coping with atomic anxiety can be discerned: one is immediately *transformative* and revolutionary in character, and the other is step-by-step *transitory* and pragmatic. By acknowledging these dissimilar reactions to atomic anxiety, we arrive at an even more in-depth understanding of the nuclear taboo's impairing interference that decision-makers experience while practicing deterrence as a strategy to ensure nuclear non-use. This is this study's second *main argument.*

Chapter 4 ends by my critically reflecting on the empirically generated insights, pondering their scope and considering possible alternative perspectives. In that regard, I argue that my work on atomic anxiety contributes a firm conceptual proposition, an initial charting of the empirical terrain and a first offer on how to think about nuclear abstinence along the lines of the novel concept of atomic anxiety. But further research is needed.

Chapter 5 summarizes this study's overall results and discusses the conclusions and implications to take away from this book. First, this is done in academic terms and with regard to possible avenues of further research, especially regarding the possibilities of additional cross-fertilization between explanatory and understanding approaches. Second, the conclusion considers nuclear policy-making, mainly by pondering what we can learn from thinking along the lines of atomic anxiety over and above the U.S. case, particularly regarding the danger of becoming complacent about nuclear abstinence.

2 Explaining Nuclear Non-Use

IR research on nuclear non-use relies on nomothetic concepts. Even though nuclear deterrence and the nuclear taboo differ in terms of their theoretical backgrounds and their conclusions about why nuclear weapons are so persistently not used, both claim to present a – more or less – far-reaching, general explanation reliant on causal mechanisms. To understand the reasons for and implications of this, a closer look is required.

2.1 Nuclear deterrence

When thinking about nuclear deterrence along the lines of 'explaining nuclear non-use', the key reference point is rational deterrence theory. The rational theory of nuclear deterrence is *nomothetically strong* because '[e]fforts to develop a robust theory... encouraged treatment of [nuclear deterrence] as an abstract phenomenon, as if it would be basically the same everywhere and at any particular time. The impact of context [was] underemphasized, even neglected' (Morgan, 2012, p. 85). In other words, the relation that rational deterrence theory postulates between deterrer and deterree, when nuclear weapons are in play, is akin to a 'covering law' (Van Evera, 1997, p. 40). However, deterrence is, of course, not only a theory but also a 'strategy of conflict management', with its practical application underway since the end of World War II (Lebow, 2010a, p. 393). So a look at both these will be required in the following passages, while the reasons for how deterrence theory came to be framed as nomothetically strong will be addressed again at the beginning of Chapter 3.

The following statement conveys why outspoken proponents of nuclear deterrence such as Kenneth Waltz (1990, pp. 732, 734) have so much confidence in the concept: 'Nuclear weapons purify deterrent strategies by removing elements of defense and war-fighting…because only a small number of warheads need to reach their targets. [C]ontemplating war when the use of nuclear weapons is possible focuses one's attention not on the probability of victory but on the possibility of annihilation.…The problem of the credibility of deterrence, a big worry in a conventional world, disappears in a nuclear one'. Consequently, Waltz (1993, p. 53), by quoting George W. Ball's famous *New York Review of Books* article, deems nuclear deterrence 'a "cosmic bluff"'. No one would *ever* dare to call this bluff – and this is why deterrence is such a reliable cause of nuclear non-use.

I will return to Waltz and why his take on deterrence is particularly interesting. At this point, the argument I aim to make is that his optimistic view neglects two fundamental problems with nuclear deterrence: one is situated at the theoretical level, and the other one unfolds when theory and practice meet.

2.1.1 Theory: from paradox to nonsense

The first of the two major problems with nuclear deterrence is a paradox in deterrence theory's logic. The basic idea of nuclear deterrence is that the threat of retaliation in kind – the threat of a second strike – will avert an enemy's attack, his first strike. Yet, already in the earliest days of the nuclear age, Frederick Dunn (1946, p. 17; cf. Morgenthau, 1964) described the problem in this way: 'Thus we come to the final paradox that while the best way to avoid atomic warfare is to get rid of war itself, the strongest present ally in the effort to get rid of war is the capacity to resort to atomic warfare at a moment's notice'.

The nub of this paradox of nuclear deterrence – having to resolutely facilitate that which one wants to avoid at all costs – kept scholars busy throughout the 'three waves' (Jervis, 1979, p. 289; Freedman, 2004, pp. 21–25) in which deterrence developed from a basic, seemingly straightforward idea into the sophisticated rational theory of deterrence we know today.

The credibility paradox

A couple of years into the nuclear age, with the first wave of deterrence theory cresting and more nuclear weapons available, deterrence theorists realized that for tackling the problem of making deterrence work, capabilities were no longer paramount. Instead, the credible demonstration of an unmistakable *will* to actually launch a second strike became their key concern.

Second-wave theorists based their work on 'systems analysis'[1] and rational choice theory (Steinbruner, 1975, pp. 225–226). And, in stark contrast to Waltz's statements at the beginning of this section, they actually took credibility to be a big problem, quintessential to the functioning of deterrence theory, *especially* in a nuclear world. After all, an enemy harboring doubts about the sincerity of the retaliatory threat can immediately exploit the fact that a threat of retaliation is no longer rational as soon as deterrence has failed. Because *hedging* the residual deterrent capacities is then the rational thing to do, while executing a massive second strike would be quite irrational then; because there is nothing more to be gained from it except revenge. Even worse, it might invite a crushing counterretaliation (Blair, 1993, p. 5; Steinbruner, 1975, p. 231). In short, 'the motives for executing the threat would, to a certain extent, have evaporated once the originally-to-be-deterred aggression actually occurred' (Kull, 1988, p. 144). It truly was a paradox.

Hence the conviction that under the assumption of rational actors the threat of a second strike could effectively deter a devastating first strike (instead of literally inviting the attacker to exploit the deterrence paradox) *only* if it was *truly credible* (Fink, 1965, p. 54).While not overcoming the paradox, this figure of thought at least allowed for getting a theoretical handle on it: 'It is a paradox of deterrence that in threatening to hurt somebody if he misbehaves, it need not make a critical difference how much it would hurt you too – *if* you can make him believe the threat' (Schelling, 1966, p. 36, Original emphasis).[2] Most of the – immensely influential – second-wave deterrence theory literature tried to further explore and solve this problem by casting its notion of rational decision-making, defined as 'a calculating, value-maximizing strategy of decision' (Schelling, 1979 [1960], p. 17), into game theoretical models.

Generally speaking, there are two models with which rational deterrence theory tries to gauge ways for the deterrer to achieve *escalation dominance*. In an ideal-typical scenario, nuclear deterrence works and causes nuclear non-use because the deterrer succeeds in dominating the escalation of *risks* or *violence,* in this way manipulating the opponent's cost-benefit calculus and thus his behavior in turn. In a nutshell, this is what the rational theory of nuclear deterrence is all about.

Risk escalation

According to this model, crises – not necessarily but also in the form of conventional wars – become competitions about driving the risk of a nuclear war higher and higher through escalatory measures, without actually triggering the fatal outbreak of nuclear war. The overall goal of this brinksmanship is to unsettle the opponent as well as to force upon him the burden of the impossible final decision, thus forcing him to back down by appearing more 'reckless, oblivious to the danger or out of control' (Kahn, 1962, p. 47; cf. Schelling, 1966, pp. 37–43). Thomas Schelling (1979 [1960], pp. 187–203; cf. Schelling, 1966, pp. 92–125) captured the essence of this model as the 'threat that leaves something to chance'.

So, to hasten his resignation, the opponent has to believe that during a crisis there is a dramatically increasing risk of false alarms, technical malfunctions or simply a trigger-happy general unleashing a first strike (Powell, 1985, pp. 77–79). Consequently, under the assumption of rational actors, having the opponent believe in fake deficiencies of one's own deterrence apparatus or the growing risk of an accidental launch turns out to be a recipe for success. The model thus draws on the notion that *real* deficiencies of the deterrence apparatus force decision-makers to succumb to the pressures of striking first in a situation of 'use them or lose them' ('anticipatory retaliation') because the gains of action – as long as command and control can still be exercised – outweigh the costs of inaction (Blair, 1993, p. 116). Furthermore, the threat that leaves something to chance also seems to remedy the paradoxical second-strike problem because it keeps the attacker in doubt as to whether, should he execute his first strike, the reckless victim will in fact 'stay rational' and really abstain from a by now senseless full-blown retaliation.

At this point it becomes obvious that this model is in contradiction with itself. For one, the occurrence of accidents implies a heavy element of unpredictability that seems incompatible with an otherwise neat and orderly model. But more importantly, the model treats rational actors as *the* core assumption on the one hand, while on the other hand relying on completely reckless, irrational actions to guarantee credible deterrence (Powell, 1985, p. 80; Snyder, 1960, p. 173; Jervis, 1979, p. 300; Lebovic, 1990, p. 146). Therefore, by relying on the risk that 'things can get out of hand', deterrence conceptualized as the 'rationality of irrationality' (Kahn, 1962, p. 48) does not escape from the credibility paradox.

The problem with the rationality of irrationality is, of course, that if rationality can also be irrational, there is nothing left to separate one from the other. But when the two concepts – one of which is said to be vital for the model to work – cease to be distinguishable in any meaningful way, they lose all discriminatory function, and the logic of the risk escalation model collapses. In short, if the logic that rational is rational because rationality is the opposite of irrationality is lost, a tautology results.

While risk escalation correlated – in terms of military strategy – with the doctrine of 'massive retaliation' (implying city/countervalue targeting and the holding of entire populations as hostages in a nuclear stalemate), an alternative model was soon formulated, corresponding with the U.S. strategic shift during the Cold War toward a conventionally bolstered 'flexible response', featuring only limited nuclear options (and implying no city/counterforce targeting).

Both theoretically and strategically, this second model promised to get around the existing contradictions and the credibility paradox. The groundwork for it was laid in the 1950s by William W. Kaufmann and his 'limited war' school. Henry Kissinger, at least for some time, was one of its outspoken proponents, and it also featured prominently in the writings of other strategic thinkers like Bernard Brodie and Robert E. Osgood.[3] The model picked up on the second-strike problem and faced the fact that threatening massive retaliation is not credible because states – still assuming they are rational actors – do not pull through when push comes to shove, thus threatening to render, as seen above, the whole idea of deterrence and second-strike threats self-defeating. Limited war, or counterforce targeting, promised a workaround for this because it dispensed with the 'distasteful alternatives' of having 'either [to] put up or shut up' (Kaufmann, 1956c, pp. 24–25), hence providing genuine choices. This model rendered obsolete the massive, exaggerated and, consequently, *incredible* threat of completely wiping out an enemy's population centers in retaliation by providing a spectrum of threats short of general war, options a decision-maker might actually carry out, for example, tailored responses against the enemy's military assets or, in other words, 'a response which delivers direct benefits and is therefore more credible' (Steinbruner, 1975, p. 232).

Violence escalation

This alternative deterrence theory model takes the destructive arsenals on both sides into account by accepting the possibility of mutual destruction at any given time. However, against the backdrop of this paralyzing state of nuclear parity, the model excludes this possibility from the deterring threat in order to retain (or rather regain) political and military freedom of action. This warrants a more in-depth explanation.

While Kaufmann (1956b, pp. 118–121, especially p. 121) did not categorically rule out the use of nuclear weapons, he, in weighing the pros and cons, reached the conclusion that due to their indiscriminate and 'eerie' nature they increase uncertainty and irrationality on the battlefield to such a degree that it becomes 'desirable to consider foregoing the [first] use of atomic weapons for tactical purposes' (for some time, Brodie [1959, pp. 319–327, 329–331] made a very strong case along the same lines). Other nuclear thinkers of that era such as, most prominently, Kissinger, took 'limited war' to explicitly also mean 'limited use' of (tactical) nuclear weapons (Kissinger, 1957, pp. 174–202). But Kaufmann's preference clearly was for a limited war fought only with *conventional* means (Kaplan, 1983, p. 198).[4] Hence, in this original sense, violence escalation is in fact a deterrence model for the *non*-use of nuclear weapons (and it is worth noting that Kissinger revised his opinion and also adopted this stance later on [Freedman, 2000, pp. 19–20]). After all, the model was meant to function toward this exact goal in political practice. It was supposed to (re-)establish a spectrum of political and military options in the European Cold War theater, including, most importantly, a 'firebreak' between conventional and nuclear weapons, thereby forestalling the contingency of having to use the latter (Osgood, 1979, pp. 19, 22; cf. Brodie, 1966, pp. 6, 8, 103–111; Lebovic, 1990, p. 149). Yet, the eventual step across the nuclear threshold had to be carefully planned – a key issue that section 4.2 will deal with again in light of empirical sources.

So with the goal of nuclear non-use (or 'as-late-as-possible use') in mind, this model bases the manipulation of an opponent's expectations on discretely scalable 'options' of violence, most prominently embodied in Herman Kahn's (1968 [1965], p. 39) 'escalation ladder'. Upping the ante by gradually inflicting damage upon the opponent and burdening him with steadily rising costs, he is denied his original goal by eventually rendering it unbearably expensive and thus unreasonable to continue in light of the issue originally at stake (Osgood, 1979, p. 11).[5] The notion of escalation in this model is thus diametrically opposed to the one in the risk escalation model. Demonstrating control, rather than threatening to lose control, is pivotal. It is not superior risk tolerance, but rather the demonstration of determination, willpower, endurance (given the destruction oneself has to face during the gradually escalating violence) and especially massive 'deliberate restraint' (Brodie, 1959, pp. 309–310) that are essential. The model promises that flexible options allow for shifting the burden of 'responsibility for escalation' (Kissinger, 1962, p. 518) to the opponent, so that he is forced to eventually cease the fight *despite* the fact that both sides are retaining the option of unleashing an all-out (mutually destructive) nuclear strike. 'We must be clear... that the curtailing of our taste for unequivocal victory is one of the prices we pay to keep the physical violence, and thus the costs and penalties, from going beyond the level of the tolerable' (Brodie, 1959, p. 314; cf. Powell, 1985, p. 83).

So this model derives the deterrent effect not from the risk of total devastation and the death of millions of civilians but from the ongoing destruction of military hardware and especially all such further costs an opponent has to expect in the future, or, in Schelling's (1979 [1960], pp. 190–191; cf. Schelling, 1966, pp. 1–34) words, '[t]he threat of what is yet to come'. With the existential risk removed from the equation, the relationship between adversaries in the violence escalation model becomes, according to Osgood (1979, p. 11), one of politically 'bargain[ing] with each other through the medium of graduated military responses, within the boundaries of contrived mutual restraints, in order to achieve a negotiated settlement short of mutual destruction'.

The more sophisticated violence escalation model has its benefits over the blunt risk escalation model, but it is far from compelling due to some rather keen built-in assumptions. Unlike with risk escalation, there absolutely *has* to be the use of physical force in order to manipulate the opponent's cost expectancy, deter him from further escalatory steps and reach a settlement. Violence thus accumulates on both sides, gradient by gradient according to the model, similar to moves in a chess game.[6] The first assumption is thus that, like in a chess game, actions in war and even in the heat of an ongoing battle can be executed in an orderly way, in controlled and graduated steps, all done in accordance with a strict set of rules mutually agreed upon by both players. It is implied, furthermore, that the resulting coercive signals are always interpreted correctly by the opponent and that they achieve the intended effect (namely his giving in, thus stopping further escalation), which is an even more dubious, second assumption. The 'chess pieces' cannot be neatly rearranged in their original positions on the board afterward, however. After all, death, destruction and suffering cannot simply be 'de-escalated'. The consequences of violence persist even after one belligerent backs down. Seen in this light, and given the ease with which nuclear weapons allow almost limitless damage to be inflicted, why should a nuclear-armed opponent accept a quick end of combat? The escalation of violence might just as well torpedo any willingness of the opponent to agree to the violently negotiated settlement, and instead have him strife for payback, hence completely foiling the model's intent. And while, as Steven P. Lee argues, wars before the nuclear age were 'self-limiting' because limited capabilities for inflicting damage did not allow the loser to deny the winner the overall advantage in terms of costs and benefits, nuclear weapons remove all such limitations. This is why the third and most problematic assumption of the violence escalation model is that the reliance on 'restraint' in effect means that the *winner* is forced to 'rely on the *loser's* restraint' (Lee, 1996, pp. 14, emphasis added; cf. Kissinger, 1962, p. 521; Jervis, 1984, pp. 19, 26, 35), a bet that appears ludicrous in light of the existence of powerful strategic nuclear weapons but that is actually quite typical for the logic-bending twists and turns of the 'Cold War rationality' (Erickson et al., 2013) underpinning deterrence theory.

Finally, pursuing the model's logic further despite all these objections means ending up in yet another paradox. After all, if a stable situation regarding mutual nuclear destruction is assumed per a common conduct of restraint, a more volatile situation between adversaries regarding lower levels of violence is bound to result. This link between simultaneous stability and instability became subsequently known as the 'stability-instability paradox' in deterrence literature (Jervis, 1984, p. 31; Lebovic, 1990, pp. 146–150).

To sum up, while it preserves the rationality of actors in formal terms and is thus less obviously in contradiction with itself than the risk escalation model, the violence escalation model relies on fallacious assumptions and also winds up in paradox.[7] This makes it implausible from a theoretical point of view and even more problematic in regard to its practical applicability, a point to which I will return.

This discussion of the two deterrence models points to a much larger suspicion, namely that the elegant assumptions about decision-making as a tidy, rational process of weighing costs against benefits might not actually apply in nuclear decision-making. Further delving into the practical problems and implications of the paradoxical theorizing of deterrence, Lynn Eden (2004, p. 276) in her review of the 'self-contradictory world' of U.S. nuclear target planning comments, 'What many comfortingly call the "paradox" of nuclear strategy is perhaps better understood as the "nonsense" of nuclear strategy – literally, that which does not make sense'. The notion of deterrence's paradox logic resulting in the 'nonsense of nuclear strategy' in practice is a suitable departure point for reviewing the second problem with nuclear deterrence.

2.1.2 Strategy: the theory-practice divide

The translation from abstract theory into concrete practice is the second major problem related to deterrence as an explanation for nuclear non-use. This notion was also central to the critical, third wave of deterrence theory. Drawing on cognitive psychology, third-wave deterrence theory moved the role of perception and misperception as well as other rationality-constraining factors into the center of the debate surrounding the theory-practice divide. The result was a heightened awareness of the potential *failing* of deterrence (Jervis, 1982; 1985; 1989; Kull, 1988, pp. 120–126; Lebow/Gross Stein, 1989).

And while scholars evaluated for the first time empirically whether decision-makers acted in accordance with theory (Jervis, 1989; George/Smoke, 1974; 1989), it came to light that the calculus of costs, benefits and probabilities as assumed in deterrence models was no adequate representation of nuclear policies (Jervis, 1979, pp. 310–311). Regarding the application of limited war strategy in Europe, for instance, Osgood (1979, p. 22) concluded that '[o]ne problem with all strategies of local war in Europe is that the Soviet Union has shown virtually no inclination to be a partner to them'. In other words, the two opponents were not even engaged in the same bargaining game. The U.S. played chess, while the Soviets played checkers.

The examination of real-life decision-making pretty much thwarted the strict rationality assumption as well as the neatly developed models that assumed a highly risk-tolerant and benefit-maximizing aggressor. Not even the roles of aggressor and defender were clear-cut in the real world. Frequently, they were not distinguishable at all. Political practice turned out to be much more complicated, muddled and opaque than what theory would have one expect (Freedman, 2004, p. 56; Lebow/Gross Stein, 1989, pp. 209–211, 221; George/Smoke, 1989, p. 173; 1974, pp. 503–504; Gray, 1999b, p. 12). Richard Ned Lebow and Janice Gross Stein summed all this up provocatively: 'Rational deterrence theory may be elegant but irrelevant' (Lebow/Gross Stein, 1989, pp. 218, see also 208, 213), they suggested.

A working strategy nevertheless?

But what if decision-makers simply took the basic idea of deterrence, not minding theory, and somehow managed to make deterrence work? The notion of deterrence working in some shape or form cannot easily be explained away by pointing to the theory's logical flaws or a few critical case studies. So despite deterrence theory being 'premised on a litany of unwarranted assumptions, improvable assertions and logical contradictions' (Butler, 2006, p. 766), nuclear deterrence might *in practice* nevertheless have prevented the 'war nobody wanted' (Quester, 1988, p. 127). After all, '[p]eople sometimes successfully apply what they do not understand' (Morgan, 1977, p. 26).

In that regard, McGeorge Bundy wrote in a *Foreign Affairs* article in 1969 some passages that are worth quoting at length: 'In light of the certain prospect of retaliation, there has been no chance at all that any sane political authority, in either the United States or the Soviet Union, would consciously choose to start a nuclear war. This proposition is true for the past, the present and the foreseeable future. For sane men on both sides the balance of terror is overwhelmingly persuasive... Think-tank analysts... are in an unreal world. In the real world of real political leaders – whether here or in the Soviet Union – a decision that would bring even one hydrogen bomb on one city of one's own country would be recognized in advance as a catastrophic blunder; ten bombs would be a disaster beyond history; and a hundred bombs on a hundred cities are unthinkable.... The object of political men – quite rightly – is that these weapons should never be used' (Bundy, 1969, pp. 9–10, 12).

Bundy's statement and the notion of a 'working deterrence strategy in practice' are intriguing, but a closer look reveals three caveats. For presenting the first two caveats below, I assume that risk-aversion indeed has decision-makers deterred, i.e. that deterrence 'works' on them. But I contrast this assumption with the quirks of deterrence in practice and how it can fail in unforeseen ways. In other words, the first two caveats are formulated under the assumption that deterrence has the decision-makers at the top of the command chain acting with the utmost hesitation and caution due to 'the awesome risk of executing the strategy in practice' (Kaplan, 1983, p. 306). For fleshing out the third caveat, however, I take a step back to review a couple of reasons for doubting that this risk aversion of decision-makers, and thus reliable deterrence, is even created in the first place. Hence I return to the notion of some of the third-wave deterrence theorists by acknowledging the possibility of deterrence failure. With this third caveat, it must seem that I suddenly base my remarks on arguments that I established to be the opposite with the first two. Also, the conclusions to be taken from all this seemingly point in opposing directions: Either the relationship between the theory and practice of deterrence is problematic because decision-makers are *too cautious* and not as bold as deterrence models suggest they would have to be for deterrence to work, or they are *too reckless* and not as cautious as the 'awesome risk' instilled by deterrence would have one expect. To make a coherent and compelling case about the theory-practice divide, these two statements seemingly cannot both be true at the same time. However, I argue that this is exactly the case here. What is more, I argue that this is in fact the key point to take away from a discussion of the theory and practice of deterrence. So my goal is to demonstrate the practical manifestations of the deterrence paradox as well as how complicated and variable deterrence practice can be and, consequently, that the apparent contradictions in my remarks on the three caveats about 'working deterrence' derive not from my sloppy argumentation but from the collisions and contradictions that are produced by a *nomothetically strong theory clashing with a checkered strategic practice.*

Caveat 1: Normal accidents and close calls

First, there is an inherent characteristic of all complex systems to take into acccount: namely that, over time, due to unforeseen system failure or human error, even highly unlikely events will materialize at some time, which is why accidents are inevitable, and frequent, serious accidents less frequent but still inevitable, and catastrophes very rare but just as inevitable. A system as complex as the deterrence apparatus of a nuclear power is no exception to the fundamental insight that accidents are 'normal' (Perrow, 1984).

Albeit no accidental nuclear explosion has been set off up to today, the issue is a matter of perspective. Scott D. Sagan (1993; see also Schlosser, 2013) convincingly argues for the example of the U.S. nuclear arsenal that the catch-22 of close calls, namely that the closeness of the call that demonstrates the system working safely, is in fact *not* a counterargument against the theory of normal accidents. After all, an accident has not taken place because the system worked but rather because of other factors *outside* the system (Craig, 2012, p. 293). So, in short, even while assuming that 'the awesome risk of executing the strategy in practice' has decision-makers deterred, there are still a million things that can go wrong in a deterrence apparatus, simply due to human error or unforeseen system failures. And the fact that no accidental nuclear explosion has been set off up to today does not disprove this. Accordingly, even with the U.S. and Russia having comparably much smaller arsenals today, an intentional but erroneous retaliation remains a possibility. Numerous examples of 'close calls' are documented for the Cold War era as well as after, from training tapes being mistaken for reality to weather rockets being misinterpreted as a nuclear launch (Sagan, 1993, pp. 99–100, 130–131, 228–230; Rhodes, 2008, pp. 145–146; Dobbs, 2008, pp. 132–134). The lesson is that even if decision-makers are risk averse and deterred, there are still myriads of things that can go wrong – from technical malfunctions to honest mistakes – while practicing deterrence, rendering it a fickle guarantor of nuclear non-use.

Caveat 2: Loss of control and recklessness

Second, and in close connection to the first caveat, the nuclear powers' constant struggle for both negative and positive control over their deterrence system has to be taken into account (Blair, 1993). The dilemma here is that 'the ability to use nuclear weapons whenever necessary works at cross purposes with the desire never to use them accidentally' (Lewis, 2007, p. 8; Brodie, 1959, pp. 272–273).

Two scenarios of positive control loss are possible. In scenario one, the enemy learns of a loss of positive control which immediately invites his disarming first strike. In other words, a 'window of vulnerability' opens up. Retired general and chairman of the Joint Chiefs of Staff Hugh Shelton, for instance, disclosed in his memoirs that during the Clinton administration in the year 2000, the authorization codes for launching nuclear weapons were 'missing for months'. Neither the president's aide nor the president himself could find them, and they had to be replaced with new ones. In this case, the U.S. dodged a silver bullet, in Shelton's (2010, pp. 392–393) words (arguably overstating things since the chain of succession would eventually have made a launch possible, albeit with considerable delay).

In scenario two, the enemy's strike is already underway or has taken place, and positive control is lost in the attempt to retaliate. Here, the case of U.S. Air Force Major Harold Hering, a nuclear missileer, is instructive. He questioned his mission of launching nuclear retaliation upon receiving an authorization code (Rosenbaum, 2011). Again, total failure to use nuclear weapons despite the intention to do so would not have resulted from only Major Hering's refusal.

But Hering's case illustrates loss of positive control. And political decision-makers face – on a much greater scale – the same problem that bothered Major Hering: as seen above, executing the second strike becomes rather illogical as soon as the enemy's attack is underway or has happened (because it serves nothing but revenge). Consequently, reducing the time to think and allowing the U.S. president no 'cooling-off period' was seen as an enhancing factor for deterrence during the Cold War because 'it increase[d] the certainty that the American President would react angrily' (Kull, 1988, p. 186). So the idea was to constrain a president's choices 'so that he would not be tempted to "ride out" an attack' and shy away from retaliating (Eden, 2010, p. 385).

The Soviet PERIMETR system took this idea further by delegating the retaliation decision to a group of duty officers in case the Kremlin was destroyed (Rosenbaum, 2011, pp. 88–93). But would some random lieutenant colonel of the Soviet Armed Forces, after half the planet had already gone up in smoke, carry the burden of finishing the job (Hoffman, 2009, p. 153)? A tentative answer to this question is provided by the case of Stanislav Petrov. In 1983, the ongoing NATO exercise ABLE ARCHER 83 was misperceived by the U.S.S.R. as a cover for an actual attack with tactical nuclear forces. On top of that, a malfunctioning Soviet early-warning satellite registered first one, then a couple of more U.S. ICBM launches (Rhodes, 2008, pp. 165–166; Blair, 1993, p. 181; Hoffman, 2009, pp. 94–95). Lieutenant Colonel Stanislav Petrov, the Soviet officer in charge, decided on his own (correctly) that this had to be a false alarm and gave the all clear up the command chain. This was a heroic decision in hindsight. Within the deterrence paradigm, however, it was a problematic loss of positive control. It was a control loss that averted an accidental World War III, as some suggest today, since the already extraordinarily tense situation between the superpowers at that time might have left little to no room for hesitation by the Soviet leadership (Hoffman, 2009, pp. 6–11; Rosenbaum, 2011, p. 7).

Turning, next, to the loss of negative control, the focus rests on the illegitimate use of nuclear weapons. Here, the history of the Cold War holds dozens of hair-raising episodes about close calls on the U.S. side. Many of these situations came about because for a period of time after World War II – before the introduction of the president's nuclear football – nuclear authority was delegated to the lower echelons of the deterrence apparatus in case presidential communication broke down (Blair, 1993, pp. 46–55; cf. Lebovic, 1990, pp. 153–156; Allison/Zelikow, 1999, pp. 197–199). Additional examples, such as Permissive Action Links with their supposedly 'secret unlock code' widely known and set to 'all zero digits' (Blair, 2004), as well as the two-key system of nuclear missileers being cheatable with a string and a spoon, underline the possibility of negative control loss, that is, a nuclear launch without proper authorization (Rosenbaum, 2007; cf. 2011, pp. 61–62).

Finally, reckless behavior by decision-makers in light of the risks involved goes hand in hand with the loss of negative control. To give but one example, Strategic Air Command (SAC) general Curtis LeMay infamously started 'raising the ante' in 1954 by ordering spy plane flights over Soviet territory – 'covertly and extra legally' (Rhodes, 2005, p. 564). If the Soviets had detected these flights, they likely would have taken them for acts of war.

In sum, risk aversion may have decision-makers at the top of the command chain deterred, but to use nuclear weapons when it is intended and to not use them when it is not produces a fundamental tension that is trickier to deal with in practice than theory acknowledges. This undermines the basic tenet of guaranteed threat execution on which deterrence theory relies.

Caveat 3: Contemplating use and deterrence failure

The third caveat is the discrepancy between the hesitation and caution that deterrence supposedly instills in decision-makers and the de facto issued threats. Take, for instance, the vociferous Cold War threats of nuclear use voiced by the U.S. to keep the numerically superior Red Army in check in Western Europe. Against the background of these very unambiguous postures by officials and convictions held by the general public ('better dead than red') during the early Cold War, can it really be safely assumed that American presidents never *really* considered using nuclear weapons?

The easy way to deal with this is to dismiss the respective policy documents (NSC-162/2 and JCS 2101/113, quoted in Rosenberg, 1983, p. 31 [fn. 96])[8], declarations and threats as 'cheap talk': threatening nuclear war for the purpose of deterrence, yes, but actually *meaning* it, no. Claiming that presidents are all talk and no action is an elegant way out. But if the deterrence paradigm is to be kept intact, it is not a logically sound argument.

Assuming that the credibility of the threat is indeed the cornerstone of deterrence, we have to deduce that Cold War threats like those in the early 1950s and 1960s were in fact believed by (most of) the Soviet and (most of) the American decision-makers. Otherwise, if we assume that few people or no one actually believed the threats, we cannot at the same time keep crediting deterrence with explaining non-use. This is why Waltz errs in describing deterrence as a simple 'bluff'. To guarantee credibility, the goal of deterrence must be to credibly 'communicate that fact that it is *not* a "mere threat", a bluff or a gambit' (McCanles, 1984, p. 15, emphasis added). Clearly, 'an effective policy of nuclear deterrence [can] *not* be based on bluff, because, given the institutional nature of the policy, the absence of a retaliatory intention could not rest in a single mind but would have to be reflected in the military organization supporting the threat, and thus might easily be discovered by the opponent' (Lee, 1996, pp. 30, emphasis added). A logically coherent perspective in hindsight would thus require that, if working Soviet deterrence and the according constraints on an American 'decision to use' are to be assumed, one in turn has to assume that the U.S. tried to establish a political and military posture that guaranteed credible threats as well, that is, a posture that credibly manifested the *genuine intention* to strike first against the Red Army on European soil. Consequently, as long as we are not ready to scrap deterrence as an explanation for non-use, we *have* to assume that the Cold War threats of using nuclear weapons were considerably more than just 'cheap talk' – with constraints on the initial 'decision to use' consequently being much lower, at least during certain phases after 1945.

It gets more complicated because, ironically, the declassified documents and war plans of the time indicate that the Soviet threat after World War II was overestimated. The Soviet Union had in fact neither the mobilization capability nor, apparently, the intent to stage an overwhelming conventional attack on Western Europe – the scenario that Western nuclear deterrence posturing was designed to forestall (Evangelista, 1998; cf. Karber/Combs, 1998). Seen in this light, the early Cold War strategy debates at that time seem like a Western soliloquy. But while interesting in hindsight, this does not dispute the fact that *at the time* Western political and military decision-makers did not know about these Soviet documents and had to be convinced otherwise. Consequently, the argument against 'cheap talk' holds. If anything, an even bigger question mark remains regarding whether deterrence 'worked' during this period of time since there apparently was not much to deter in the first place.

Even if one grants that deterrence strategy 'worked' on other occasions during the Cold War, the point made here is that planning, proclaiming and all in all just being dead serious about the 'decision to use' is certainly not ruled out or rendered 'unthinkable' by it. On the contrary, a feature of the deterrence logic's paradox put into practice is that a deterrence strategy inevitably begets both non-use *and* use. To put this ambiguity in a nutshell: the more *un*thinkable you want the use of nuclear weapons to be, the more deterrence makes you think about using them (Brians, 1987, pp. 2–3).

Lastly, there is deterrence failure. Deterrence failure means the deliberate use of nuclear weapons – no accident, positive and negative control intact. Here, the Cuban Missile Crisis is instructive. After Nikita Khrushchev had approved the warheads on Cuba to be moved closer to their delivery vehicles, Robert McNamara saw an increasing risk that the Soviets might 'use their nuclear forces rather than to lose them' (quoted in Rhodes, 2008, p. 100). As Arthur Schlesinger Jr. later noted, Soviet field commanders in Cuba were in fact authorized to use tactical nuclear weapons in case communication links with Moscow were severed. McNamara 'almost fell out of his chair', according to Schlesinger (quoted in Kennedy, 1968 [1999], p. 8) when he learned about this for the first time during a Missile Crisis conference on Cuba in 1992. Also, and most importantly, the Cuban leadership was not deterred. Fidel Castro stated at the same conference in Havana: 'Would I have been ready to use nuclear weapons? Yes, I would have agreed, in the event of the invasion you are talking about, with the use of tactical nuclear weapons' (McNamara/Blight, 2002, p. 13). The Cuban leadership was hell-bent that in the case of an invasion and the destruction of Cuba, 'the Soviets should take the Americans down with them' (McNamara/Blight, 2002, p. 12). It is important to notice that the statement of Castro is not just him bragging at a conference 30 years after the events. Rather, his testimony turns out to be consistent with the cable found in both Cuban and Soviet archives in which he, on October 27, 1962, requested from Khrushchev an all-out nuclear strike against the United States in case of an invasion, calling this 'an act of legitimate self-defense' (McNamara/Blight, 2002, p. 12). The fact that the U.S. government did not know about the cable at the time (it was not made public until 1990) also eliminates the possibility of Castro's merely doing saber rattling for deterrence purposes. Rather, the Cuban situation apparently created so much despair on Castro's side that he would not have been deterred from using nuclear weapons. And Ernesto 'Che' Guevara also declared himself prepared 'to walk by the path of liberation even when it may cost millions of atomic victims' (McNamara/Blight, 2002, p. 12; Dobbs, 2008, p. 245). 'Going to war is not necessarily a rational process', Schlesinger laconically notes with regard to Khrushchev's extremely risky nuclear predelegation orders for Cuba (Kennedy, 1968 [1999], p. 8).

This cautionary tale suggests that statements like 'it's been proven without exception that whoever gets nuclear weapons behaves with caution and moderation' (Waltz, quoted in Sagan et al., 2007, p. 137) or that '[o]ne can describe the way all nuclear states have behaved in one word: responsibly' (Waltz, 2011) are strangely one-sided. Even if deterrence had decision-makers shy away from the 'awesome risk' involved, they or the apparatus they rely on could still be in error and deterrence could fail. They also might lose control, causing deterrence to fail due to the reckless behavior of subordinates. Finally, and most importantly, the deliberate use of nuclear weapons seems to be ruled out less *necessarily* in practice than nomothetic deterrence theory suggests. So, in sum, there remains ample reason for skepticism about the notion of risk aversion rendering deterrence a 'working strategy in practice' and a law-like guarantor of the non-use of nuclear weapons.

2.1.3 Concluding remarks

The central paradox of nuclear deterrence so aptly described by Frederick Dunn – that the superpowers had to resolutely facilitate that which they wanted to avoid at all costs, putting at great risk what they actually meant to protect – could not be resolved at the theoretical level, but was merely replaced with new contradictions. For a nomothetic approach that claims an almost law-like validity, being 'plagued with internal paradox' (Steinbruner, 1975, p. 224) certainly is a problem. And regarding deterrence as a non-use guaranteeing strategy, there are so many caveats that no one can say for sure whether the Cold War progressed the way it did *because of* the rational theory of deterrence being applied in practice, or rather, *despite* it (Gray, 1999b, pp. 19, 88–91).

Against the backdrop of this review of rational deterrence theory, its interactions with practice as well as the critique arising from all this, it is safe to conclude, I argue, that we suffer from a lack of more detailed understanding of *how deterrence* – with and despite all its theoretical flaws – *plays out in practice* and, consequently, whether and how we can keep using it as an explanation of nuclear non-use. In short, the question is whether deterrence in practice is even the same thing that rational deterrence theory claims to describe. Because if (some sort of) deterrence is at work, it oftentimes seems to be running contrary to what models of rational deterrence theory state. After all, if the 'balance of terror is overwhelmingly persuasive' and instills a strong need for *caution* in decision-makers due to the 'awesome risk' involved, how can they at the same time be practicing either risky brinksmanship (via deterrence by risk escalation) or gradually but relentlessly punish their opponent in an upward spiral of conflict (via deterrence by violence escalation)? I will return to this train of thought in Chapters 3 and 4.

For now, having demonstrated that the paradox of deterrence means that for nuclear weapons not to be used, one constantly has to think about *using* them, I will unfold in the next section the argument for why nuclear use might be *un*thinkable after all.

2.2 Nuclear taboo

Compared to rational deterrence theory, the norm-based concept of the nuclear taboo is *nomothetically weak*. Its explanation for non-use is not as law-like as the one postulated by deterrence theory for the constellation deterrer versus deterree. Nevertheless, this explanation implies a high degree of regularity by pointing to a very powerful force guiding, steering and regulating the behavior of decision-makers.

It was primarily Nina Tannenwald (1999; 2005b; 2007) who offered a new take on nuclear non-use – by focusing on morality. Her work provides both an alternative theoretical explanation for non-use as well as policy thinking outside the box of the straitjacketing deterrence paradigm. It promises answers to several questions left unanswered by deterrence theory. For example, if the essence of deterrence is that '[n] uclear weapons have never been used in a world in which two or more states had them' (Waltz, 2003a, p. 16), then why were they not used in conflicts in which only *one* state had them? And why have nuclear weapons never been used when retaliation was not a credible threat? U.S. nuclear superiority in the late 1940s is an example. Furthermore, there is the flip side of the argument: why did nuclear weapons not deter attacks by nonnuclear weapon states against nuclear weapons states, for example China's attack on U.S. forces in Korea or the North Vietnamese attack in Vietnam (Tannenwald, 2007, pp. 2–3, 33)?

Generally speaking, the answer the nuclear taboo provides to such questions is that the possessors of nuclear weapons do not allow themselves to use these weapons because they are stigmatized as immoral weapons of mass destruction. Due to the nuclear taboo, a strong normative understanding ensures that no civilized nation would ever again dare to bring such destruction and suffering as in Hiroshima and Nagasaki upon another people. In a nutshell, it is this normative factor, the strong social norm in the minds of decision-makers that simply renders a first-use of nuclear weapons *wrong*, from which the nuclear taboo derives its explanatory power.

Tapu, from which the word 'taboo' derives, is a Polynesian word that does not translate easily. But the term's basic concept is twofold. On the one hand taboo means 'holy', while on the other hand it means 'forbidden'. Sigmund Freud tried to capture that notion in German as *heilige Scheu*, meaning 'holy awe'. A taboo conveys a very strict prohibition to protect people from the dangerous consequences of disobeying it. Because breaking a taboo poses such great risk to not only an individual but also society as a whole, deeming something taboo is considerably more than just labeling it 'forbidden'. Taboo means it is neither to be done, nor touched, nor said, and sometimes not even thought of. Strong taboos mark what is unnatural, abnormal, *unthinkable* within the framework of a society; consequently, taboos are basically unquestionable and go along with threats of automatic and severe punishment in case of a violation (Tannenwald, 1999, p. 436; 2005b, p. 8; 2007, pp. 10–14; Paul, 2009, pp. 5–6).

Should a violation occur nevertheless, typically a taboo does not cease to exist. Incest, for example, is deemed a taboo in most societies and even while there almost regularly do occur violations of this taboo, its 'taboo-ness' is not fundamentally called into question. Quite the contrary, oftentimes violating a taboo even strengthens its prohibitive quality (Tannenwald, 2005b, pp. 7, 36–38; 2007, pp. 14–16; Quester, 2005, p. 83; 2006, p. 131).

But qualifying neither as a norm in a legal sense nor as a prohibition against the acquisition of taboo objects (Tannenwald, 2007, p. 12; cf. Walker, 2010),[9] how does the nuclear taboo prevent the use of nuclear weapons? Drawing on the social constructivist body of literature on the relevance of social norms, Tannenwald ascribes regulative and constitutive effects to it.

The first effect regulates the actions of political decision-makers. It does so in two possible ways. First, it increases political costs by one's having to justify one's action vis-à-vis the domestic or global public. Second, it becomes internalized through repetition as a genuine inhibition threshold that decision-makers, who are themselves convinced of the existence and moral value of the taboo, no longer dare cross (for the notion of different stages or degrees of norm internalization, see Wendt, 1999, pp. 268–278; Finnemore/Sikkink, 1998, pp. 895–905). This means that in the latter case, pressure by public opinion is displaced by an inherent conviction about what is right and wrong – and the obligation to act accordingly. This effect is enforced by the fact that the nuclear taboo is perceived as a 'bright line norm' separating two worlds. The use of only *one* single bomb means the opening of Pandora's box, thus irrevocably crossing over into a new world (Tannenwald, 2007, p. 11), an utterly inacceptable prospect that the nuclear taboo rules out categorically. So by establishing a strong, socially shared standard for distinguishing 'right' (non-use) from 'wrong' (use), the regulative effect of the nuclear taboo suppresses the deviant choice of 'use' and forcefully directs actors toward the decision of non-use.

The constitutive effect of taboo is twofold as well. First, the categorization of certain weapons as 'weapons of mass destruction', which cause excessive destruction and indiscriminately kill combatants and non-combatants alike, goes along with the nuclear taboo, separating them from 'normal', conventional weapons. Second, state identities are shaped by this stigmatization of nuclear weapons, such that abstaining from their use becomes an important characteristic for the behavior of nuclear weapon states that deem themselves 'civilized nations' (Tannenwald, 1999, pp. 462–463; 2005b, pp. 9, 11, 13–14; 2007, pp. 18–19, 44–51, 58–59, 64–67; Farrell/Lambert, 2001, p. 312). So when states heed the nuclear taboo and thus reproduce the norm in their ongoing practice, they reproduce an essential aspect of their identity (Wendt, 1992, pp. 412–415).

Tannenwald (2007, p. 13) traces the evolution of the nuclear taboo in her work, gathering the accumulating 'evidence for the taboo... in discourse, institutions, and behavior'. She demonstrates that the taboo originated from the first *use* of nuclear weapons against Japan in 1945. Of course, the U.S. population was mostly clueless about the horrors on the ground at that point. At first, people were mainly joyous and relieved about the end of the war (Rose, 2001, pp. 14–15; Weart, 1988, p. 107). More than 80 percent of Americans supported Harry S. Truman's decision (Bundy, 1988, pp. 132–133; cf. Boyer, 1994 [1985], p. 183). Protests were few and far between (Boyer, 1994 [1985], pp. 196–210). There was no stigma attached to nuclear weapons yet, and a taboo did not exist either (Tannenwald, 1999, pp. 442–443; 2005b, p. 14; 2007, pp. 74, 89–91; Bernstein, 1991, p. 151).

But John Hersey's article 'Hiroshima', published by *The New Yorker* on August 31, 1946, and soon reprinted in many papers and read aloud on the radio, depicted the gruesome fate of several people in the city. It was one of the kick-starters for the public's (re-) assessment of the bomb from a distinctly moral perspective (Franklin, 2008 [1988], p. 157; Rose, 2001, pp. 52–53; Tannenwald, 2007, pp. 92–93; Weart, 1988, pp. 107–108).

So explaining non-use through the nuclear taboo hinges on the insight that the Japan bombings and more and more people learning about the effect of nuclear weapons laid the foundation for a political and societal process that ended up shifting the 'burden of proof'. Over time this process put proponents of nuclear use under increasing justification pressure (Tannenwald, 1999, pp. 440–442; 2007, pp. 52–53).

Consequently, when nuclear attacks were considered during the Korean War, the emerging taboo was already in effect – if only to protract the decision-making process and gain some more time for the ceasefire to arrive (Tannenwald, 2007, p. 150). In addition, a stigmatization process that would change nuclear weapons from 'just another weapon' into 'weapons of last resort' and eventually even 'weapons of mass destruction' (WMD) had begun as well (Walker, 2004, p. 22).

After these two steps forward, the taboo took a step back due to Richard M. Nixon's obsession of ending the Vietnam War with a final 'knockout blow'. The influence of the taboo on the administration shrank from an internalized moral threshold to mere considerations of possible reputation loss (Tannenwald, 2007, pp. 227–230). But the already furious worldwide protests against the Vietnam War gave a foretaste of what to expect if the decision-makers were to go forward with their nuclear plans. Also, Nixon's détente policy to mitigate tensions with the Soviet Union and China would have been jeopardized by the poisoned political climate in the aftermath of a U.S. nuclear attack in Vietnam. Nixon dreaded, first and foremost, the *political* fallout (Bundy, 1988, p. 540). So while Presidents John F. Kennedy and Lyndon B. Johnson before him had deemed it genuinely *wrong* to use nuclear weapons in Vietnam, Nixon – at least in his rhetoric – was far less scrupulous. But he, too, was faced with the shifted burden of proof (Tannenwald, 1999, pp. 455–458; 2007, pp. 238–240).

Lastly, the 1991 war against Iraq provides an especially interesting and important case for the nuclear taboo. It demonstrates how nuclear weapons were still politically relevant, but also how much the conviction not to use them had matured into a shared, taken-for-granted norm, sturdily anchored in institutionalized conventions and practices of U.S. nuclear decision-making. And because deterrence was out of the equation for the first time since the beginning of the Cold War due to the Soviet empire's no longer being in existence, and with the international community standing united against a nonnuclear Iraq in a desert scenario that would have allowed the use of tactical nuclear weapons on the battlefield with few if any civilian casualties, Tannenwald's case study of the Persian Gulf War is the litmus test for explaining non-use exclusively with the nuclear taboo (Tannenwald, 1999, p. 458; 2007, p. 294).

While U.S. government officials sent mixed signals, publicly employing only thinly veiled nuclear threats against Iraq (Atkinson, 2010, pp. 845–846), then denying these and suggesting that the U.S. would not answer an Iraqi chemical attack with nuclear weapons, actually using nuclear weapons never came up for discussion behind closed doors. Neither did nuclear weapons appear in the war plans of U.S. Central Command nor did President George H.W. Bush have anything but conventional means in mind. Despite his administration's calculated ambiguity and its public threats, the president had actually decided at Camp David in 1990 not even to retaliate with nuclear weapons against an Iraqi chemical attack. Nobody at the political level seemed to discuss, let alone engage in serious considerations of the nuclear option (Tannenwald, 1999, pp. 458–459; 2007, pp. 62, 294, 297–298; Halperin et al., 2009, pp. 40–41). Colin Powell (quoted in Tannenwald, 2007, pp. 299, see also 300–301), then chair of the Joint Chiefs of Staff, had a particularly strong aversion against using tactical nuclear weapons on the battlefield: 'Let's not even think about nukes. You know we're not going to let that genie loose', he decided. So the constraining effect of the taboo was clearly visible during the Persian Gulf War – using nuclear weapons had literally become 'unthinkable' for the most part. And the term 'nuclear taboo' had become part of everyday language.

So far, the nuclear taboo seems just as much a political success story as a convincing explanation for non-use. Two problems have to be recognized nevertheless. Prior to discussing those, however, a controversy needs to be addressed, namely, whether the taboo is in fact a taboo.

2.2.1 Taboo versus tradition

Thinking about nuclear non-use in terms of a 'tradition' goes back to Schelling (see e.g. Schelling, 1979 [1960], pp. 260–261, 264–265; cf. Bundy, 1988, pp. 586–588). What is the difference between a 'tradition' and a 'taboo'?

While not excluding the material considerations for non-use from her argument, Tannenwald especially stresses the pivotal role of non-material factors, of social norms, in her analysis. According to her, we are in fact dealing with a socially constructed taboo, and *not* 'simply a "tradition"' (Tannenwald, 2007, pp. 14–17). T.V. Paul on the other hand, by adopting an argument of Scott Sagan, who suspects non-use to be grounded in prudence-based considerations about 'longer-term material factors' such as 'concerns about precedent-setting' (quoted in Tannenwald, 2007, p. 14), disputes the notion of non-use being primarily grounded in a strict prohibitionary social norm.

Paul (2009, p. 1) conceptualizes his explanation as a mere 'accustomed obligation'. While granting non-material norms an 'intermingling' effect, Paul (2009, pp. 1–3, 22–36) refers to Sagan's material factors, such as the horrendous impact of a nuclear explosion and considerations of reputation loss or detrimental precedents, as the 'primary causal factors' for non-use. This is what deterrence theorists call 'self-deterrence', a shying away from the 'unpredictability and enormity of nuclear weapons' (Paul, 2009, p. 2) resulting in non-use, either rightly so or because imagination runs wild (Freedman, 2004, p. 30; Jervis, 1982, pp. 14–19). A continuous feedback loop of self-deterrence formed the tradition of non-use – a process deliberately fostered and deemed beneficial by both the U.S. and the U.S.S.R. in Paul's mind, since it kept the peace through upholding and enforcing mutual deterrence and preventing the proliferation of nuclear weapons (Paul, 2009, pp. 3, 26).

According to Paul, not using nuclear weapons is not (yet) taboo (but merely traditional) for a couple of reasons. First, there is no severe punishment for breaking the alleged taboo. Since the norm is not legally enshrined, unlike, for example, the norms against using chemical or biological weapons, it is an informal norm at best and definitely not a taboo (Paul, 2009, p. 4). In 1996, the International Court of Justice gave its advisory opinion on the legality of using or threatening the use of nuclear weapons (ICJ, 1996). In its statement it found the threat or use of nuclear weapons to be 'generally...contrary to the rules of international law' (ICJ, 1996, p. 44). However, for the 'extreme circumstance of self-defence [sic!], in which the very survival of a State would be at stake' the Court could not 'conclude definitely whether the threat or use of nuclear weapons would be lawful or unlawful' (ICJ, 1996, p. 44). Paul argues that this ICJ ruling clearly represents the lack of legal sanctions (see also Farrell, 2010, p. 826). Other forms of sanctions such as shame and humiliation he deems uncertain at best. In addition, Paul argues that states *do* in fact keep contingency plans for using nuclear weapons, while sane individuals would not even consider breaking a strong social taboo (Paul, 2009, pp. 7–9; cf. Lee, 1996, pp. 319–320, 407, fn. 42; Tannenwald, 2007, pp. 369–370).

However, there are in fact stronger taboos than the nuclear taboo – such as those against incest, cannibalism or pedophilia –, and even these very robust social norms get broken in society on an almost regular basis (Eden, 2010, pp. 832–833; cf. Paul, 2010, pp. 857, 860). And oftentimes the taboo breaker plans the deed meticulously and is not declared a psychopath during trial. So it is unclear why considerations of breaking a norm should be absolutely inconsistent with its still being a taboo, an unthinkable thing for most people most of the time. And making the legal formalization of a norm a necessary precondition for accepting it as a taboo also raises the bar fairly, arguably too high since, as Tannenwald's argument goes, an informal social norm such as the nuclear taboo can very well be in existence and effect even though it has not (yet) been legally codified.

In essence, the dispute between Paul and Tannenwald is actually about prioritizing one logic of action over another (Fearon/Wendt, 2002, pp. 60–62). Tannenwald recognizes that a full-fledged, fully internalized taboo is an ideal-type situation. Then, and only then, '[t]here is no weighing of benefits and costs; we simply reject the idea without further thought', as George H. Quester (2006, p. 12) put it. Tannenwald recognizes the 'intimate link between rational self-interest and morality', and thus deems *both* 'strategic interests' and 'moral opprobrium' as being in play. Nevertheless, her overall argument deems the *logic of appropriateness* as pivotal in regulating action and creating widely internalized patterns of behavior via a social norm (Tannenwald, 2007, pp. 25, 53–55). In other words, the nuclear taboo sets a standard of appropriateness for 'proper behavior of actors with a given identity' (Katzenstein, 1996, p. 5) and marks what is normal, that is, 'appropriate' for an actor conceptualized as a *homo sociologicus* with a social identity.

In contrast, the thrust of Paul's argument, while also 'eclectically' combining the two logics of action, gives priority to the *logic of consequences* via a process of *Realpolitik* and rational decision-making by a *homo economicus* in light of reputation, which he deems a material factor (Paul, 2009, p. 21). In his words, 'Moral and legal considerations are subsumed in the reputational variable' (Paul, 2009, p. 197). But although Paul argues that Tannenwald undervalues material factors, he occupies a position in between a purely rational-functionalist stance and a normative stance by not explicitly taking exception to Tannenwald's statement that '[n]orms are templates for interests and thus for what counts as "rational"' (Tannenwald, 2007, p. 25).

So both agree that the relation between the two logics of action is indeed not a mutually exclusive one but one of gradual succession on a spectrum of possibilities (Paul, 2009, p. 19; Tannenwald, 2007, pp. 50–52; cf. Fearon/Wendt, 2002, pp. 61–62). In other words, the stronger and the more internalized a social norm is, the more the *logic of appropriateness* kicks in when an actor conducts a cost-benefit calculus during what is then deemed a rational decision according to the *logic of consequences*. Since not even Paul disputes the existence of the norm per se, the controversy between him and Tannenwald boils down to the question of how far the nuclear taboo has progressed on the 'internalization scale' – and thus how predominant or decisive it is in 'rational' decision-making – in any given case. So their difference is in fact, as Paul (2010, p. 854) concedes, 'a matter of degree', a gradual, not an absolute one.

Since both authors admit that a final answer to the question of norm internalization is tricky and can only be come by when dealing with the interpretation of actual empirical material, such as historical documents on a case-by-case basis (Paul, 2009, pp. 27–28; on this problem in regard to Paul's study, see Gill, 2009, pp. 867–877), their dispute resembles an – albeit important – footnote in light of the bigger picture dealt with here, namely the development of a full-fledged explanation for nuclear non-use that is not deterrence. This is important to note with regard to how this chapter further progresses in terms of unfolding a critique. A few more remarks are thus in order.

In terms of the big picture, Tannenwald concludes from her research that political leaders found themselves constrained by a taboo (and not just a mere tradition or a 'rule of prudence' (Tannenwald, 2007, pp. 14, 367)) and that 'a taboo can be distinguished from a tradition by the fact that a tradition depends on precedent and reciprocity and is easily disrupted by a violation' (Tannenwald, 2007, p. 367). That means that if non-use *were* largely explainable via a prudence-based tradition and the morality-based and socially enforced convictions of a taboo were mere accessories, the case for non-use in this explanatory line of thought would be a weaker one. After all, if Paul is right, and societal pressure, stigmatization and moral convictions factor in less, changing material factors might suggest a prudent use of nuclear weapons by tomorrow – and the tradition might find an abrupt end *despite* the fact that it has held for seven decades. Or, in his own words, '[i]f the absolute destructive nature of the weapon changes radically, the reputation costs will decrease and hence the probability will increase for use' (Paul, 2009, p. 26). He backs this up by referring to plans for more '"usable" mininuclear weapons' that might 'erode' the tradition (Paul, 2009, p. 26). Here, Paul uses the same notions as Tannenwald by stating that a tradition can be in danger of 'eroding' or being 'undermined' (Paul, 2009, p. 111), just as she observes with respect to the nuclear taboo. But this does not fit his picture that well, I argue.

Times change, and so do the circumstances for rational decision-making according to Paul. Consequently, traditions can be disrupted or deemed outdated and done away with rather quickly. As Paul (2010, p. 861) concedes, traditions 'are more open to challenge and mutation than taboos'. That is what sets a tradition apart from a taboo conceptually. And for the idea of a tradition of non-use to have any analytical value over the nuclear taboo, it has to be distinguishable from it. But to conceptually grasp processes of 'erosion' and 'undermining', the tradition does not do as good a job as the taboo does, conceptually speaking. After all, if not the taboo but rational considerations of material facts are dominating nuclear decision-making, why is the U.S. dragging its heels and why does it *not* build these undoubtedly very handy mininukes? To explain the strong political inertia against the development of mininukes or to conceptualize a process of erosion, that is, how that peculiar force that keeps decision-makers from using nuclear weapons is indeed only slowly eaten away and *not* just momentarily interrupted, Paul's line of argument appears less convincing than the one provided by the nuclear taboo.

Lastly, Paul attempts to put forward a competing narrative to the nuclear taboo by drawing on many of the same empirical cases that Tannenwald uses. But weaknesses of his argument show especially in the discussion of war initiation cases by nonnuclear versus nuclear states. He deems the '[n]onnuclear initiators...to believe that the nuclear defender is self-deterred through the operation of the tradition' and to 'calculate that the nuclear state would be reluctant to use nuclear weapons, as it would be breaking the global tradition against nuclear use' which 'could involve high reputation costs, especially in terms of world public opinion' (Paul, 2009, p. 144). He continues by asking, 'If there existed neither an explicit legal ban nor a deterrent capability to prevent possible nuclear retaliation, what else could explain the belief among the decision-makers of nonnuclear states that nuclear weapons would not be used against them in their impending conflict' (Paul, 2009, p. 144)? The answer is actually quite simple: the nuclear taboo. For one, Tannenwald's work already documents the influence of the nuclear taboo as an inhibitive factor in such cases (as, for example, the Chinese entering combat against the U.S. in Korea). And in addition, what is more reassuring from a nonnuclear attacker's point of view? A deeply ingrained social taboo that strictly forbids nuclear retaliation *or* the notion that nuclear use might result in bad public relations? In a situation in which a nonnuclear state puts nothing less than its existence on the line, it seems implausible that it should be relying on the latter.

Judging from the amount of first-order critique against the tradition explanation, it appears that building a case against the more coherent and conclusive taboo explanation means building a stronger case overall. Consequently, when formulating my critique in the next subsections, the tradition of non-use thus need not be dealt with separately. For my more general second-order critique at the beginning of Chapter 3, the tradition of non-use and the nuclear taboo are dealt with together as well, because this critique also applies to both. However, I will pick up the difference between the taboo and the tradition later on, proposing in section 3.3.1 how the 'matter of degree' discussion can play a role for empirical analysis. For now, I will stick to the notion of a nuclear taboo and return to seductive developments such as mininukes and the notion of 'erosion'.

2.2.2 Taboo erosion

For dealing with the first problem of the nuclear taboo as an explanation for nuclear non-use, it is worth remembering that over time it brought about both regulative and constitutive effects. Societal pressure and normative convictions of decision-makers gradually raised the inhibition threshold against the use of nuclear weapons. And their categorization as WMD as well as the institutionalization of non-use in the context of non-proliferation eventually constituted their stigmatization.

However, the evolution of norms is not a one-way street. It is a long-standing critique against IR norm research in general that not enough theoretical concern for the possibility of even internalized social norms fading away again was mustered for the longest time. The literature suffered from a progress bias, dealing with norms only in terms of successfully traversing an upward 'spiral' or 'cascading' toward internalization through a 'norm life cycle' (Finnemore/Sikkink, 1998, pp. 895–905; Risse/Sikkink, 1999). But the taken-for-grantedness of even strong and widely internalized norms – such as the prohibition against torture and the use of nuclear weapons – *can* be, and is in fact being, challenged, despite being a cornerstone of the identity of a 'civilized' nation such as the U.S. (McKeown, 2009; Panke/Petersohn, 2012). Perceived threats such as those by so-called rogue states or terrorist networks might eventually 'seduce' decision-makers into reconsidering nuclear use of state arsenals – at the cost of the taboo (Quester, 2006, p. 19; Farrell, 2010, pp. 826–827).

Plans for developing the Robust Nuclear Earth Penetrator (RNEP) are a prominent case in point. The RNEP is a low-yield nuclear weapon – a mininuke – with earth-penetrating capabilities. It is designed to destroy deeply buried and hardened targets and keep the radioactive fallout contained underground, thus allowing it to limbo through right beneath the inhibition threshold of decision-makers – an instrument to 'break the ice' (Quester, 2006, p. 35) and make nuclear weapons usable again. Even though its technical feasibility is debatable and the U.S. Congress denied funding for the RNEP twice during the George W. Bush administration, the possibility for future technical breakthroughs to satisfy the effectiveness criterion, making the weapon usable, is now no less unthinkable than before.

Tannenwald (2007, p. 59) concluded in 2007 that the nuclear taboo – although strong and widely internalized today – is *not yet* a 'fully robust norm' and that it might unravel in processes such as the one surrounding the RNEP. A recent study by Daryl G. Press, Scott D. Sagan and Benjamin A. Valentino (Press et al., 2013) reinforces this concern. They conducted a survey experiment on a representative sample of U.S. citizens to probe the current stance on nuclear-use by the U.S. public. According to their findings, while there is in fact a public aversion against using nuclear weapons, it is only a relatively weak one. In fact, Press, Sagan and Valentino note that 'the U.S. public's preference for nuclear options seems to grow steadily as a function of perceived utility' (Press et al., 2013, pp. 189, 202).

An unrivaled U.S. hegemony and an unchecked mind-set of exceptionalism could not only have U.S. military and political leaders believing they are exempt from the common set of international norms. Rather, U.S. hegemony could also foster horizontal proliferation among states that feel threatened and view nuclear weapons as the only available balancer against U.S. conventional superiority. North Korea and Iran come to mind. The technical effort it takes to build nuclear weapons and their slow proliferation in the past 'bought time' for the taboo to take hold (Tannenwald, 2007, p. 365). But further proliferation of nuclear weapons might put the norm under further pressure on both the U.S. side and on the side of its competitors, especially since accelerating proliferation might carry nuclear weapons into regions where the nuclear taboo is not yet an established rule and might not have the time to become one. Already in 1996, Peter Gizewski (1996, pp. 417–418) wondered in this regard 'whether the norm is up to such challenges'. This points to the second problem with the nuclear taboo.

2.2.3 Taboo limitation

The aforementioned fact that the Polynesian *tapu* does not translate easily into the concept of a *taboo* points to a fundamental caveat. As James Davis (2005, p. 13) puts it, 'most conceptualization takes place within complex preexisting yet evolving symbolic structures and bears no direct, one-to-one correspondence to mind-external phenomena'. So without a socially constructed and shared 'worldview' (Davis) on which a particular notion of 'taboo-ness' rests, there could not even be a common understanding of a certain situation being a case in which deciding between a certain 'wrong' and a certain 'right' is required. In short, social norms are necessarily culturally specific (Tannenwald, 2007, p. 361).

The nuclear taboo profits from the characteristic features of democracies (Tannenwald, 2007, p. 366) since those are said to be characterized by a stronger adherence to human rights and feature a decisive role for public opinion. Consequently, Tannenwald deems 'most Western democracies, with the possible exception of France' even more 'antinuclear' than the United States. Most other countries in the world also 'have forsworn nuclear weapons', which is why Tannenwald concludes that the taboo is shared by 'the vast majority of states' and is thus 'probably not universal' but 'certainly widespread' (Tannenwald, 2007, pp. 23, 59, 377, 381). Illustrative examples, such as the United Kingdom's conduct of the Falkland War support her assumption (Farrell, 2010, pp. 820, fn. 4).

Nevertheless, there are six specific mechanisms on which the nuclear taboo thrives: societal pressure; normative power politics; norm entrepreneurship by state leaders; iterative behavior over time; institutionalization in formal rules and conventions; historical contingency (Farrell, 2010, pp. 823–824). While numerous examples of how such mechanisms play out in the United States – societal pressure, for instance – are documented, it is unlikely that these mechanisms would develop comparably in, say, North Korea or Pakistan (Tannenwald, 2007, pp. 380, 381). So far the U.S. case remains the only thoroughly explored case, and thus, judging from this current state of research, '[t]he fact that the taboo matters in the United States does not necessarily mean that it matters elsewhere' (Tannenwald, 2007, p. 376). As William Walker

(2010, p. 867) critically adds, 'the empirical evidence beyond the US and (perhaps) the Soviet Union is too thin and selective to support a confident generalization'.

By definition, social norms are a regulative mechanism tied to social and cultural context. Their scope is thus necessarily subject to limitations. The nuclear taboo is not exempt from this basic fact. With regard to explaining nuclear non-use, this leaves questions unanswered and, albeit different from those regarding deterrence, doubts are shed on the taboo as a reliable guarantor of non-use as well.

2.2.4 Concluding remarks

Tannenwald presents a powerful and in many ways extremely compelling narrative for how the nuclear taboo caused U.S. nuclear abstinence after 1945. Nevertheless, the nuclear taboo is bound by both time and space. So the norm, even in the case of the United States, might wither away. And there might be cases other than the United States that escape Tannenwald's analysis, cases in which the norm just does not apply in the same fashion.

It is worth emphasizing in connection to this that the nuclear taboo is a concept based on the nomothetically weak foundations of social constructivist norm theory; hence, these limitations are practically innate and not to blame on Tannenwald's work. She is aware of these issues and deals with them in a reflective manner. That said, an additional critical remark could be raised with regard to the methodology of Tannenwald's book.

In her historical analysis she traces the development of the taboo 'through a set of decisionmaking studies and a broader process-tracing narrative' (Tannenwald, 2007, p. 17). By investigating the explicit references to the norm suspected in play – or what Tannenwald (2007, pp. 51, 55) calls 'taboo-talk' – she demonstrates empirically the shifting burden of proof regarding the employment of nuclear weapons and does so across a variety of different sources (Tannenwald, 2007, pp. 23–24). Yet, some questions remain unanswered or are not addressed as systematically or transparently as they could be. How is the burden of proof operationalized as a 'useful measuring device' to indicate 'where the normative presumptions in a discourse lie' (Tannenwald, 2007, p. 52), and why is there no explicit concept of 'discourse'? What were the source selection criteria? Why is the research process not more transparent regarding, for instance, negative instances in the material? In other words, how were findings contradicting the taboo hypothesis (or ones consistent with competing explanations) dealt with? Tannenwald's overall compelling case would have been even stronger, in my mind, if these considerations had been included and reflected upon more systematically in the book's chapter on research design and method. I suspect, however, that some of these characteristics are owed to the particular type of research style Tannenwald chose to apply. This points beyond what has so far been laid out in terms of critical remarks. In the next chapter I will focus on this notion and flesh out a more general critique applying to *both* existing explanations of non-use.

3
Understanding Nuclear Non-Use

Chapter 2 surveyed the existing body of research on nuclear non-use. On the one hand there is the notion of nuclear deterrence, with the rational theory of nuclear deterrence at its center and deterrence strategy as the theory's translation into practice. On the other hand there is the nuclear taboo. Both lines of thought approach their subject matter by trying to explain it. However, rational deterrence theory is plagued by its paradoxical conceptual core. And its awkward translation into practice leaves a bad aftertaste, raising severe doubts about the applicability and ultimately also the vast explanatory power to which nuclear deterrence lays claim. And the nuclear taboo, while making a strong case regarding U.S. nuclear non-use since 1945, leaves open the question of whether other cases of non-use can also be explained by it. Furthermore, it is unclear whether and how its explanatory power will stand the test of time.

This current state of knowledge is thus not entirely satisfying. Considering the deficiencies of deterrence theory and the nuclear taboo, and the open questions that remain, it is fair to say that there is still plenty to try to comprehend about 'the single most important phenomenon of the nuclear age' (Tannenwald, 2007, p. 1). In other words, the question still persists concerning what explains the continual non-use of nuclear weapons after 1945, and how can we better understand (the causes of) this abstinence.

3.1 Explanatory synthesis?

One possible avenue to go down from here is to aim for a *synthesis* of deterrence theory and the concept of the nuclear taboo. Attempting to conceptually synthesize the two existing explanations is not a far-fetched idea. In fact, it represents an important element of the current debate about the next step of explanatory research on nuclear non-use.

While Nina Tannenwald treated the relation between deterrence theory and the nuclear taboo as almost mutually exclusive in her earlier writings (Tannenwald, 1999, p. 433), she later saw the two concepts embedded in a larger 'complex interrelationship' (Tannenwald, 2007, p. 19), with the taboo 'helping to stabilize the practice of deterrence itself', the taboo-explanation thus analytically 'illuminating the normative and institutional bases of deterrence' (Tannenwald, 2007, p. 71). The argument there is that the non-use norm's coagulation in formal agreements and institutions (the Moscow-Washington hotline and Permissive Action Links come to mind) buttressed the day-to-day practice of negative control over nuclear arsenals and deterrence as a strategy, thus helping create the pattern we observe today as the 'politics of non-use' (Tannenwald, 2007, pp. 19, 36, 53–54, 71–72, 371; cf. Morgan, 2011, p. 151). Hence there is the idea to combine the two concepts analytically as well as an attempt to produce a better or more sufficient explanation, since 'any sufficient explanation must synthesize material and normative factors' (Tannenwald, 2007, p. 53). 'Thus the question [...] is not one "norms" *vs.* "deterrence", but rather one of norms *and* deterrence – that is how norms are part of the practice of deterrence itself' (Tannenwald, 2007, pp. 19, original emphasis).

On the other side of the aisle, deterrence theorists such as Lawrence Freedman (2005, p. 791) are open to conviction, pointing out that a norms-based approach on deterrence 'may better reflect how deterrence actually works in practice' (Freedman, 2004, pp. 5, 60–74; Tannenwald, 2007, p. 36). Patrick Morgan (2005, pp. 751–752) concurs and deems synthesis 'a stimulating notion because it blends two concepts one might otherwise consider antithetical, internalized norms and internalized deterrence'.

So an interesting case seemingly awaits its making: deterrence and the nuclear taboo not only interact with each other in practice but this interaction is also in fact a 'stabilizing' or 'positive' one for nuclear non-use. After all, from a deterrer's perspective, it comes close to a best-case situation if the deterree over time internalizes deterrence as a norm-based conviction that executing a first strike is simply out of the question. A conceptual synthesis might explain this process more comprehensively. Even the differences between the two concepts' theoretical backgrounds might not be a hindrance, as growing numbers of IR scholars are now deeming 'paradigm incommensurability' outdated and 'synthesis' in IR theory in general both feasible and desirable.[1]

I would add that synthesis optimism is fueled further when considering the research logic the two existing explanations share (more on that soon). Both base their claims on 'explanatory factors', on distinct 'causes of non-use' – one material, one normative. With each one explaining the phenomenon quite well already on its own, the two of them together will likely produce a clearer and more comprehensive picture.

So far this notion of synthetic compatibility has not met much objection, save for the questions marks that William Walker raised most pointedly: 'It seems self-evident that a principal goal of policy should be to strengthen, worldwide, inhibitions on the use of nuclear weapons. Yet this goal, if too successfully pursued, is inimical to nuclear deterrence' (Walker, 2010, p. 875; cf. Rosenbaum, 2011, p. 255; similar: Perkovich, 2009, p. 11). This suggests that, at a policy level, deterrence and taboo might actually work at cross-purposes. After all, deterrence is a two-way street, and practicing deterrence requires constantly thinking about what is declared *un*thinkable by the nuclear taboo. In that sense deterrence actually 'relies upon [the taboo's] constant denial' (Walker, 2012, p. 82).

These considerations clearly complicate things at the conceptual level, too. If the relation between deterrence and the nuclear taboo is in fact not as cut and dried as 'one stabilizing the other', a plausible conceptual synthesis might be harder to come by. In any case, it is now more questionable that a 'sufficient explanation' is feasible by simply combining 'material and normative factors' (Tannenwald, 2007, p. 53). Things could well be much more complicated than that.

Nevertheless, both lines of thought have some plausibility. Definitively choosing one over the other would be premature at this stage. So, with an eye on the second part of my research question – how to better understand the causes of abstinence – I will keep the notion of synthesis, especially 'how norms are part of the *practice* of deterrence' (Tannenwald) and how 'deterrence actually works *in practice*' (Freedman),[2] firmly in mind. But I will discuss it in more detail only later, in light of empirical results in Chapter 4. Also, since my critique challenges the current state of research in a different, more fundamental sense – as the upcoming section will highlight – the question of synthesis can be put on the back burner.

3.2 Explaining non-events

I will now review deterrence theory and the taboo one more time, this time with a specific focus on their attempt to *explain* nuclear non-use. This closer look at the theoretical and methodological groundings of the two explanations and their respective history of development confirms that there exists a methodological misfit between them and their subject matter.

3.2.1 Nuclear deterrence, one more time

Deterrence started out as a practical, policy-oriented enterprise. The interest of first-wave deterrence scholars like Bernard Brodie (1946a) was to prevent a potentially cataclysmic use of nuclear weapons against the U.S. Since the new weapon had removed the element of defense from the equation, resorting to deterrence to forestall this danger seemed like the next best alternative. After all, threatening retaliation to manipulate an opponent's behavior is a very basic, instinctive notion (Freedman, 2004, pp. 6–7). It panned out particularly well at the time because the dominant intellectual paradigm for dealing with questions of international relations – such as deterrence – was Realism.

There was an alternative position. The 'nuclear one worlders' considered the more sustainable and less dangerous answer a 'world government of some sort' (Deudney, 1995, p. 89; cf. Walker, 2012, pp. 2, 41–42). Yet, this was utterly incompatible with Realist political *zeitgeist*. 'Remorselessly dissected' (Boyer, 1994 [1985], pp. 43–44) in public by influential Realist thinkers such as Reinhold Niebuhr, the idea of putting nuclear weapons under international control faded into the background, and the deterrence idea became accepted as 'the next best bet' (Morgan, 1977, p. 11).

The experience of World War II and the writings of Realist IR scholars such as Hans Morgenthau had converted Realism into 'a popular and fully articulated interpretation of world politics, everywhere and any time' (Rothstein, 1972, p. 349; cf. Guzzini, 2004). And not only because Realism 'paints a rather grim picture of world politics' (Mearsheimer, 1995, p. 9) could the idea of a deterrence theory be cast in Realist vocabulary so nicely. It also provided the quasi-mechanical notions of balance, action, reaction, cause and effect. States, power, anarchy, uncertainty, constant threats and the qualitative and quantitative balance of military forces, it was all there. Deterrence made perfect sense in a Realist post–World War II world of competition and mistrust in which even 'today's friend may be tomorrow's enemy' (Grieco, 1988, p. 487). In short, 'because most American scholars accepted Realism, it is not surprising that they found deterrence theory congenial' (Jervis, 1979, p. 289).

Deterrence also catered to the theorists' claim to advise decision-makers. The abetting factor was that Realism was the accepted paradigm among practitioners as well. It 'encapsulated what they took for granted... especially during the height of the cold war' (Rothstein, 1972,

p. 348; cf. Hollis/Smith, 1991, pp. 27–28). In the Realist narrative of international politics as a 'great drama in which wise statesmen made "hard choices"' (Rothstein, 1972, p. 351), nuclear weapons and deterrence provided the greatest drama and hardest choices of all. So deterrence held the theoretical and practical answers for dealing with the nuclear question in a world in which Realist orthodoxy was already practiced as *Realpolitik* (similar: Hellmann, 2010, p. 161; Campbell, 1992, pp. 20–21, 31). In this chicken-and-egg-situation, politicians who already thought in Realist categories such as the balance of power were introduced to notions like the 'strategic balance' by Realist deterrence theorists. These ideas not only felt intimately related. For some practitioners it was 'all the same thing' (Kull, 1988, p. 49; cf. Jervis, 1979, p. 290; Guzzini, 2004, p. 555) – the perfect kick-off for a self-fulfilling prophecy (similar: Jervis, 1984, p. 40).

Early 20th-century Realist thinkers such as Morgenthau and E.H. Carr are usually said to be among the first scholars advocating objective and scientific thinking about international relations (Hollis/Smith, 1991, pp. 20–28, 45). They did so in opposition to what they themselves deemed the 'utopist' or 'alchemist' (Carr, 2001 [1939], p. 8) follies of Idealism. While Carr and Morgenthau declared their writings a quest for the discovery of the 'objective laws' of politics (Morgenthau, 2005 [1948], p. 4; cf. Carr, 2001 [1939], p. 10), their Realism was actually steeped in questions of morality, heavily reliant on the elusive notion of individual 'prudence' and neither theoretically nor methodologically conformed to the ideal of objectivity and science (understood as natural science). Especially 'Morgenthau's theory is best viewed as a manual for state leaders' (Wight, 2002, p. 28; cf. Guzzini, 2004, pp. 546–548; Oren, 2009, pp. 290–291; Jackson, 2011, pp. 4–5). So both he and Carr actually stood for an interpretive and practically oriented tradition of classical thinking.

Behavioralists wanted to shed this classical heritage to make the discipline as theoretically and methodically scientific as the natural sciences by importing 'positivism' from the philosophy of science (Bull, 1966; Kaplan, 1966; cf. Hollis/Smith, 1991, pp. 28–32, 98–99; Wight, 2002, pp. 28, 30). The second wave of deterrence theory was strongly influenced by this approach. Enter Kenneth Waltz. His 'Neo-Realist' critique of Behavioralism as 'reductionist' (Waltz, 1979) was the prominent, resounding Realist answer – with lasting effect (Wæver, 2009, pp. 214–216).[3] Many deterrence theorists embraced his 'structural realism' as fervently as the rest of IR did. And while Waltz at first did not take nuclear weapons to have any profound effect on what he identified as the 'perennial forces of politics', considering them as merely another element of a nation's power capabilities (Waltz, 1979, pp. 173, 180–181), he quickly became an influential author on deterrence theory himself with his *Adelphi Paper* (1981) on why 'more' nuclear proliferation 'may be better' – and he revised his stance on the impact of nuclear weapons further and further over time.[4] He ended up stating that the sum of all his theoretical work 'has been an attempt to theoretically deal with the implications of the invention and application of nuclear weapons' (Waltz, 2011).

The majority of IR scholars misread Waltz's *Theory of International Politics* – deterrence scholars no exception – and embedded Waltz's Realism in the existing positivist scheme of thought in IR and its 'if-then' propositions (Jackson, 2011, p. 113), even though Waltz never was a positivist (Jackson, 2011, p. 205; Wæver, 2009). This misunderstanding reached textbook status. Jack Donnelly's (2000, p. 30) *Realism and International Relations,* for example, described Waltz as 'the key figure [...] of a new generation of scholars who sought to establish realism on the foundations of positivist social science'. Of course, some deterrence theorists remained classical in their thinking. Colin S. Gray (1999b, p. 61), for instance, remained famously skeptical about Waltz's 'rigorous semi-nonsense' that treated 'actors in world security politics largely as if they were black boxes'.

Nevertheless, the irony is that not *because* but *despite* Waltz's influential writings on both IR theory and deterrence, the overall majority of deterrence theory literature became wedded to Realism *and* positivism (Williams, 1992, pp. 69–70) within the rationalist (Fearon/Wendt, 2002, pp. 54–56, 59) framework of IR, thus fueling the transition of deterrence from a practical enterprise to a general scientific explanation of nuclear non-use.

Waltz (1979, pp. 8–9), for instance, unequivocally states that a theory cannot be compared to reality. Hypothesis can be falsified. But theories cannot. According to him, theories cannot be proven 'untrue' empirically. They can only be overthrown by a better theory, that is, a better 'picture, mentally formed, of a bounded realm or domain of activity', one that is 'useful' in explaining and predicting what goes on in this isolated realm (Waltz, 1979, p. 8). Strangely, however, mainstream (U.S.) deterrence theorists, almost all of them card-carrying Realists and positivists, were all about pitting theories against each other. Testing competing theories in empirical case comparisons or large-n studies was their bread and butter, the idea being that there is a mind-independent reality out there to test against, and that theories, such as deterrence, 'develop as people test them and examine their internal dynamics and causal linkages' (Jervis, 1979, p. 301).

For deterrence theory this meant an emphasis on the impact of (anarchic system) structure on agency ('akin to a field of forces in physics' [Waltz, 1979, p. 73], a notion Waltz [1986, pp. 343–344] would later question himself), parsimony, and especially yet another insistence on objectivity. In this last regard, deterrence research came to be based on material variables and testing hypotheses that, 'if confirmed quite conclusively, [...] are called laws', following the contorted yet canonized reading of Waltz's notion of theory (1979, pp. 7–8; cf. Hollis/Smith, 1991, pp. 50–55; Fearon/Wendt, 2002, p. 59; Wæver, 2009, pp. 205, 211).

Rationality, too, was dealt with in an odd fashion in deterrence research. While Waltz was clear about his ideas about theory, his microeconomically informed take on rationality was anything but straightforward. Whereas he did not make it a core assumption for his Neo-Realist theory at the beginning, he later admitted that the cost sensitivity of units (states) had at least been an implicit starting point, 'which for convenience can be called an assumption of rationality' (Waltz, 1986, p. 331). But he also stressed explicitly that deterrence does *not* depend on rationality in any way because common sense and the supreme survival interest of states suffices for it to take effect (Waltz, 1981, p. 21; 2003b, p. 154). Yet, like Thomas Schelling and earlier deterrence scholars, who had simply assumed actor rationality for the sake of devising escalation models, deterrence theory largely abided by the assumption of rational expected-utility maximization in unitary actors (see e.g. Huth/Russett, 1984, pp. 498–499; cf. Morgan, 2003, pp. 119–120) – which made deterrence theory's inner contradictions such as the 'rationality of irrationality' only more awkward.

I will return to why Waltz's writings were influential for and at the same time quite out of tune with mainstream deterrence theory in subsection 4.3.2, delving deeper into the rationality assumption. For now, it seems clear that Realism's scientific turn did not help deterrence theory. Rather, the pursuit of a scientific seal of approval hurt it. With the two terms positivism and science practically interchangeable (Wight, 2002, pp. 25, 30), couching deterrence in the scientific framework of (the new) Realism meant it was no longer just a practical question of coming up with successful nuclear policies. Rather, with the Cold War continuing, there arose 'the impetus for elevating deterrence as a practice into an elaborate strategy and generating an elaborate theory to go with it' (Morgan, 2011, p. 150). Creating this elaborate, 'scientific' theory meant 'quantification, formal models, and general propositions' (Jackson, 2011, p. 6). As Patrick Morgan (2003, pp. 116, original emphasis) confirms, 'Deterrence theory developed in line with social *science* [...]. Hence it was subjected to three broad efforts at instilling positivist rigor: the assumption of rationality, quantitative empirical studies, and detailed case studies'.

The rational theory of deterrence had to be validated as a properly scientific explanation, with hypotheses (statistically, rigorously) tested against an independent reality, over as many cases as possible, hopefully resulting in the confirmation of a general law of cause and effect.[5] In this particular reading of a scientific approach, deterrence theory was now the Realist *explanation* for nuclear non-use: 'Rational deterrence theory, associated with the "neorealist" perspective in international relations, claimed to provide both a general explanation for the US-Soviet nuclear standoff and a set of guidelines for putting deterrence into practice' (Tannenwald, 2007, p. 31).

To take the step from mere statecraft to science, instilling positivist rigor into a research design requires empirical 'data' to be *subsumed* under the predetermined template deterrence in order to isolate the explanatory 'variable' and to 'prove' deterrence to indeed be the cause of nuclear non-use. The problem in this particular case of something *not* taking place is, of course, that there is no tangible empirical 'evidence' produced to reliably establish the link between cause and effect. Well aware of that fact, deterrence literature generally tends to argue that 'absence of evidence is not evidence of absence'. Can this matter be brushed aside so easily?

The positivist-subsumptionist notion of deterrence as a variable causing an effect in objective reality faces a serious question: when a causal chain cannot be completed because at its supposed end point there is nothing but an elusive non-event, no clearly visible effect, no place at which to definitively pinpoint the cause to have successfully run its course, how can an inference about the causal relation between deterrence and non-use ever be reliably established? Strictly speaking, the empirical void renders impossible any attempt to falsify (or verify, for that matter) the proposition 'if deterrence, then non-use'. In other words, when rigorously (mercilessly?) judging deterrence theory against its own positivist benchmark, it falls flat. As Gary King, Robert Keohane and Sidney Verba, whose seminal book *Designing Social Inquiry* (1994, pp. 24, see also 134–135) represents the 'ur text for how to do social science' (Mearsheimer/Walt, 2013) in the positivist tradition, concede, '[S]ufficient good data on deterrence in international politics is lacking'. In light of this it is less surprising that literature on deterrence theory in general can be described as 'more than ample, [while] the results are uneven and satisfaction is underwhelming' (Morgan, 2003, p. 116).

I am by no means the first one to point this out (see, for example, Morgan, 1977, p. 23; Freedman, 2004, p. 29). That with 'no empirical reference points and data banks, it cannot be falsified' was grounds enough for Emanuel Adler (1992, p. 107) to call the entire 'science of nuclear strategy [...] imaginary'. Michael Rühle (2009, pp. 10, original emphasis) also admits: '[S]ince one can never prove for certain why an event has *not* occurred, the war-preventing function of nuclear weapons remains, strictly speaking, a mere assumption'. Bruno Tertrais (2011, p. 9) is even more straightforward in conceding that '[i]t is by definition impossible to prove that deterrence has worked, and correlation is not causality'. But deterrence theorists conceding this point while at the same time trying to uphold the claim that their theory is scientific in a positivist sense means wanting it both ways (and sure enough Tertrais [2011, pp. 9–13] continues unimpressed by his own declaration by referring to 'quantitative studies' and 'test cases' while scrambling for 'evidence', pronouncing 'alternative explanations' as 'not satisfying'). But I contend that for positivist deterrence scholars, keeping an unprovable yet supposedly still scientific theory is a clear case of having your cake and eating it too (similar: Oren, 2009, p. 290).

It now also becomes clear that, with no validation outside the level of theoretical reasoning to empirically back the assumption that deterrence is in fact the cause for why something did *not* happen, large parts of deterrence theory not only preferred but literally *had* to stay abstract and self-referential. It stayed confined to contests about 'the nature and meaning of the concepts that comprise nuclear strategy' (Williams, 1992, p. 71) at the level of analytical logic, mathematical equations and computer models. But with leading theorists repeatedly changing their viewpoints (Jervis, 1984, pp. 52–54), for example, with regard to the merits of the violence escalation model, no sort of agreement could be reached. The question of which of the two deterrence models presented above was logically sound and which one was flawed remained unresolved and a constant bone of contention. 'Thinking about the logic of strategy and deterrence has thus come to resemble a closed circle. No sooner has the question been resolved by one form of analysis than it is claimed to be resolved in a completely contradictory way by another. [...] Rather than being characterized by the sort of clarity central to analytic-empiricism, [deterrence theory] is dominated by acrimony, dispute, and division' (Williams, 1992, p. 78).

So, even while deterrence was practically implemented as advocated by the early scholars, no real empirical 'evidence' could later be gleaned from practice. Hence it was (and is), strictly speaking, *impossible* to validate in the so-called scientific sense the assertion that deterrence works: 'One of the great ironies of contemporary strategic relations is that a field which champions its own "realist" heritage should find itself, in the postwar era, so devoid of observable and empirically verifiable material regarding the operational utility of nuclear deterrence' (Klein, 1994, p. 29, cf. 75; cf. Jervis, 1984, p. 38).

Unlike the 'nuclear one worlders' who critically and fundamentally called the relationships of states and institutions into question during the dawning nuclear age, aiming at a transformation, deterrence scholars, equipped with a Realist worldview, approached theorizing deterrence as a mere 'problem-solving' enterprise (Cox, 1981, pp. 128–130). And by trying to transform deterrence from statecraft into a generally valid (yet unprovable) explanation for nuclear non-use, the Realist/positivist enterprise exposed the theory's inherent and insoluble paradox as well as its awkward translation into practice. Deterrence is thus a prime example for the failed attempt of Realist scholars to 'translate the practical rules or maxims of European diplomacy into the scientific laws of a US social science' (Guzzini, 2004, pp. 546, see also 554–558). It is in this sense that the attempt to *explain* nuclear non-use via a scientific theory of deterrence underlies the two problems outlined in Chapter 2. Reexamining the nuclear taboo will allow me to clarify the problem with explaining non-events further.

3.2.2 Nuclear taboo, one more time

By lowering some of the un-Realistic theoretical standards, the nuclear taboo tries to avoid the fate of 'scientificated' rational deterrence theory. Nevertheless, a comparable case can be made.

First, there are important differences to note. The taboo implies a different stance on questions of materialism, rationality and even causality. As a typical example for middle-ground norm constructivism (Adler, 1997; Wendt, 1992; 1999; critical: Patomäki/Wight, 2000, pp. 214–215), the nuclear taboo is based upon ontological assumptions different from those of deterrence theory, allowing for immaterial norms and relational identities to be taken into account. Both shape the behavior of actors through constitutive and regulative effects, in line with Peter Katzenstein's (1996, p. 5) standard definition of norms as 'collective expectations for the proper behavior of actors with a given identity'. Accordingly, it bears repeating that Tannenwald argues in a two-track fashion of both causal and constitutive logic. The stigmatization of nuclear weapons as WMDs is, for example, a constitutive process (Tannenwald, 2007, pp. 368, 371).

Second, however, the regulative effect of the taboo norm is clearly the decisive element in inhibiting the use of nuclear weapons. Alexander Wendt (1999, p. 82; programmatically also Finnemore/Sikkink, 1998), on whose seminal writings the norm-based approach of the nuclear taboo rests, sums up the role of social interaction, norms and identities as follows: 'All of these phenomena involve rules and self-understandings ("ideas"), but this does not preclude their having causal effects [...] Norms are causal insofar as they regulate behavior'. So eventually, in a nomothetically weaker fashion but not unlike deterrence theory, the gist of Tannenwald's take on the nuclear taboo is that she bases an explanatory claim on the logic of a causal mechanism, with a normative structure as the *explanans* and nuclear non-use as the *explanandum* (see especially Tannenwald, 2005a).

While trading the logically flawed yet sweeping theory of deterrence and its unclear translation into practice for a logically more consistent concept of overall smaller, spatial and temporal scope, Tannenwald ends up, conceptually speaking, with a less convoluted and much more coherent explanation of nuclear non-use on the one hand. But on the other hand she adopts a common practice of constructivist mainstream research. First, while assuming agents and structures to be co-constitutive, norms, especially internalized ones, are treated akin to a structure. Then, while replacing the logic of consequentialism with the logic of appropriateness, she proceeds (as does T.V. Paul [2009, p. 23] who stresses the 'casual linkage' behind the tradition of non-use) in a mode of positivism and subsumption (on the structural bias in the logic of appropriateness itself, see Sending, 2002). The agent's behavior, observed in mind-independent reality out there, is subsumed under the social 'norm structure', which is deemed to cause specific ('appropriate') outcomes in agency, in this case a political decision-making process with the effect of non-use at its end. Equipped with this vocabulary and the overly hygienic research logic of this approach, it is not surprising that sources or irritating 'evidence' refuting or not corresponding with the taboo hypothesis are largely ignored, as I already alluded to in the short discussion of Tannenwald's method and research design at the end of the last chapter.

Tannenwald is well aware of the absence-of-evidence trap. Consequently, she (2007, pp. 6, 29) is quick to add that 'causes of "non-events" are notoriously difficult to pin down', thus posing 'special challenges for analysis'. And she unequivocally states, 'In reality, there is no such thing as explaining a non-event. Any such perception arises simply from our theoretical predispositions, which affect how we frame the issue' (Tannenwald, 2007, p. 30).

However, by ascribing causal effects to social norms and subscribing to the idea of discovering a cause for a non-event, the taboo adopts the same problematic research logic as positivist deterrence research. Tannenwald draws on *Designing Social Inquiry* (1994) as a methodological reference and on 'process tracing' to produce a 'coherent account of causality [that] specif[ies] how its effects are exerted' (King et al., 1994, pp. 85–86), and speaks of 'causal factors' and 'mechanisms', 'causal arrows', of use and non-use as 'dependent variables', of the taboo's 'autonomous effect', of 'measurements', of a 'competitive test' between materialist and normative explanations as well as of empirical sources as 'evidence' (Tannenwald, 2007, pp. 4, 7, 17–18, 47, 51–52, 69 [fn. 119]). This is certainly in line with Wendt's mainstream-friendly version of constructivism (Kratochwil, 2006), but to restate and deliberately stress the point somewhat for the sake of the argument: a non-event means that there exists no palpable effect, and thus, strictly speaking, it makes no sense to deduce the existence of a preceding cause to which one could trace a causal path back. Insisting, however, on the applicability of a logic of causality despite the 'special challenges', Tannenwald points to 'the dog that did not bark' in the famous Sherlock Holmes story *Silver Blaze* to highlight the importance of non-events for causal reasoning – because the dog did not bark, Holmes concluded that the dog knew the perpetrator, thus allowing the detective to reliably identify the latter by a process of elimination. Referring, in addition, to an article by James Fearon (1991) that probes the possibility of reconciling a causal research logic via 'hypothesis testing' with the study of non-events, Tannenwald (2007, p. 30) declares that what is actually studied and 'explained is a contrast between an actual event and a possible alternative or counterfactual event'. Fearon (1991, p. 170), it is worth noting, does not give 'a firm answer' to the question of whether a 'counterfactual argument [is] a viable means of assessing causal hypotheses'. But positivist research has dealt with events, such as war (Ripsman/Levy, 2007), not occurring in other contexts as well, and scholars (Mahoney/Goertz, 2004) put further thought into how to best deal with what they call 'negative cases' in positivist, variable-based research. Thus, is the absence-of-evidence trap really not that big of a problem?

Tannenwald states that what a positivist researcher studies about a non-event is the 'contrast between an actual event', that is, the non-use of nuclear weapons by relying on 'conventional munitions (or diplomacy)', 'and a possible alternative or counterfactual event', that is, the use of nuclear weapons which is plausibly assumed as just as well likely in that same situation (Tannenwald, 2007, p. 30). An (empirically derived and substantiated) thought experiment about a counterfactual event does not strike me as the primary problem here, even though it is irritating that an explicitly fictional event is ascribed a decisive a role in a research logic that usually touts to base its arguments on (and to 'test hypotheses' against) a measurable, 'objective reality out there', the 'real' reality that is, with actual cases and dependent variables, not imagined ones, which actually *does* create discomfort for positivist scholars, at least according to Fearon (1991, p. 173) and is reason enough for King, Keohane and Verba (1994, p. 25) to explicitly advise not to let 'unobserved or unmeasurable concepts get in the way' and strictly '[adhere] to the data' (which in this case, of course, does not exist and thus needs to be created counterfactually). Be all that as it may, the bigger problem with regard to nuclear non-use is that with non-events such as the one at hand, the one, clear-cut and measurable *actual* event seldom (if ever) exists. According to Tannenwald, the actual event is to represent the non-event ('non-use') as a sort of stand-in to be contrasted with the counterfactual event ('use'). Therefore, what research on the phenomenon of nuclear non-use is interested in, and what both existing explanations actually aim to base their claims on, is measurable, traceable 'evidence' in social reality, in which one of these two options manifests in a clearly recognizable way. But unfortunately, while the use of nuclear weapons *does* leave unmistakable traces, non-use is much less prone to do so. It is thus, and I am overstating this again to get the point across, highly unlikely that anyone will ever come up with a state leader's announcement, stating unequivocally and on the record that 'now is the moment my country X decides not to use nuclear weapons and turn to other means such as conventional munitions because it is *deterred* and/or because it finds that course of action to be *taboo*'.

Consequently, the 'actual events' that positivist scholars are forced to interpret, isolate and utilize as plausible stand-ins are always prone to a fair amount of second-guessing. In other words, the 'data' collected is not 'reliable' in a strictly positivist sense. While one scholar might find Tannenwald's selection and interpretation of 'actual events' plausibly functioning as proxies, another one might less so, a third one not at all. That in itself does not have to be a problem, at least from my scholarly perspective, as will get clearer when I present my alternative methodology further below. However, it *is* a problem when the positivist benchmark is taken seriously. Because according to positivists, reliability means that 'applying the same procedure in the same way will always produce the same measure' independent of time and of which researcher is doing the measurement, as King, Keohane and Verba (1994, pp. 25–26) explain. And this is clearly not the case here.

A reasonable step in reaction to all this, one that helps mitigate the problem of objectionable interpretive wiggle room remaining where crystal clear 'evidence' *should* be, is to amass numerous cases. With enough pertinent incidents compiled, an argument for upholding the suggested causal mechanism can be made in light of a now stronger empirical base, moderating the logical and methodological issues involved. This is, in fact, routinely done, not only in taboo research. And all these procedures are reasonable, at least within the confines of research that keeps insisting on causality. They can, however, not be called immaculate when judged against the quality criteria to which Tannenwald herself refers, namely those for conducting positivist research.

In sum, it is without too much exaggeration fair to say that the taboo's positivist research design – by that latter's very nature and its adherence to reliable measurements, empirical evidence and causality chains with causes and effects – remains in quite a pickle when analyzing nuclear non-use.

Judged against IR's history of development (and the significance of strategically labeling research in IR), Tannenwald makes a clever move by situating her constructivist research on social norms within the accepted epistemological framework of the discipline. Analyzing nuclear non-use equipped with the nuclear taboo differs from a deterrence perspective by allowing a widened ontological commitment, including the recognition of immaterial norms and relational identities. Yet, it is at the same time not too far out and sticks to the notion of a mind-independent, objective reality against which the 'testing' of hypotheses is possible in a mode of pure subsumption under a preformed template. The newly identified 'cause' thus cannot be easily ignored by peer scholars (and since positivist deterrence scholars are faced with the same, awkward absence-of-evidence trap, my observation is that few of them are making a big fuss about it). The nuclear taboo has thus been 'discovered' and 'proven' while adhering to the same, widely approved standards of research with which deterrence scholars work. The downside is, of course, that despite its comparatively innovative theoretical argument, the taboo is ultimately unable to avoid the methodological trap into which deterrence theory already fell. This is why it is fair to say that, despite all their efforts, both existing explanations of non-use suffer from a misfit between themselves and their subject matter. So what is the alternative?

3.3 Understanding non-events

Since there is 'no such thing as explaining a non-event', and 'theoretical predispositions' are 'affect[ing] how we frame the issue' (Tannenwald, 2007, p. 30), a change of theoretical dispositions might have certain benefits, such as avoiding the absence-of-evidence trap. But developing an alternative perspective has to avoid the mistake of dismissing existing knowledge lock, stock and barrel. After all, even while knocking down its own positivist bar, existing research has yielded a rich and multifaceted body of literature on nuclear non-use by amassing so many 'cases' in the effort to remedy the absence of evidence.

But by focusing on the employment of templates that 'prove' the existence of preconceived causal chains over numerous cases in a big-picture effort, explanatory research also developed very similar *blind spots* regarding the actual, small instances in which abstinence comes about in nuclear decision-making, the *practice* of nuclear non-use, with all its complexities, intricacies and sometimes inconsistencies involved. These blind spots are why the effort to develop more or less wide-ranging general explanations can carry only so far. They resemble fishing nets cast widely over the empirical phenomenon in a top-down move, with an important aspect of the elusive non-event, namely *how it is actually coming into the world through agency*, slipping through the mesh. This is why, when scrutinizing practice more closely, deterrence and the taboo leave us with some question marks and puzzles – from the open question of their interaction, to deterrence failure, to the taboo either not applying or eroding. In short, I argue that 'we *still* lack' in '*understanding* [...] *how* this tradition [of non-use] arose and is maintained' (Tannenwald, 2007, p. 1) in practice.

This is the research gap my alternative perspective focuses on. And instead of narrowing the empirical inquiry down right from the start in another attempt to only subsume material under a preconceived and to-be-validated explanatory template, a promising start is to dial down the positivist research logic and the insistence on causality and explanation, to step back, reopen the inquiry and embrace the complexity of the phenomenon – while keeping the existing knowledge in mind. The goal of this approach is twofold, namely to arrive at additional insights about existing explanations as well as at ideas for new notions to emerge from *within* the empirical study of practice, from the bottom up so to speak. In other words, the goal is to mix elements of subsumption derived from existing knowledge with an overall *reconstructive* inquiry. This change in perspective satisfies the need to *understand* nuclear non-use by diving into its *meaning* for decision-makers.

Making the distinction between explaining and understanding is bound to evoke Martin Hollis and Steve Smith's (1991, pp. 1, 6–7) old and famous dictum about 'two stories to tell' in IR: explaining, as seen above, from an outsider's perspective by deducing hypotheses and identifying (generalizable) causal laws – the result being a story geared to natural sciences or economics, versus understanding from an insider's perspective by tracing social meaning interpretively – the result being a story geared toward history. Hollis and Smith go so far as to suggest that these two are incommensurable (Hollis/Smith, 1991, pp. 210–216; cf. Jackson, 2011, pp. 9, 28–30). And while there is 'a lively tension' (Hollis/Smith, 1991, p. 1) between them, the stern epistemological divide between either a positivist effort to isolate *causes* or a hermeneutic effort to make sense of *reasons* is quite an artificial one (Kurki, 2006, p. 202; Wendt, 1999, p. 82; Wight, 2002, p. 38).

In my mind, there is no paradigm war to be fought here. I do not see explanations and understandings of the same social phenomenon in a zero-sum relationship. Rather, they can inform and complement each other. Understanding how nuclear non-use comes about in decision-making practice thus allows for employing, complementing and refining existing knowledge derived from thinking about nuclear non-use in an explanatory way – and vice versa. So while I turn away from positivism and causality, the idea here is dialectics, not dualism. I will now explain how to retain key elements of existing knowledge and employ them – subsumptively – in a reconstructive research process.

3.3.1 Methodology: making sense of abstinence

I will argue below that understanding a non-event requires an analytical focus on meaning, language and agency by prioritizing reconstruction over subsumption. I will first present this methodology and the assumptions underlying it, clarifying how it differs from hitherto approaches. I will then discuss how I reconceptualize the existing explanations to include them as subsumptive elements in a reconstructive analysis. Lastly, I present my research method, a mix of deductive and inductive software-aided coding.

Understanding and reconstruction

My first assumption is that natural phenomena are not the same as nor can easily be likened to social phenomena. A city could get hit by a hurricane or an atomic bomb. Would the weather be deemed 'responsible' in the same way an attacker with a nuclear weapon would be? No. Therefore, it seems there are good reasons to assume that '[i]nternational affairs are at least less independent of what human beings believe about them than are the shifts of weather' (Hollis/Smith, 1991, p. 68; cf. Friedrichs/Kratochwil, 2009, p. 704; Oren, 2009, p. 289). Social reality is generated by reasoning agents – humans – and this reality is thus dependent on the beliefs we hold about it because we are 'meaning-making creatures' (Yanow, 2006b, p. 9). And since 'subsumption under a covering law does not explain anything' and successful subsumption 'simply states regularity' (Guzzini/Leander, 2006, p. 81), a regular social phenomenon is only 'explained' if it also is 'understood' in terms of its social meaning – and vice versa (Baert, 2005, pp. 42, 46–47; cf. Wight, 2002, pp. 32–33).

Understanding what nuclear non-use means to decision-makers requires double hermeneutics, that is, interpreting their firsthand interpretations and *making sense* of how nuclear abstinence came about (Jackson, 2006; Bevir, 2006, p. 283; Yanow, 2006b, p. 20). Since meaning is primarily generated via language (Davis, 2005, p. 42), an analysis of language is key.

In deterrence theory, even though communication and meaningful signaling of resolve are essential, its Realist heritage allows for no systematic consideration of the role of language. It merely mirrors the given 'world out there' and is considered cheap talk or, at best, a stone pit for illustrative empirical factoids. Tannenwald, in contrast, insists that 'taboo-talk' is *not* cheap talk (Tannenwald, 2007, pp. 370–371). However, she (2007, p. 13) also assumes an 'objective reality', with 'discourse' merely providing the 'evidence' for the nuclear taboo's real-world effect on changing thinking and behavior over time. While not as stepmotherly a treatment of language as in the deterrence case, in the end this is not so different.

Also, Tannenwald's approach to language tends to desensitize the analysis to the inevitable recalcitrance of all empirical material. After all, it is set up for seduction by the favored variable 'taboo', thus nullifying the chance for something unforeseen emerging. With my main concern being that both existing approaches are top-down and ought to be contrasted and complemented with a bottom-up analysis, I have to deal more open-mindedly with what there is to find in the empirical sources, hopefully resulting in a less 'filtered' glimpse into the phenomenon.

I consequently assume language to be performative, to construct social reality. More precisely, I assume that meaning-making takes place via *speech acts* in *(public) discourses*. This means adopting the viewpoint that, while nuclear weapons and missile silos, for example, do exist outside our minds, '[n]othing speaks for itself, not even a missile silo' (Klein, 1994, p. 116; cf. Hellmann, 2010, p. 154). So it is not to say that 'brute material conditions [...] have no role whatsoever, but rather that their impact is always mediated by the ideas that give them meaning' (Fearon/Wendt, 2002, p. 57; cf. Wendt, 1992, pp. 396–397; Wendt, 1995, p. 73; Hollis/ Smith, 1991, pp. 68–71). Hence meaning attributed to events in the world via language at the same time discursively constructs social reality – because '[t]he world is out there, but descriptions of the world are not [...]. The world does not speak. Only we do' (Rorty, 1989, pp. 5, 6).

With this in mind, it becomes clear why I am interested in the use of language as an action in its own right, thus leaving the separation between 'what people say (cheap talk)' and 'what people actually (read nonverbally) do' behind definitively. James L. Austin (1962) and many drawing on his seminal work have convincingly argued that saying can also be doing because 'speech acts' in discourse are the primary way for human beings to attribute meaning to events in the world through language.

So the literal impact of a nuclear warhead can thus be said to be *real*. No discussion there. But what makes it interesting analytically is the social meaning ascribed to this event via language in a discursive praxis. And that ascription, I argue, could potentially range from 'a provocation that must be met with resolve' to 'a cataclysmic tragedy that must never repeat' – depending on the social context and with respective, widely differing implications. I will return to the example of the exploding warhead.

Attaching this kind of importance to discourse, language and its performative role in an IR study is no longer considered 'dissident' (Campbell, 1992, p. 4), 'deviant' (Milliken, 1999, p. 227) or controversial in IR. And I leave it up for the reader to decide whether this approach renders this study a radical constructivist, poststructuralist, critical realist, pragmatist or whatever-ist analysis of nuclear non-use, doubting myself whether the current plethora of labels in IR still clarifies or rather has started confusing and impeding things (Wight, 2002, pp. 35, 37, 40–41; cf. Lake, 2011).

On a less serious note, one might briefly consider that the whole phenomenon in which I am interested is 'fabulously textual' anyway. Because no actual use of nuclear weapons in war took place after 1945, 'one can only talk and write about it' (Derrida, 1984, p. 23).

So simply because it is adequate to the subject matter, an approach focusing on language to *reconstruct* (Herborth, 2010; 2011) the meaning of nuclear non-use and how it came about in practice – *including* the causes identified by existing literature but *principally* keeping an eye out for so far overlooked facets as well – is a plausible alternative way to go.

The goal of this reconstruction is not simply to state that 'things could have come differently'. Instead, it is that if human action is not simply 'effected' but rather takes place due to reasoning, this means that decision-makers could also have reasoned *differently* (Bevir, 2006, p. 285). Consequently, this necessitates taking *agency* and *contingency* more seriously. These are two especially hefty concepts in need of unpacking.

A good way to start the discussion of agency is by noting how a stronger focus on it sets my analysis apart from the existing explanations of non-use. For deterrence to work everywhere, every time and for everyone (without near misses and failures), decision-makers would have to resemble billiard balls *all* of which *always* behave the same law-of-physics way when subjected to the same deterrent force. But I have already rejected the notion that deterrence *necessarily causes* (Hawthorn, 1993, pp. 19–20) nuclear abstinence. Furthermore, actors can deviate from 'normal' behavior. In other words, there are always degrees of freedom (Sending, 2002, pp. 455, 458); otherwise, there would never be any conflicts with any norms or taboos anywhere, actor identities would never change and no new 'norm structures' would ever emerge. So decision-makers are neither billiard balls subdued to a law-like logic of mechanical consequentialism nor are they preprogrammed norm-obedient automatons subdued to a somewhat softer logic of constant appropriateness.

Instead, even a process of an existing norm's eroding never ends up in *nothing*; rather, every reasoned decision creates *something* new – in this case eventually even a new norm to replace the old one or even entirely new social structures to be populated with numerous norms later on, none of which would be possible without 'creative agency' (Hellmann, 2002, pp. 22–23) and its '"transformative capacity"' (Anthony Giddens, quoted in Sending, 2002, p. 458). Putting the analytical focus on agency leading up to a reasoned decision to use or not use nuclear weapons thus means lowering the positivistic emphasis on the structuring regularity of conditioning or determining exogenous factors – such as deterrence or the taboo – affecting the agent. The overall perspective change from pure subsumption under regulating structures and more toward a reconstruction of agency as proposed here thus requires being more susceptive to *contingency* because the notion that things could have come differently is inextricably linked to the thought of agency in social practice (Hellmann, 2010, p. 165; Jackson, 2006, p. 267).

So acknowledging contingency is not so much an assumption in its own right as merely a logical consequence of conceiving nuclear non-use as an outcome of agency at the outset, as a choice by a reasoning actor rather than merely an 'effect' caused by law-like perennial forces of international politics, such as deterrence explaining all cases of nuclear non-use always and everywhere. After all, as Richard Ned Lebow (2010b, p. 10) points out, 'If major historical events are so inevitable, [i]f events are overdetermined, the underlying conditions responsible for these events should have been apparent at the time to scholars and policy-makers alike, making them [...] to some degree predictable'. The Cuban Missile Crisis serves as a case in point. If deterrence is such an overwhelmingly powerful determining force, why was humankind, including the key decision-makers at the time, so deeply worried that the crisis might escalate into a nuclear war?

Before returning to the example of the exploding nuclear warhead, I need to, lastly, discuss the concept of agency and the focus on practice employed here. My thought process in this regard begins with the notion that, despite the formalized structure and systematic planning of nuclear command and control, a situation that demands a definitive answer to the question of whether nuclear weapons should or should not be used can be conceived of as a *crisis*. This might sound rather self-evident regarding the severe 'foreign policy crisis' outside of which the nuclear question would probably never arise. But crisis here also means a 'crisis of thought and action'. This is a helpful figure of thought because it emphasizes how reflections – let alone decisions – about nuclear use are cardinal questions and out of the ordinary for decision-makers. They require extra effort in order to successfully cope with them. From the vantage point of a 'nuclear decision-maker', a crisis means that habitual routines are challenged, maybe even fundamentally called into question.

The concept of agency I adopt here holds that decision-making is about (re-)interpreting and defining a situation to ascribe meaning to it – to 'speech-act' – in order to allow further sensible, subsequent action. A focus on agency – one that acknowledges that actors make genuine *choices* (Sending, 2002, p. 458) – consequently goes hand in hand with the notion of reconstructing how things turned out one way and not the other, what situated choices were made by actors to cope with reality in a given social context. That social context is composed of discourse that holds a history of evolved interpretations and shared usable meanings, as well as established useful practices. From an actor's perspective it, in short, makes up the experience-saturated system of *beliefs that provide the rules for action* (Hellmann, 2009, p. 639; Franke/Weber, 2012, pp. 675–680).

Practices and beliefs are in a constant interplay according to that perspective on agency: 'Practices could not exist if people did not have appropriate beliefs; and beliefs or meanings would not make sense in the absence of the practices to which they refer' (Bevir, 2006, p. 284). In other words, a decision-maker will routinely draw on beliefs to ascribe meaning to situations in the world in order to act upon that in a fashion that 'makes sense' according to his or her experience. Since the majority of practice situations are routine situations, beliefs offer a relieving function by allowing habitual action. However, beliefs are never fully stable, and a crisis is characterized by posing an unexpected challenge to an existing belief. It is characterized by doubt. Crises can thus not be dealt with by applying the usual day-to-day problem-solving practices. *Creative* agency is key when routines break down and a decision-maker is forced to (speech-)act on (and cope with) a challenging decision. So agency can be genuinely creative, yet situated and adequate in a given social context at the same time, that is, trying to avoid choices that are senseless, absurd, wrong, forbidden, suicidal and so forth. Moments of creative agency are neither decoupled from their social environment and discourse nor from past experiences. Creative agency thus creates something new, but not out of thin air; rather, since agency is situated and socially contextualized, it is best described as agents *re*-constructing (via language) the way they ascribe meaning to and cope with the world in problematic situations of crises, in other words a *readjustment* in the ever ongoing process of experience and practice. And *if* this readjustment turns out to be helpful in successfully coping with the crisis, a new routine can – temporarily – be established (Franke/Weber, 2012, pp. 676–677; Hellmann, 2010, pp. 146–153; Hellmann, 2009; 2002, pp. 5–12).

Now recall the impacting nuclear warhead. If this event is interpreted as a first step of the escalatory ladder in a nuclear shooting war and portrayed as a provocation that must be met with resolve, then, arguably, firing one or two nuclear missiles in return is a plausible thing to do. However, if it is interpreted as a cataclysmic tragedy that must never be repeated and is taken to be the trigger for a process directed toward that exact goal, then it stands to reason that working toward conflict settlement and nuclear disarmament is a sensible action.

Since I defined agency as not consisting in solitary actions but rather as a process, an ongoing experience stream of routine, crisis and creativity, this illustration is not meant to suggest that agency is decoupled from social context and that radically individualistic agents can randomly decide how to interpret their environment and act on it (because social life would then be utterly chaotic and not as more or less well ordered as it usually is, most of it being, as I said, habitual routine within the confines of social context, that is, at least temporarily stable beliefs, discourses and practices). Quite the contrary, the illustration only shows the range of possibilities. And, depending on its specific social context (and the stockpile of usable meanings it contains), not every decision is equally *likely*. But there is almost always more than one decision *possible*. And every single one of these decisions would be contingent and determined by agency, which means neither overdetermined nor random, but rather situated and dependent on the potentialities of the respective social context that provides the framework for the processes of creative agency – and choice. This is why I use the term 'nuclear abstinence'. Only because choice is pivotal for agency, is it possible and meaningful to abstain from one possible path of action in favor of another.

With language under analysis, some will take this study to be a discourse analysis – and rightly so because there are many similarities. Of course, discourse is providing the structures of meaning, thus establishing the conditions without which the ascription of meaning and intelligible actions would not be possible in the first place (Jackson, 2007, pp. 420–421). Nevertheless, the two following empirical chapters focus on the micro and the meso level of meaning attribution processes in an attempt to identify and understand the meanings and beliefs involved. 'Mapping' the macro level of discourse in its entirety, as the overall horizon for what agents can know and say, is not my focus. That said, this study does share a crucial feature with discourse analysis, summed up nicely in a remark by Ole Wæver (2002, p. 27): 'What is often presented as a weakness of discourse analysis – "how do you find out if they really mean what they say?", "what if it is only rhetoric?" – can be turned into a methodological strength, as soon as one is conscientious in sticking to discourse as discourse. One often finds a confusion of discourse analysis with psychological or cognitive approaches, or a commonsensical assumption that the "real" motives must be what we are all interested in, and texts can only be a (limited) means to get this. Not so! Structures within discourse condition possible policies'.

Because we cannot see into the heads of decision-makers to decide whether the reasons given by them were really why they opted for nuclear abstinence, we cannot know intentions for sure or, simply put, whether a speaker 'really meant' what she said. While I certainly should and will reflect on speakers, settings and contexts in Chapter 4, in the end, the documented concatenation of chosen speech acts, reasons given and decisions made – publicly available in texts with nothing hidden about it – remain the decisive elements of the analysis. Because no matter if they were 'really meant' that way, they (re-)establish the beliefs and conditions that, through discourse, are in turn reflected in future action, making them the only thing empirically identifiable and traceable. So not only because inferences about alleged 'real motives' are not reliably researchable but also simply because it does not matter in the end, it is of little to no interest whether speakers 'really meant what they said'. (In addition, it is noteworthy that the sources used for the first empirical inquiry in section 4.2. minimize the likelihood of speakers deploying 'only rhetoric' anyway).

With these methodological considerations laid out, I now turn to how the existing knowledge about the causes of non-use can be included in the effort to better understand nuclear abstinence. Similar to what Jarrod Hayes and Patrick James (2014, p. 401) have recently argued for IR theories in general, I will conceptualize deterrence, the nuclear taboo and the tradition of non-use as *beliefs that rule action* that 'embody shared patterns in how actors understand the world' to analyze them as 'modes of thought [...] reflected in the thought processes of policymakers' in practice.

Reconceptualizing existing explanations

First, the above-mentioned notion of rules forestalling 'senseless' or 'wrong' action obviously resonates with the constructivist approach of explaining non-use via a prohibitive norm (Tannenwald, 2007, p. 10; Sending, 2002, pp. 449–450; on the contingency of norm-governed behavior, see Davis, 2005, p. 144). Regarding the aspect of causality, however, there is a debate among scholars about the effect of norms and positivist epistemology. It is important to point out that the objections in this debate go further than my discussion of the absence-of-evidence trap. They lend even more plausibility to some of the arguments I made, however, because they straightforwardly ask whether social norms can be submitted to positivist causal analysis *at all* (Davis, 2005, pp. 132–153).

Some scholars, like Friedrich Kratochwil and John Gerard Ruggie (1986, p. 767), have long argued that the regulative effect of norms can simply not be grasped by causal analysis because they do not cause effects in the same way that 'a bullet through the heart causes death', but merely 'guide', 'inspire', 'rationalize' and 'justify' behavior. So even without the absence-of-evidence problem, there could never be a causal chain to discover. As Davis (2005, pp. 134–135) points out, the fact that norms do not 'cause' behavior in a causal sense is why they can be counterfactually valid in the first place, meaning in the context of this study that the taboo does not necessarily cease to exist if it is broken. Tannenwald (2007, p. 371), again, is well aware of these considerations and states that '[n]orms do not simply work as triggers for a single kind of behavior but rather are part of complex sets of meanings, including permissions and prohibitions, through which people understand, and act in, the world'. Nevertheless, her analysis is driven by positivist methodology and causality.

In contrast, I suggest to reconceptualize the taboo by shifting the analytic focus onto the role that norms play in terms of people's 'meaning-making' in practice, that is, from their regulative to their constitutive function, namely as part of a belief system and the convictions 'through which people understand, and act in, the world', in Tannenwald's own words (cf. Franke/Weber, 2012, p. 679). Drawing on the nuclear taboo in this fashion is thus a pretty straightforward affair, one that does not denigrate but merely differs from Tannenwald's chosen methodology and analytical focus.

Second, the tradition of non-use and its middle position between rationalists and constructivists Chapter 2 can now be reactivated – with still no need for a discussion about which concept, the taboo or the tradition, explains non-use better or more comprehensively. Instead, with the difference between the two being one of degree and with them distinguishable in a meaningful way only by dealing with the interpretation of actual empirical material on a case-by-case basis, this procedure is exactly what I propose. I will provide more on the details of that after I have dealt with, thirdly, deterrence.

So far, from a theoretical vantage point, the possibilities opening up for reconceptualization are not entirely surprising because the notion of creative agency is considered by some a third, even an overarching, alternative to rational and norm-oriented models of action (Franke/Weber, 2012, p. 677). But the question remains: are beliefs not totally alien to hard-nosed 'rational deterrence theory'? Even though critical third-wave deterrence theorists such as Robert Jervis or Richard New Lebow and Janice Gross Stein pointed to the importance of taking history and psychology, including belief systems, into account when deterrence practice is scrutinized, some might demand a more argumentative effort to reconceptualize rational deterrence theory as a belief. A final look at the development of deterrence and its hybrid character of both theory and strategy is thus in order.

I criticized deterrence – understood as a positivist explanation – as strictly speaking unable to account for a non-event. Its trajectory toward this ironic state of scientification might be one of the reasons why deterrence in parallel also developed into a 'theology' (Quinlan, 2008, pp. 13–14; cf. Rosenbaum, 2011, p. 45; Lebow/Gross Stein, 1994, p. 348; Cohn, 1987, p. 702).[6]

In this way, nuclear deterrence could, for those unmoved by critical objections, persist and outlast all its critics. The important note to take is, however, that a leap of faith was required for this to take hold. One had to believe it to be true that deterrence and nuclear strategy somehow work their magic, all the criticisms and caveats notwithstanding (similar: Derrida, 1984, p. 24). For deterrence believers this is the way to deal with the 'paucity of evidence' (Jervis, 1984, pp. 37–41). As the aforementioned Michael Rühle (2009, p. 10) concedes, '[Q]uestions of nuclear weapons and deterrence are questions of faith, beyond "hard" empirical science'. In their quest for theorizing the truly credible, believable deterring threat, unable to validate their theory in rigorous empirical testing, the only way out for deterrence theorists was for them to faithfully believe crucial theoretical assumptions before they safely could believe that it is actually deterrence that explains nuclear non-use (Müller, 2013, p. 548).

At the practical level, 'it may seem counter-intuitive to conclude that such ontological beliefs play such a significant role on the highly secular world of defense policymaking' (Kull, 1988, p. 310). But it actually makes sense to ascribe a significant role to them, especially in the realm of practice. Because they offer cohesion to policymakers, the defense community and the military in what Michael C. Williams (1992, p. 88) called 'a closed abstract system of idealism' (see also Cohn, 1987, p. 709), an instrument of collective psychological suppression and self-affirmation. After all, 'it was psychologically and politically reassuring to think that the bogey of nuclear war could be kept at bay by the rational practice of deterrence' (Lebow, 2010b, p. 13).

A critical stance toward nuclear weapons and deterrence as, for example, during the nuclear freeze movement in the 1980s is thus not a serious critical argument to be reckoned with but the equivalent of a 'loss of faith'. For '[i]n the still alien world of nuclear weapons, it is only faith in deterrence that preserves continuity with a familiar past' (Tucker, 1984, p. 2). Yet, already 40 years ago, Fred Charles Iklé (1973, p. 267) was deeply concerned about the consequences: '[W]e do in fact assume nuclear immortality. We believe, or we act as if we believe, that thanks to a certain international order, the existing arsenals of nuclear weapons with their almost incomprehensible destructiveness will never be used'. Iklé (1973, p. 281; cf. Cohn, 1987, pp. 711–712) likened the ensuing 'jargon of American strategic analysis' to a 'narcotic' that 'dulls our sense of moral outrage', blinding 'us to the fact that our method for preventing nuclear war rests on a form of warfare universally condemned since the Dark Ages – the mass killing of hostages'. Strangely, this ultimately 'vulgar psychology' (Derrida, 1984, p. 24) of theories on deterrence and nuclear war coexists with the extreme level of technical sophistication found necessary for the strife to make deterrence work in practice.

Also, an additional reason for the persistence of deterrence can be sought in Robert Cox's (1981, p. 128, original emphasis) by now proverbial saying that '[t]heory is always *for* someone and *for* some purpose'. Because sure enough, being able to speak the pertinent jargon with virtuosity was (and still is) a way of attaining influence in political and military circles, a source of power for an elite preacher caste, in the know and conversant with the arcane doctrine of nuclear deterrence. Thus, there are clear incentives to believe and to proselytize. As Colin S. Gray stated in the context of the U.S.-Soviet arms race, 'Military meaningless weapons are significant politically if political leaders *believe* them to be important' (Gray, 1974, pp. 215, emphasis added; cf. Jervis, 1984, p. 41).

Finally, some odd behaviors that should not go unmentioned go along with the belief in deterrence. They are especially eye catching regarding the Realist stance of most deterrence thinkers. For example, when nuclear weapons and deterrence come into play, Realists such as Waltz suddenly turn into cheerful utopists, firmly believing that nuclear weapons herald the perpetual peace for which proponents of *Realpolitik* such as himself usually ridicule their liberal colleagues (Betts, 2000, p. 52; cf. e.g. Waltz, 2003a; Waltz, 2003b). Waltz believes in deterrence so fervently that he goes so far as to state in pseudomathematical lingo that '[t]he probability of major war among states having nuclear weapons approaches zero'. *He* believes that '[a] nation will be deterred from attacking even if *it* believes that there is only a possibility that its adversary will retaliate' (Waltz, 1988, pp. 51, 50, emphasis added; see also Quinlan, 2008, p. 16). Believing is required to take care of the rest of remaining uncertainty that Waltz means when he carelessly describes deterrence as a 'cosmic bluff', enabling the believer to trust that deterrence 'has worked 100 percent of the time' (Waltz, in Sagan et al., 2007, p. 138). How else to cope with the troubling possibility that there could someday be an actor that decides not to be deterred (Gray, 1999b, pp. 89–90)?

A dyed-in-the-wool believer *cannot* doubt the truth claim of theory or that deterrence worked in practice (heresy!) regarding, for instance, the international order of the Cold War. He would rather lament that tensions, arms races and instabilities are merely due to 'misperceptions on both sides of what mutual assured destruction (MAD) means, and how the world works' (Van Evera, 1984, p. 694). This completes the deterrence development cycle from a practical craft via a scientific project through to a creed. At that stage, 'how the world works' stops being a question of empirical inquiry, answerable by taking a careful look at how the world actually 'works'. Rather, empirical inquiry is (again) replaced by the scholarly postulate of how he *believes* MAD and the world *should* be working.

This is especially irritating since the strict separation between normative and analytical theory, between statements about what is and what ought to be, is commonly held to be one of the hallmarks of scientific enterprise within the Realist/positivist paradigm. But apparently even the most fundamental Realist principle 'to see the world as it is, not as we would like it to be' (Mearsheimer, 2001, p. 4) goes out the window when the belief in deterrence kicks in.

In his popular introductory textbook *Guide to Methods for Students of Political Science*, Stephen Van Evera (1997, pp. 14–15, original emphasis) states that a '"theory" that cannot be arrow-diagrammed is *not a theory* and needs reframing to become a theory'. 'If deterrence, then non-use' can easily be arrow-diagrammed and is thus a theory by that definition, a very parsimonious one even (Jervis, 1979, p. 290). But since '[p]olitics has the nasty habit of not always behaving as even the most plausible and rigorous theories suggest it should', as Jervis (1991, p. 40) puts it, the believer's conclusion that it is the world that needs reframing to accord with his theory is only consequential. Conceiving of deterrence as a belief thus helps to understand the strange self-contradictory practice that is Realist/positivist deterrence theorists issuing strategic advice. After all, if the theory merely explains a world independent and impervious to human thought (in analogy to nature) and if talk is cheap, why even bother with trying to influence policy (Oren, 2009, p. 283; Guzzini, 2004, p. 542)?

So Realist/positivist deterrence theory's 'doctrines and beliefs [...] shape, rather than describe, reality' (Jervis, 1984, p. 38) – and this way, the tautological claim to exclusive policy advice inherited from the olden days' classical Realists can come full circle. After all, if 'everyone believes that someone else believes, [...] a behavior that might otherwise appear illogical is justified as rational' (Harrington de Santana, 2009, p. 329). The law-like mechanics of cause-and-effect deterrence theory's cold logic of science supposedly 'discovered' in 'reality out there' from a neutral observer's point of view are fed back right into political practices as descriptions of the world and prescriptions for how to act on it, completing the ongoing exercise of circular, self-referential reasoning and practice that makes up the deterrence paradigm. The history of deterrence theory and strategy as a self-fulfilling prophecy comes to mind again (Lupovici, 2010, p. 716).

Thus, a deeply held conviction, a belief, to sum this up, is *vital* to deterrence by providing the needed assumptions on which theory rests on the one hand, and by being nothing short of the *conditio sine qua non* for strategy to work in practice on the other. Conceptualized as a belief that rules action and helps make sense of the world, rational deterrence theory constructs reality, rather than merely describing and explaining it.

Returning to my original train of thought in this segment, it seems that all three causes of nuclear non-use proposed thus far, including deterrence as framed in rational deterrence theory, can indeed be conceived of – or reconceptualized as – beliefs ruling action. In this way, the focus comes to rest on their main functions for decision-makers: helping them to make sense of the world, providing rules for routine action, offering meaningful building blocks for creative use in crises.

With the groundwork laid, the questions that can now be directed at the material are not which explanation best explains nuclear non-use, but rather *how* these beliefs are invoked in practice, how prevalent they are, how stably they play out as rules and how they interact with each other. So the three formerly explanatory concepts are preserved and integrated into my approach as heuristic tools for empirically reconstructing their role in situations in which agents make sense of the world. As recently proposed by numerous authors who favor such an 'analytic eclecticism' (Katzenstein/Sil, 2008; Friedrichs/Kratochwil, 2009; Sil/Katzenstein, 2010), the rationale here is to preserve and adapt three discrete concepts from various research traditions to integrate them in a pragmatic fashion into a novel research perspective on a real-world problem.

In sum, shifting the perspective from a top-down to a bottom-up one focusing on language, meaning and agency in a reconstructive analysis needs not abandon existing knowledge but opens up a chance for gaining new insights into it. And it additionally allows accounting for less preconceived facets of the phenomenon.

3.3.2 Method: deductive and inductive software-aided coding

With the change of perspective explained and my methodology set up, the following subsection will present the research method with which the research process for this study was conducted. Most importantly, I will explain the mix of deductive and inductive software-aided coding that allows an overall systematic and transparent qualitative analysis of the source material while coupling subsumptive concepts with a reconstructive inquiry.

With this book I join the growing number of interpretivist scholars who challenge the positivist claim that understanding research is 'neither rigorous nor objective' (Yanow, 2006a; Bevir, 2006). Contemporary authors describing themselves as explicitly postpositivist, such as Lene Hansen (2006) or Eva Herschinger (2011), are calling for the disentanglement of 'science' from 'positivism' in IR. For example, in her post-structuralist analysis of the constitutive role of identity in foreign policy, Hansen (2006, pp. 5, original emphasis) underlines that *'adopting a non-causal epistemology does not imply an abandonment of theoretically rigorous frameworks, empirical analyses of "real world relevance", or systematic assessments of data and methodology'.*

The 'protocol' (Lebow, 2010b, p. 37) I followed for the empirical research was to orient it strictly toward the specific characteristics of the non-event while observing procedural systematicity and striving for transparency, the overall goal being a presentation of the material, the analysis and its results that is intersubjectively comprehensible – to allow for peer scholars to develop a substantiated, intrinsic critique of my inquiry and thus maintain the conditions for an open, fruitful scholarly conversation to be facilitated about the subject matter.[7] None of this strikes me as controversial. After all, 'how to' conduct research in IR might be a subject of debate, but what I call my 'protocol' should be met with approval by the majority of peers in IR, considering that intersubjective comprehensibility is the cornerstone of what most practitioners agree constitutes 'good' science.

Following my double interest of what explains the persistent non-use of nuclear weapons after 1945 *and* how this abstinence can be better understood, including its known causes, a balance needed to be struck. After all, this research interest implies respecting and employing the existing knowledge *as well as* allowing for new insights to emerge in at least an equal measure. Consequently, I chose the middle way of *both* deduction *and* induction, navigating in-between the two extremes of either staying chained to the reproduction of preformed hypotheses or risking to drown in impressions accumulated from within the material. This 'reasoning at an intermediate level' (Friedrichs/Kratochwil, 2009, pp. 709, 715), as originally formulated by Charles Sanders Peirce, is called 'abductive' thinking (Franke/Weber, 2012, pp. 672–675) and has more recently, differences in details notwithstanding (Hellmann, 2009, p. 641), been advocated as a research style by a number of scholars in IR (Jackson, 2011, pp. 82–83; Rytövuori-Apunen, 2009, p. 644; Friedrichs, 2009, p. 647).

From coding to an analytic narrative

To keep the interrogation of empirical sources transparent, I used the coding software MAXQDA. Mixing deductive and inductive coding procedures enabled me both to inquire into the known causes of non-use and to develop new facets of the phenomenon. Two basic deductive codes (head codes) were distinguished at the very beginning: *Use* and *Non-Use*. *Use* is, of course, derived from the possibility of using nuclear weapons that is to be reconstructed more systematically in this study. Being a 'negative' in terms of the overall research interest, that is, making sense of *non*-use, made this 'misfit' all the more interesting to explore and the coding method that was applied allowed for systematically tracing it in the material (Coffey/Atkinson, 1996, p. 47). The second head code, *Non-Use*, contained three codes (main codes): *Deterrence, Tradition* and *Taboo,* deduced from my reconceptualization of known explanations of non-use. I defined subsumption as sorting empirical material under preformed concepts. This is exactly what this set of deductive codes served for, bringing the existing knowledge to fruition for my own analysis. However, they were embedded in an overall reconstructive research process, meaning in particular the generation of many additional, inductive codes from within the material. This process is what allowed me to inquire more deeply into the specific meaning of preformed concepts and add complexity to them, *as well as* to crystallize other facets of the phenomenon out of my sources. A glance into the MAXQDA project files shows the two resulting code systems that developed over the course of my two empirical inquiries (Coffey/Atkinson, 1996; Weitzmann, 2000; Mason, 2002).[8]

For the actual coding process, the source texts were imported into the software first and, of course, carefully read. Along the way short notes were attached to the text, and sometimes passages were hyperlinked to connect them within or across documents. Only pertinent passages in the material used for the following analyses in Chapter 4 were coded. For example, I reserved the deductive main code *Deterrence* for those passages in the material in which the potential costs of retaliation in kind were the primary concern regarding the use of nuclear weapons. John F. Kennedy, explaining in a conversation with General Maxwell Taylor '[t]hat we're so slow about using nuclear weapons in Europe [...] because we're against a nuclear force [...]' (WHT, 2001c, p. 162), would be an example. Furthermore, trying explicitly to *apply* deterrence to prevent military, possibly nuclear, escalation was coded *Deterrence*. And in very much the same vein, I applied the main code *Tradition* in situations in which reputation loss or detrimental precedents seemed pivotal, and *Taboo* when nuclear weapons use was rejected by decision-makers who stated moral concerns.

However, not all coding decisions are as easy and clear cut as the *Deterrence* example above might suggest. I will quote a longer passage from the Kennedy material as an example for a more recalcitrant bit of text regarding *Taboo* and *Tradition*.

> **Robert Kennedy:** I think just the whole question of, you know, assuming that you do survive all this, we don't have, the fact that we're not...what kind of a country we are. The fact that you just don't [*unclear*].
>
> **Rusk:** This business of carrying the mark of Cain on your brow for the rest of your lives is something [*unclear*].
>
> **Robert Kennedy:** The fact that they'll be mad. We did this against Cuba. We've talked for 15 years that the Russians being [planning for] the first strike against us, and we'd never do that. Now, in the interest of time, we do that to a small country. I think it's a hell of a burden to carry.
>
> **Thompson:** By far the strongest argument against this is that, killing the Russians, which to my mind means you are going to end up the whole way, and [*unclear*].

The focus here rests on what to make of the statement by Secretary of State Dean Rusk: 'This business of carrying the mark of Cain on your brow for the rest of your lives is something [*unclear*]' (WHT, 2001c, p. 547). The group is discussing the possibility of attacking Cuba surprisingly and without prior announcement during the Missile Crisis. Rusk's statement, neither in isolation nor even against the background of the surprise attack under discussion, would necessarily have to have something to do with the code *Non-Use*. After all, they could be discussing a conventional attack. But context is pivotal. And the context suggests that the surprise attack is apprehended as the prelude to nuclear escalation, evident, for instance, in Robert Kennedy's remark preceding Rusk's about 'assuming that you do survive all this' as well as Ambassador-at-Large Llewellyn Thompson's subsequent assessment that if the attack is conducted 'you are going to end up the whole way' (WHT, 2001c, p. 547), with 'the whole way' meaning general war, including a nuclear exchange and 'surviving all this' connected to just that. Interpreting the 'mark of Cain' remark in a context of nuclear weapon employment matter-of-factly would point to nothing more than a reputational problem (and I did code Rusk's statement as *World Opinion* as well, accordingly), especially in light of the fact that further context (not included in the example quote above) at first suggests that President Kennedy is worried about setting a precedent for the U.S. similar to 'Pearl Harbor' (WHT, 2001c, pp. 545–546). So in deciding about this ambiguous passage in terms of '*Taboo* or *Tradition*', the code *Tradition* seems to apply. However, focusing on the context one more time, attention is drawn to Attorney General Robert Kennedy, who immediately before Rusk worries about 'the fact that we're not...what kind of a country we are. The fact that you just don't [*unclear*]' (WHT, 2001c, p. 574). This points to questions of national identity – namely, what kind of country the U.S. *is* rather than what reputation it *has* – and furthermore to an intrinsic moral conviction as another meaningful element in play, the fact that some things the U.S. *just does not do*. These are the hallmarks of the nuclear taboo. The points of reference in Robert Kennedy's statement, the ones that Rusk was immediately answering with his 'mark of Cain' statement, point toward this line of thought. Coding Rusk's phrase *Taboo* is thus plausible and justifiable from within the material and the context in which the coded passage is situated. Lastly, the knowledge about existing explanations goes a long way in this case. Rusk had also referred to the mark of Cain during discussions about using nuclear weapons in Korea, according to interviews and Rusk's memoirs, cited by Tannenwald (2007, p. 131). She interpreted this as 'taboo-talk', which I find plausible.

A look at some of the dozens of new, inductive codes and their importance is now in order: a first example code, again taken from the upcoming chapter on John F. Kennedy, is *Alliance* (further differentiated via the inductive subcode *Turkey*). It exemplifies several things. First, it illustrates how inductive codes can be generated by using the exact terms found in the material ('in vivo codes'), for example, Kennedy's worrying that 'the alliance would disintegrate' (WHT, 2001c, p. 541). But the term does not *have* to be used literally, of course, for a passage to be coded *Alliance*, for example: 'Why don't we send an instruction to Hare to have a conversation [with the Turks], but also have the NATO meeting? We need to explain to them what's happening over here' (WHT, 2001b, p. 453). Most of the codes in my code system are in vivo codes. Some, however, are not, such as, for instance, the code *Language*, which labels passages in which decision-makers discuss wording and language to put into policy documents. Lastly, pointing to *Alliance* serves to emphasize that new head codes – such as *Use* and *Non-Use* – were inductively gained from the material. In fact, numerous such new head codes and main codes (such as *Contingency Plans* and this in turn with a subcode like *Command and Control)* were necessary to be able to structure the material (even only pertinent passages, of which, obviously, again only a fraction was directly concerned with *Use* or *Non-Use*) and systematically understand the meaning of key concepts raised by speakers.

Another inductively gained, new main code of the deductive head code *Non-Use* is *Escalatory Control*. It illustrates how deductive and inductive elements worked in combination, that is, how new insights into the meaning of subsumptively deployed concepts could be reconstructed: 'Yeah. I would think it more likely he would just grab Berlin. That's the more likely' (WHT, 2001c, p. 533), is what Kennedy stated on the escalatory risks resulting from U.S. action against Cuba. These two short phrases of Kennedy were inductively coded *Escalatory Control*. For this coding decision, again, context mattered. The conversation from which these phrases were lifted revolved around fathoming out the risks of uncontrolled escalation to ensure that nuclear weapons would *not* have to be used at the end of the expected chain of events around Berlin. Lastly, the passage under discussion here was coded not only *Escalatory Control* but also *Berlin*. And *Berlin* turned out to be an extremely important inductively gained code, crucial for understanding how the causes of non-use played out as beliefs ruling action in practice. This code helped in reconstructing what upholding a credible U.S. deterrence posture (*Deterrence*) and dreading the prospect of nuclear weapon use (*Taboo*) at the same time meant for President Kennedy. Lastly, *Fear*, yet another inductively gained main code of *Non-Use*, is worth mentioning here. Its relevance – pointing beyond existing explanations – will become clear as Chapter 4 progresses.

Coding is only the comparably mundane process of comparing, sorting and organizing larger amounts of material. Software is a helpful tool in this regard, alleviating for the researcher some of the mechanical aspects involved and allowing a stronger focus on interpreting the material systematically and working toward an analytic narrative. A few remarks on how the research process moved from coding to the analytic narrative are in order.

The analytic narrative presents the results of my reconstructive analysis. 'Narrative' here means not a fictional or subjective story; it also has nothing to do with narrative analysis of the literary studies. Analytic narratives are a common tool in IR. Most studies, no matter whether reconstructively or subsumptively conducted, necessarily present some kind of narrative to the reader to present their conclusions about how things hang together, how the nuclear taboo or deterrence led to nuclear weapons not being used, for example. In other words, what I call an 'analytic narrative' as part of the effort to understand nuclear non-use is not different from, say, the 'process-tracing narrative' that Tannenwald (2007, p. 17) deploys. Important particularities lie only in the way in which I arrive at my narrative (by trying to understand, not to explain) and, consequently, what my narrative ultimately comprises in terms of insights to take away from it.

For writing the two narratives presented in Chapter 4, the code systems provided valuable directional signs for systematically comparing, questioning and evaluating the material, especially in terms of locating and reinterpreting crucial passages. This process of renavigating the material while reading and comparing passages (and the notes attached to them) allows the meaning of specific codes to be dug into more deeply, which was essential to establish more and more meaningful connections. A software-based code system helps organize this probing process around specific threads such as, for instance, a particularly meaningful connection of two codes. The 'Berlin problem', featuring prominently below, is a case in point in that regard.

Lastly, threads of meaning that turned out to be sustainable and relevant to the research question guided the write-up process. Writing ended with the narrative being sufficiently dense, that is, compellingly presenting the results of the analysis and offering answers on how one can plausibly make sense of nuclear abstinence by inquiring into how known explanatory concepts as well as so far underexposed aspects play out in practice. This is what I turn to now.

4
Revisiting Nuclear Non-Use

Regarding the empirical analysis, it bears repeating that this book is not inquiring into the subject matter in the same way an explanatory analysis would conventionally do. Neither is a causal process postulated upfront nor are empirical sources confronted with one or more testable hypotheses. Consequently, the following 'case' selection might appear unconventional or counterintuitive as well. But if the goal is to understand nuclear non-use as a contingent phenomenon that hinges on agency at the level of decision-makers, and not to 'prove' the validity or superiority of an explanatory concept across so and so many cases, different source selection criteria apply. The pivotal question for beginning the empirical research process was thus what material is suitable and available.

4.1 Selecting sources

Recordings and verbatim transcripts of conversations between White House decision-makers – the White House Tapes – made for adequate primary sources and a sensible point of entry for beginning the empirical analysis for this book. Six U.S. Presidents used audio recording equipment in the White House. The Miller Center's Presidential Recordings Program at the University of Virginia makes them available to the public. However, 'Franklin Roosevelt, Harry Truman, and Dwight Eisenhower recorded to a limited extent' (WHT, 2001a, p. xii). While the Roosevelt tapes are of no interest for the purposes of this study, the Truman and Eisenhower tapes are of low quality, with only bits and pieces audible, let alone intelligible, as some sampling quickly confirmed. Unlike his three predecessors, John F. Kennedy made extensive and systematic use of tape recorders, which he had installed to be manually activated.

The analysis focusing on his administration, presented in section 4.2, draws on the tape transcripts published by the Presidential Recordings Program, supplemented by a few transcripts prepared by myself, as well as a few additional materials to be detailed further below.

For every analysis dealing with texts and language, the selection of sources is a crucial decision in need of justification. Especially from the vantage point of discourse theory, the problem that presents itself is that 'due to the openness of discourses' an enormous amount of possible sources might well 'be interesting and equally relevant' (Herschinger, 2011, p. 53). Even though my analysis is not a discourse analysis in a strict sense, the same question arises: why enter the research process via conversation transcripts rather than, for instance, memoirs, public speeches, policy memos or official government documents?

The first answer is *intertextuality* (Hansen, 2006, pp. 55–72). As stated above, even in a situation of crisis in which a decision-maker needs to creatively make sense of what she is confronted with, she still depends on the given social context and the stockpile of meanings it contains. The construction of meaning thus necessarily takes place 'via juxtaposition to past meanings' (Herschinger, 2011, p. 55). Practically speaking, this means that already existing meanings and texts are to a certain extent contained or reflected in the sources at hand, and thus are never completely outside the scope of the analysis. As a matter of fact, in my case it turned out that references by speakers to articles, policy documents, treaty texts, speeches, internal memos or telegrams could fruitfully be integrated into the analysis.

Second, recordings – be it of meetings with numerous attendees, telephone conversations between two people or entries in a Dictaphone diary kept by a single individual – fit my methodology by allowing me to focus on the micro level of processes in which decision-makers attribute firsthand meaning to events via language and deliberate or decide about nuclear abstinence. To reconstruct this in detail, the sources used should ideally provide direct access to the interpretation and decision-making process. And while transcribed recordings can, of course, also offer only a secondary interpretation, that is, an interpretation of the interpretation by the agent under analysis, verbatim records still are preferable over interviews, memoirs or history books. All these would cloud the access by time and by adding another layer of interpretation. In contrast, the White House Tapes provide researchers with a one-of-a-kind opportunity to become the fly on the wall. Philip Zelikow and Ernest May (WHT, 2001a, p. xxiv), the two general editors of the Presidential Recordings Program, underline this point, explaining what sets the Kennedy White

House Tapes apart from any official document, public speech or internal policy memo: '[Kennedy] had no reason to suppose that the tapes would ever be heard by anyone other than himself unless he chose to make them available. They were completely secret. [...] He often made statements or discussed ideas that would have greatly damaged him had they become public. [H]e could hardly have known just what statements or positions would look good to posterity, for neither he nor his colleagues could know how the stories would turn out' (WHT, 2001a, p. xxiii).

Third, transcripts of presidential decision-making fit a peculiarity of the subject matter, because regarding the use of nuclear weapons, political decisions in the U.S. are special. Since the 1948 National Security Council Report 30, this decision of 'highest policy' (NSC-30, 1948, p. 625) rests with the 'Chief Executive' (NSC-30, 1948, p. 628), that is, the president, and solely the president.[1] Nuclear weapons are the president's weapons, nuclear use or non-use a presidential decision (Rosenbaum, 2011, pp. 32, 34) – 'a single decision compressed into a moment, a decision that could be executed swiftly, irrevocably, and almost automatically without further political deliberation' (Osgood/Tucker, 1971, p. 14). This peculiarity, which is anything but tension free regarding democratic checks and balances (Franklin, 2008 [1988], pp. 145–146), has been referred to as 'nuclear monarchy' or 'nuclear despotism' (Deudney, 2007, p. 255; Deudney also calls this the nuclear security constitution, see Deudney, 1995, p. 105).

Some caveats apply. First, there is the period of time before the nuclear football and nuclear predelegation. Second, the extreme case in which a president is forced to decide in almost an instant about using or not using nuclear weapons rarely, if ever, occurs. This would only be the case after an enemy launch is detected, when the normal sequence in which the president's decision is needed to order retaliation leaves him or her only *minutes* – from three to around twenty, depending on the specifics of the situation (Rhodes, 2008, pp. 145–146; cf. Blair, 1993, pp. 188–191, 217). Predominantly (and luckily), the pondering of nuclear weapon use has not taken place in this setting very often (and it was, of course, only evoked by false alerts in the past). Throughout the nuclear age, the decision about using or not using nuclear weapons has thus usually been one of concocting nuclear strategy, planning for contingencies and discussing posturing. And the decision to use nuclear weapons first rather than in retaliation also became immediate in only a limited number of conflicts. However, the question of using nuclear weapons is always outside of political routine. And because it ultimately hinges on the decision of the commander in chief and is a delicate a matter, pertinent deliberations are usually exclusive in terms of participants, limited in terms of time and sometimes conducted under pressure due to a crisis situation. This is why the Kennedy tapes provide suitable source material.

4.2 Empirical inquiry #1: John F. Kennedy and the crises in Berlin and Cuba

President Kennedy's handling of the Berlin crisis and the Cuban Missile Crisis has been studied intensively in the past. In the concluding remarks (4.2.3) I will put the following analysis – especially its result regarding the 'Berlin problem' – into the perspective of that existing research.

4.2.1 Nuclear use according to plan

West Berlin was a political symbol, a bulwark of freedom. For President Kennedy, keeping his commitment to Berlin was a question of principle. It also was one of prestige and of holding the Western alliance together. However, as a bridgehead with little strategic significance but an ever-looming potential to escalate a simmering conflict to nuclear war, Berlin was a heavy burden, too.

East-West relations took a turn for the worse with the construction of the Berlin Wall in August 1961. Furthermore, Nikita Khrushchev repeatedly threatened to sign a peace treaty with the German Democratic Republic to effectively cut off Western access and expel U.S., British and French forces from the city (WHT, 2001a, p. xlvii). Against the background of the crisis, President Kennedy (1961c) in October sent a letter to Supreme Commander Allied Powers Europe General Lauris Norstad. In his letter, he requested an effort for contingency planning in connection to the declared buildup of NATO conventional forces in Europe. The use – or rather non-use – of nuclear weapons was of utmost importance to the president.

Poodle Blanket's 'selective nuclear attacks'

Upholding nuclear deterrence in the European theater to keep the Soviets in check, while using nuclear weapons only as late as possible, was Kennedy's main concern. In his letter to Norstad he reiterated his administration's policy of replacing Eisenhower's nuclear doctrine of massive retaliation with flexible response, a point he conveyed to Norstad in clear terms: 'I ask that you spell out for me with particularity your operational concepts for the command and control procedures within your command to be used in the "selective nuclear attacks" and "limited tactical employment of nuclear weapons" [...]. What I want is a sequence of graduated responses to Soviet/GDR actions [...]' (Kennedy, 1961c, p. 520).

Over the course of the following year of planning, a political mitigation of the crisis in Europe could not be achieved. The U.S. expected 'the crunch' over Berlin, as it was referred to then (see e.g. WHT, 2001c, pp. 186, 202, 494, 552), for the fall of 1962 during Khrushchev's planned visit to the United Nations. In August and September 1962, the graduated military responses of the Berlin contingency plan, known by then as 'Poodle Blanket', were reviewed by the Kennedy administration – and its pitfalls manifested (WHT, 2001a, pp. 321, 328–330). Raising the nuclear threshold for not having to use nuclear weapons in Europe and establishing the aspired firebreak between conventional and nuclear weapons was tricky. Kennedy had to uphold the U.S. display of resolve, while at the same time implementing a strategy geared toward not actually having to act upon the threat of nuclear use. The allies, however, were anxious not to lose the U.S. nuclear commitment that provided security. So the flexibility of his new strategy was problematic: it rendered the extremely dicey question of exactly *timing* the nuclear option in the contingency planning paramount. This was revealed primarily in the question of employing nuclear weapons over an escalating conflict in Berlin.

The 'Berlin problem'

In a September 1962 meeting with his predecessor, General Eisenhower, Kennedy mused further about the timing of the nuclear option. He explained that 'talking about our immediate use of nuclear weapons, it seems to me, [that] if we didn't have the Berlin problem, [...] then obviously any Soviet intrusion across the line would be a deliberate one and would be a signal for war [...]' (WHT, 2001c, p. 129).

Eisenhower was skeptical about the new, cautious strategy. He remained wedded to the notion of massive retaliation regarding the big picture, that is, the regulation of the superpower confrontation (WHT, 2001c, pp. 123, 130). Kennedy restated his qualms: '[I]f we did not have the problem, I say, of Berlin and maintaining access through that autobahn authority, then you would say that any attempt to seize any part of West Germany, we would go to nuclear weapons. But, of course, *they never will!* (WHT, 2001c, p. 130).[2] What exactly was the meaning and significance of this 'problem, [...], of Berlin'?

Militarily speaking, the enclave of West Berlin was impossible to hold in the event of war. That made the question of autobahn access so crucial and was the number one reason why Berlin was such a burden – a *problem* – in strategic terms: 'this difficulty of maintaining a position 120 miles behind their lines', as Kennedy knew (WHT, 2001c, p. 130). But regarding the use of nuclear weapons, the Berlin problem was meaningful in a more specific way as well.

In not having to resort to an immediate use of nuclear weapons, the plans for countering a Soviet conventional aggression with nuclear weapons only eventually and in the more flexible fashion of *controlled escalation* had been fixed with Poodle Blanket. And the question of the timing of the nuclear option had supposedly been addressed, too. However, during his briefing on Poodle Blanket as well as afterwards, Kennedy found it hard to come to terms with the plan's nuclear phase IV and to even *consider* the use of nuclear weapons, the reason being the Berlin problem: 'I completely agree that if you didn't have the problem of Berlin then you would say that they're right about this and then as the first Russian soldier comes across the West German border, then you'd consider using nuclear weapons' (WHT, 2001a, p. 329).

While it is, of course, safe to assume that German and all European decision-makers were themselves torn between the U.S. nuclear threats that provided security and the prospect of actually having the superpowers slug out a nuclear war on their territory, they had clearly voiced their concern for a security-diminishing withdrawal of nuclear resolve signals. But despite that, Kennedy kept brooding over the reasons why the European allies were dragging their heels regarding the meeting of conventional buildup targets – the best possible way, according to his favored logic of flexible response, of maximally prolonging the conventional phases of conflict (WHT, 2001c, p. 140).

His enormous uneasiness with unequivocally stating the U.S. would initiate a nuclear exchange over Berlin became especially apparent in an exchange with Paul Nitze and McGeorge Bundy about the language to be used in a paper for the North Atlantic Council (WHT, 2001c, p. 141). Here, Kennedy insisted on dialing down the language on 'the initiation of some form of nuclear action'. This made sense from a diplomatic point of view, to undercut the European overreliance on U.S. nuclear guarantees and enforce the shared conventional buildup. Yet, especially against the background of Kennedy's thoughts about the prospect that his carefully planned steps of escalation might eventually escalate into a nuclear exchange, a further interpretation of this discussion and the Berlin problem at large, not necessarily contradicting this first one, seems at least as plausible. It suggests that Kennedy's Berlin problem was connected to more principled concerns over and above the strategic quarrel with the allies or forces getting tangled up in a (nuclear) war inside East Germany. In short, to Kennedy, the tricky question of *when* to use nuclear weapons for the defense of West Berlin conjured up the more fundamental question of *whether* to employ them at all.

If 'you just had a clean line'

In a meeting with his soon-to-be chairman of the Joint Chiefs of Staff, General Maxwell Taylor, at the end of September 1962, Kennedy elaborated on the Berlin problem. Regarding the different situations in Europe and Asia, Taylor floated the idea of a study analyzing the 'pros and cons of the use of atomic weapons in the Far East. Those pros and cons are quite different from the situation in Europe' (WHT, 2001c, p. 159). Kennedy replied, 'The reason that we're so slow about using nuclear weapons in Europe is, first, because we're against a nuclear force, and second, because of Berlin. Well, you see, if you didn't have the Berlin problem, you just had a clean line, you would use nuclear weapons almost from the beginning if they came across in force' (WHT, 2001c, p. 162).

Several things are remarkable about this statement. First, by pointing out to Taylor that 'we're against a nuclear force', Kennedy repeated almost literally a phrase of Robert McNamara, making an explicit reference to the logic of nuclear deterrence, few of which were otherwise to be found in the material. Second, and more importantly, a careful listening of the original audio recording reveals that Kennedy's emphasis here is not on the part in which he merely repeats McNamara's words but on the second part of the sentence, on *Berlin* (Kennedy, 1962d, time code 14:33).[3] Kennedy's formulation 'if you didn't have the Berlin problem, you just had a clean line' is key to understanding his qualms.

Generally speaking, Kennedy's emphasis on Berlin's being responsible for the lack of a 'clean line' can, in a first step, be interpreted as the missing of a definitive tactical threshold. If there were such a clear threshold, a decision to use nuclear weapons (if the Soviets 'came across in force') would be easier to make. In other words, an unmistakable 'signal for war', a tripwire for a quasi-automatic initiation of 'considering' nuclear actions would be available. But with Berlin remaining behind enemy lines, this was clearly problematic in Kennedy's eyes. By inquiring further into this in a second step, the interpretation can be expanded, especially by focusing on the lack of the 'cleanness' of the 'line'. In this line of thought, the lack of a 'clean line' *of fire* is pivotal.

With this in mind, and applying the vocabulary derived from the existing explanations of non-use, Kennedy's statement about the Berlin problem can be interpreted in two steps. One, it is another justification for his shift in deterrence strategy. After all, without a clean line for a nuclear 'shot', it is even more imperative to provide more conventional capabilities for delaying the use of nuclear weapons as long as possible. However, from a U.S. perspective, rationally speaking, a few tactical nuclear weapons in Germany, regardless of whether they were used only after intense and lengthy conventional battle or 'almost from the beginning', were clearly preferable to a massive nuclear exchange. That made up the European concern about the faltering nuclear resolve of the U.S. in the first place, that is, that Kennedy might have decided to not sacrifice New York for Berlin. So since Kennedy's whole point was avoiding the risk of a conflict over Europe immediately escalating into an all-out – messy – nuclear conflagration, why still wonder about a 'clean line' of fire in a scenario in which even the best case would have meant intense conventional fighting would have taken place? Clearly, the Berlin problem figuring so strongly in Kennedy's parlance and the notion of a missing 'clean line' transcend the boundaries of escalation models and the rational deterrence paradigm.

Two, it thus stands to reason that the consequences of using nuclear weapons for the defense of (access to) West Berlin (and Western Germany in general) in terms of civilian casualties inhibited the use of nuclear weapons. In Kennedy's view, the German civilian population literally stood in the way – rendering a shot along an unobstructed, *clean line of fire* impossible. So what made the nuclear option for Berlin one to be dealt with in these categories to begin with were *moral* considerations about the civilian death toll and the potentially cataclysmic consequences implied – consequences Kennedy was hell-bent on avoiding.

In this two-step reading, the Berlin problem is interpreted as a mix of deterrence and the nuclear taboo. It is an interesting example of how deterrence and the taboo *interact* as rules for action in a decision-making praxis. But the Berlin problem is no example of the two of them supporting each other in explaining why Kennedy was 'so slow about using nuclear weapons in Europe'. Quite the opposite.

For the sake of contingency planning, Kennedy was forced to decide on the timing of the nuclear option in Europe. Sure, against the conventionally superior Soviet forces, he would have to use nuclear weapons eventually, maybe even against his initial plan 'almost from the beginning if they came across in force'. But this not only evoked the deterrence paradox, that is, a strategy geared toward raising the nuclear threshold in order not to have to resort to nuclear weapons that forces the decision-maker at the same time to constantly worry about using them nonetheless. What made matters worse was that his sense of taboo-ness caused Kennedy to remain uneasy about using nuclear weapons in this according-to-plan fashion. The resulting hesitation naturally carried the danger of running contrary to the U.S. deterrence posture, especially in light of the already existing nervousness of European allies about the credibility of the U.S. nuclear commitment. Consequently, regarding Khrushchev's repeated threats to challenge the status quo in Berlin, special adviser to the president and expert on the Soviet Union Charles E. Bohlen reminded Kennedy during a meeting on the Soviet Union on September 29 that '[Khrushchev] has been telling everybody that the United States is too liberal, et cetera, et cetera, to fight. And I must say the general feeling, I think is that, among the demonologists, is chances are he believes this' (WHT, 2001c, p. 185).

So what the 'demonologists' were telling the U.S. president was that Khrushchev could lose his belief in deterrence if he, Kennedy, especially when overly inhibited and hesitant due his sensitivity to the tabooness of nuclear weapon use, raised the nuclear threshold *too* high. If the Kremlin's belief that the U.S. would not fight ever came to be fixed, extended deterrence in Europe would vanish into thin air and the door would be ajar for Soviet expansion. Bohlen continued with respect to the defense of Berlin: 'Well, he believes [...] that in view of public opinion and [*unclear*] of the horrors of a nuclear war that the United States would not...would back away from that point. Therefore he's got a situation with all the advantage on his side where he can proceed. And there'll be a great whooping and yelling around but that nothing will happen. But the thing he's interested in, which is the only thing you worry about, is a nuclear war. And this is cockeyed, I think' (WHT, 2001c, p. 186).

These 'beliefs' and 'worries' about nuclear use in the Kennedy material empirically substantiate the interpretation of the planned nuclear option in Berlin as nuclear deterrence being practiced as a strategy, with the nuclear taboo interfering. This contradicts the assumption that the two explanatory concepts stabilize each other in practice (cf. section 3.1). Granted, seen as cumulatively injecting more and more logic of appropriateness into the rational cost-benefit calculus about the already deemed costly consequences of nuclear use, the idea of stabilization makes sense at first glance. But while plausible in hindsight and regarding the resulting big picture (i.e. the repeating historical pattern of nuclear abstinence), the reconstructive analysis of Kennedy's actions regarding the Berlin problem so far, by asking how non-use comes about rather than trying to explain it ex post, yields a more differentiated picture. The taboo actually made struggling with the deterrence paradox only more tantalizing because, in deterrence parlance, it amplified *self*-deterrence and threatened to undermine the necessary practice of signaling resolve. Hence, while deterrence and the taboo were interacting, from Kennedy's perspective and at the time, the taboo was more of a hindrance than a help in his trying to ensure nuclear non-use. I will discuss this in more depth in the concluding remarks (4.2.3).

While the Berlin crisis was merely simmering, the Cuban Missile Crisis boiled over quickly. With the ominous risk of escalation becoming suddenly palpable and events putting pressure on the decision-makers to take the next step here and now, without the comfort of a blueprint for action, their nuclear worries reached nightmarish proportions. When using nuclear weapons went from a required hypothetical to a dreaded but likely prospect, 'escalation control' in Cuba came to mean the opposite of what it had meant in Berlin.

4.2.2 Nuclear use as final failure

President Kennedy still expected the 'crunch' over Berlin to come in the fall of 1962. Then, on the morning of October 16, he was presented with the information that the Soviet Union had stationed medium-range ballistic missiles (MRBMs) on Cuba. Reviewing the photographs taken the previous day by U-2 reconnaissance flights, the president was assured during the first minutes of the cabinet room meeting on the unfolding Cuban Missile Crisis that the objects in the photos were in fact missile trailers, launchers and nuclear-capable missiles with a range of up to 1,100 miles. 'Is this ready to be fired?' (WHT, 2001c, p. 399) was the President's reaction. It became clear that the installations were not yet complete, however. Also, nuclear warheads could not be identified on the photographs.[4] But it was patently obvious now that the Soviet statements about the military buildup in Cuba being conventional and purely defensive in nature had been false. Kennedy's warning not to station 'offensive' – meaning nuclear – weapons on Cuba had been blatantly ignored.

Options for dealing with the missiles on Cuba were discussed, ranging from diplomatic probes to limited airstrikes against the missiles only, to an extensive bombing campaign including antiaircraft installations and airfields, up to a full-fledged invasion of the island. However, since the debacle of the Bay of Pigs invasion, Kennedy had internalized that in the event of a U.S. invasion in Cuba, the Soviets 'would just grab West Berlin' in return – after all, they easily 'could grab Berlin in two hours' (WHT, 2001c, p. 200). For him, the connection between Cuba and Berlin was unquestionable: '[T]he problem is not really some war against Cuba. But the problem is part of this worldwide struggle where we face the

Communists, particularly, as I say, over Berlin' (WHT, 2001c, p. 589), he would state on day three of the crisis.

So on the one hand, the Soviet provocation could not go unanswered for reasons of prestige and credibility. On the other hand, Kennedy knew, '[i]f we attack Cuba, the missiles, or Cuba, in any way', Berlin would be taken as a reprisal. Consequently, he was convinced that the European allies would not back a U.S. action against Cuba. 'We will have been regarded as – they think we've got this fixation about Cuba anyway – we would be regarded as the trigger-happy Americans who lost Berlin' (WHT, 2001c, p. 581), Kennedy worried. After all, Europe had been living under the sword of Damocles for quite a while. So why would the allies be particularly bothered if suddenly the U.S. were in closer range to Soviet missiles, too? As the president sarcastically remarked regarding the question of distance: 'You may say it doesn't make any difference if you get blown up by an ICBM flying from the Soviet Union or one from 90 miles away' (WHT, 2001c, p. 441).

So this is how President Kennedy came to assess the situation: respond with military action against the Soviet missile buildup on Cuba, and in Europe 'everybody would feel we lost Berlin, because of these missiles, which as I say, do not bother them [the allies]' (WHT, 2001c, p. 540). Wait and the Soviets on Cuba 'get sufficient capacity [...]. Then they start getting ready to squeeze us in Berlin' (WHT, 2001c, p. 441). In other words, let things in Cuba slide and the Soviets end up with the capacity to blackmail the seemingly risk-averse U.S. into abandoning Berlin, so that the Soviets could easily take it. Attack Cuba and the Soviets would also take Berlin, in retribution this time. From Kennedy's perspective, the dilemma was that no matter what course he of action he chose regarding Cuba, confrontation or acquiescence, in the end Berlin would be lost – and the conflict would then have to escalate, according to his own plan. In short, Kennedy realized that with Berlin set up as the tripwire for nuclear escalation, the Soviets were using Cuba as a poking stick to have *him* stumble into nuclear war.

The 'world we live in' after striking Cuba

Different options being discussed during Committee (ExComm) meetings was not a problem per se. After all, it is the job of advisers to provide the president with options (and while much has been made of categorizing ExComm members as either 'hawks' or 'doves' or 'owls' [Blight et al., 1987, p. 173], accordingly, the transcripts suggest that few of them were consistently wedded to one such camp). What *did* pose a problem was the utter uncertainty regarding the consequences of *all* conceivable options. Concerning a possible military course of action, McNamara wondered, 'I don't know quite what kind of a world we live in after we have struck Cuba' (WHT, 2001c, p. 448).

Considering, for example, that Soviet planes on Cuba could also deliver nuclear warheads to the U.S. in retribution, Kennedy saw the merits of a more extensive air campaign, including 'the advantage of taking out these airplanes [...] to protect us against a reprisal' (WHT, 2001c, p. 420). But considering the Soviet reprisal, the rifts and ambivalences in Kennedy's thinking about nuclear strategy and deterrence started to show. On October 16, he thought a reprisal with nuclear bombs after a U.S. airstrike to be unlikely, relying on deterrence and the U.S. retaliatory threat for such a contingency (WHT, 2001c, p. 440). To Douglas Dillon's question 'what if they carry a nuclear weapon?' (WHT, 2001c, p. 440), he answered, 'Well, [...] you assume they wouldn't do that'. At this early stage it still seemed clear to Kennedy: 'I would think you'd have to assume they'd be using iron bombs and not nuclear weapons. Because, obviously, why would the Soviets permit nuclear war to begin under that sort of halfassed way?' (WHT, 2001c, p. 420).

Judging from only this exemplarily cited statement (see e.g. also WHT, 2001c, p. 528), President Kennedy – at the beginning – seemed to instinctively rely on the deterrent effect of a credible threat to use nuclear weapons in retaliation. On days one and two of the crisis, he found it conceivable that the conflict over Cuba could be kept conventional. Otherwise, his conviction that a general nuclear war would not begin in some 'halfassed way' would have been impossible to uphold. However, the uncertainty regarding the consequences of his own actions had Kennedy second-guessing these assumptions. In light of these growing doubts, his initial confidence in keeping the conflict conventional by threatening retaliation 'with nuclear weapons' (WHT, 2001c, pp. 412–413) dwindled. In his newly emerging line of thought, further escalation raised not only the question 'what world' to live in afterward, but rather whether there would even be a world left to live in. By October 22, Kennedy would call the invasion of Cuba one 'one hell of a gamble' (WHT, 2001b, p. 78). And Berlin had been the catalyst for these growing doubts and worries.

The 'Berlin problem' once more

That Berlin would be lost 'anyway' regardless of his own actions had Kennedy (WHT, 2001c, p. 539) bordering on defeatism: 'Gromyko made it very clear last week [that] they're getting ready to move on Berlin anyway. [N]o matter what we do, [...] they're going to do it anyway. [T]hey're going to do it anyway' (WHT, 2001b, p. 49).

With Cuba and Berlin directly linked and the 'crunch' now potentially expedited, the implications of the U.S. commitment in Europe were discussed on October 18. This was the very same meeting in which only a couple of minutes before Kennedy had felt safe to assume that the Soviets would not retaliate from Cuba with nuclear bombs against targets in Florida. So what would happen if the U.S. took military action against Cuba? The answer was obvious. Khrushchev would try to take Berlin. But what would that mean (WHT, 2001c, pp. 540–541)?

McNamara: Well, when we're talking about taking Berlin, what do we mean exactly? Does he take it with Soviet troops?
President Kennedy: That's what it would seem to me.
McNamara: Then we have... I think there's a real possibility. We have U.S. troops there. What do they do?
Taylor: They fight.
McNamara: They fight. I think that's perfectly clear.
President Kennedy: And they get overrun.
McNamara: Yes, they get overrun, exactly.
Unidentified: Well, you have a direct confrontation.
Robert Kennedy: Then what do we do?
Taylor: Go to general war, if it's in the interest of ours.
Unidentified: It's then general war. Consider the use of...
President Kennedy: You mean nuclear exchange? [*Brief pause.*]
Taylor: Guess you have to.

Kennedy had assumed in the same meeting that in the Soviet reprisal against the U.S. after a conventional strike against the missiles on Cuba, 'they are not going to permit nuclear weapons to be used' (WHT, 2001c, p. 528). He now acknowledges that a Soviet reprisal against Berlin would require *him* to initiate nuclear action, once more evoking the Berlin problem. Because the Soviets 'just going in and taking Berlin by force' would leave him 'only one alternative, which is to fire nuclear weapons – which is a hell of an alternative' (WHT, 2001c, p. 581), as he would summarize it for the Joint Chiefs of Staff the next day.

Following this lead further, the quoted passage is worth listening to in the original audio recording (Kennedy, 1962c, time code 07:40). There is a considerable pause in the otherwise rapid conversation after Kennedy spells out general war as 'nuclear exchange'. This is followed by General Taylor sheepishly muttering 'Guess you have to' in a muted voice. After that, the conversation pauses again for almost *four seconds.* Everybody seems to hold his breath for a moment. Clearly, for once spelling out this hypothetical chain of events up to this final point discomforted Kennedy and his advisers immensely, including General Taylor. After the contemplative pause, Bundy picks up again, but the group appears a bit shaken.

Bundy: I do see your...If you go in at the same time that you do this [attack on Cuba] and you'll say to him: 'Berlin still means general war'. I don't think he will do it that way.

Unidentified: I doubt whether he would...I don't think he'd [*unclear*].

Rusk: You'd have to start at least with tactical nuclear weapons if he tried to attack Berlin [*unclear*] a blockade.

Taylor: I think they'd use East German forces, rather than bringing their own troops in.

President Kennedy: Let me ask you. It seems to me we have been talking about the alliance, you've got two problems. One would be the problem of the alliance when we say to them that the presence of these missiles requires a military action by us. There's no doubt that they will oppose that, because they'll feel that their risks increase, and this is a risk to us. [...]. If we don't take any action, then of course there will be a more gradual deterioration, I suppose. Isn't that the argument?

Rusk: I think that will be very fast.

Dillon: Very rapidly.

Bundy: Very rapid.

Dillon: Very rapid.

President Kennedy: After my statement, and then, I mean...Somehow we've got to take some action because we couldn't...Because the alliance would disintegrate. Now, the question really is to what action we take which lessens the chances of a nuclear exchange, which obviously is the final failure [...].

In light of the Cuba-Berlin-dilemma, October 18 became a turning point regarding Kennedy's confidence in keeping an escalating crisis conventional. He had now spelled out an additional, third guideline for his decision-making. One, something had to be done about the missiles on Cuba. Two, the Berlin crunch would certainly be evoked by it. But three, whatever he decided this 'something' to be, ending up with a nuclear exchange would be the final failure. Continued reliance on U.S. nuclear deterrence to keep the Soviets or Fidel Castro from using nuclear weapons in turn after an attack on Cuba was beside the point now. Because Kennedy had realized that *he himself* could easily become the one making the step toward the 'final failure' – by keeping his commitment to defend Berlin with nuclear weapons. This had rendered deterrence (its idea being the prevention of a Soviet invasion and Soviet nuclear first-use) pointless.

Kennedy's adjusted stance showed clearly over the course of the unfolding Cuba situation after October 18. For instance, an October 22 conversation with ex-president Eisenhower demonstrates the influx of doubts into the process of Kennedy's interpreting and managing the situation with the help of deterrence (WHT, 2001b, pp. 14–15):

President Kennedy: [...] As I say, we will, I don't know, we may get into the invasion business before many days are out.

Eisenhower: Yeah.

President Kennedy: But...

Eisenhower: Of course, from the military standpoint that's the cleancut thing to do, now.

President Kennedy: That's right. That's right.

Eisenhower: Because you've made up your mind you've *got* to get rid of this thing.

President Kennedy: Right.

Eisenhower: The only real way to get rid of it, of course, is the other thing [military attack]. But, having to be concerned with world opinion and –

President Kennedy: And Berlin.

Eisenhower: – of others, why you've got to do it a little slower.

President Kennedy: Well, Berlin is the...I suppose, that may be the...what they're going to try to trade off.

Eisenhower: Well, they might. But I, personally, I just don't quite go along, you know, with that thinking, Mr. President. My idea is this: The damn Soviets will do whatever they want, what they figure is good for them.

President Kennedy: Yeah.

Eisenhower: And I don't believe they relate one situation with another.

President Kennedy: Uh-huh.

Eisenhower: Just what they find out they can do here and there and the other place.

President Kennedy: Yeah. Yeah.

Eisenhower: And, we're already standing as a unit with NATO, that if they go into Berlin, that's all of it.

President Kennedy: Right.

Eisenhower: That means they've got to look out that they don't get a terrific blow to themselves.

President Kennedy: Right. Right.

Eisenhower: And I don't...It might be, I could be all wrong. But my own conviction is that you will not find a great deal of relationship between the two.

President Kennedy: Let me ask –

Eisenhower: They'll try to *make* it that way.

President Kennedy: Yeah. General, what about if the Soviet Union – Khrushchev – announces tomorrow, which I think he will, that if we attack Cuba that it's going to be nuclear war? And what's your judgment as to the chances they'll fire these things off if we invade Cuba?

Eisenhower: Oh, I don't believe that they will.

President Kennedy: You don't think they will?

Eisenhower: No.

President Kennedy: In other words you would take that risk if the situation seemed desirable?

Eisenhower: Well, as a matter of fact, what can you do?

President Kennedy: Yeah.

Eisenhower: If this thing is such a serious thing, here on our flank, that we're going to be uneasy and we know what thing is happening now. All right, you've got to use something.

President Kennedy: Yeah.

Eisenhower: Something *may* make these people [the Soviets] shoot them [their nuclear missiles] off. I just don't believe this will.

President Kennedy: Yeah, right. [*Chuckles resignedly*]

The conversation ended quickly afterward. Eisenhower could not exactly say why, but it sufficed for him to know that the Soviets, moving on Berlin or firing their missiles off Cuba, would receive 'a terrific blow to themselves'. Consequently, these things simply could not happen. In short, Eisenhower believed in deterrence more than Kennedy did. Eisenhower also saw Berlin and Cuba as not connected the same way Kennedy did. General Taylor, on the other hand, saw that connection, but in the opposite fashion. He had already stated on October 18 that 'the credibility of our response in Berlin is enhanced by taking action in Cuba, rather than being diminished' (WHT, 2001c, p. 544). Similarly, in a meeting with the Joint Chiefs of Staff on October 19, Curtis LeMay had pointed out to the president that the lesson of 'history' regarding the Soviets has been that '[w]here we have taken a strong stand they have backed off' (WHT, 2001c, p. 585). Accordingly, he was 'sure' that '[i]f you lose in Cuba you're going to get more and more pressure right on Berlin' (WHT, 2001c, p. 589).

But Kennedy could not be swayed, neither by his military advisers nor by his predecessor in office. To him, the Cuba-Berlin dilemma persisted. To LeMay he replied, 'They can't let us just take out, after all their statements, take out their missiles, kill a lot of Russians and not do anything. It's quite obvious that what they... I would think they would do, is try to get Berlin' (WHT, 2001c, p. 585). And the Soviets trying to get Berlin meant general war. And general war meant nuclear war.

Consequently, on October 23 and in light of his growing doubts about deterrence prevailing, the president had long begun thinking about civil defense and evacuation measures as preparations for a nuclear attack, specifically for Florida. Regarding the Soviet reaction to a U.S. invasion, he nevertheless insisted that 'we're not going to have an all-out nuclear exchange. If we were going to have an all-out nuclear exchange, then we'd have a different problem. Let's say we're going into Cuba, and there's maybe some bombs back, 10 or 15 [missiles launched against the United States]. That kind of fallout. Not the usual – I don't know how many megatons' (WHT, 2001b, p. 171). So the president had gone from 'assuming they wouldn't do that' to assuming that most likely 'we're not going to have an all-out nuclear exchange' but only '10 or 15' missiles in return.

Not only could the missiles on Cuba be fired in retaliation against a U.S. military action in answer to which the U.S. in turn would have to retaliate in kind. With Cuba and Berlin so inextricably linked, the Berlin problem came on top. Miscalculations, losses of control and human errors – stuff the Cuban Missile Crisis was ripe with – leading to a nuclear war erupting inadvertently were one thing. But the conflict around Cuba would certainly involve the German powder keg. And that carried along with it the contingency of Kennedy's having to initiate a nuclear exchange against the conventional Soviet forces – deliberately and according to his own plan starting the use of nuclear weapons, with all the risks of a nuclear conflagration in turn. From Kennedy's perspective it had to seem like the general war nobody intended and wanted was nearly inevitable. With Berlin on his mind, he spoke of containing the situation, provoking as little escalation as possible and thus preventing this catastrophic development into 'final failure'.

Starting October 18, Kennedy focused on a naval blockade against Cuba as the best first step. A blockade carried less escalatory risk than any form of attack and also bought time. Kennedy summed this up to himself by dictating into the machine in the Oval Office his views and decisions in light of the discussions of October 18: 'I was most anxious that we not have to announce a state of war existing, because it would obviously be bad to have the word go out that we were having a war rather than that it was a limited blockade for a limited purpose' (WHT, 2001c, p. 577). For 'not having to have a war', the State Department and Secretary Dean Rusk presented a solution on October 20. Calling the blockade a 'quarantine', a suggestion by legal adviser Leonard Meeker (WHT, 2001c, p. 575), was the way to creatively circle around the undesirable declaration of war.

Having announced the 'quarantine' around the Caribbean island on television, Kennedy spoke to UK prime minister Harold Macmillan on the phone. Kennedy had had to defend his decision to Congressional leaders (WHT, 2001b, pp. 70–89) and admitted that he did not know 'where Khrushchev wants to take us' (WHT, 2001b, p. 89) and that while the U.S. would 'start here' he did not 'know [...] where we're going to take ourselves' (WHT, 2001b, p. 90). He reiterated to Macmillan the persisting and torturing uncertainty regarding the future: 'We don't know what's going to happen in Berlin. We don't know what's going to happen anyplace else. This seemed to be the action we could take which would lessen the chance of an immediate escalation into war, though of course it could bring that result' (WHT, 2001b, p. 99).

The vexing issue of 'control'

Kennedy was not entertaining the notion of using nuclear weapons against Cuba at any point. But a deliberate first use was not out of the question for everyone. House Minority Leader Charles A. Halleck asked in the heated debate with Congressional leaders 'with what kind of bombs' potential sorties against Cuba would be flown. That the U.S. Air Force could be planning to use nuclear weapons was thus obviously not completely unthinkable. Yet, McNamara quickly confirmed: 'Initially iron bombs' (WHT, 2001b, p. 76). General Taylor did, however, when pushing for an air strike over a naval blockade in a final attempt during the National Security Council (NSC) meeting on October 20, insinuate a nuclear first strike against the Soviet missiles on Cuba. He stated (according to the notes taken by NSC executive secretary Bromley Smith) that 'he did not share Secretary McNamara's fear that if we used nuclear weapons in Cuba, nuclear weapons would be used against us' (WHT, 2001c, p. 605). Also, the chiefs of staff were at least as skeptical as some Congressional leaders regarding the quarantine. But Kennedy once more pointed to the Cuba-Berlin dilemma and the looming consequences: '[T]there's bound to be a reprisal from the Soviet Union, there always is – of their just going in and taking Berlin by force at some point. Which leaves me only one alternative, which is to fire nuclear weapons – which is a hell of an alternative – [...] that's what has made this thing be a dilemma for three days' (WHT, 2001c, pp. 581–582). President Kennedy added, 'The argument for the blockade was that what we want to do is to avoid, if we can, nuclear war by escalation or imbalance. The Soviets increase; we use [force]; they blockade Berlin. They blockade for military purposes. Then we take an initial action so that... We've got to have some degree of control' (WHT, 2001c, pp. 593–594).

In short, Kennedy's dilemma was that nuclear war could result from both controlled and uncontrolled escalation. In his televised speech, for instance, Kennedy mentioned 'the brave people of West Berlin' to whose 'safety and freedom' he renewed his commitment, assuring them that any hostilities would 'be met by whatever action is needed' (WHT, 2001b, p. 95). However, he also affirmed that the U.S. 'will not prematurely or unnecessarily risk the costs of worldwide nuclear war in which even the fruits of victory would be ashes in our mouth' (WHT, 2001b, p. 94). Similarly, he wrote in a letter accompanying a copy of his televised statement to Khrushchev that the U.S. could not 'tolerate any action on your part which in a major way disturbed the existing overall balance of power in the world' (WHT, 2001b, p. 97), and described in a letter to Macmillan the Soviet move as 'so deep a breach in the conventions of the international stalemate that if unchallenged it would deeply shake confidence in the United States, especially in the light of my repeated warnings' (WHT, 2001b, p. 98). Yet, in the letter to Khrushchev, Kennedy stressed in contrast that 'in our discussions and exchanges on Berlin and other international questions, the one thing that has most concerned me has been the possibility that your Government would not correctly understand the will and determination of the United States in any given situation, since I have not assumed that you or any other sane man would, in this nuclear age, deliberately plunge the world into war which it is crystal clear no country could win and which could only result in catastrophic consequences to the whole world, including the aggressor' (WHT, 2001b, p. 97). This underlines how much Kennedy was torn between making sense of the crises situation in a paradigmatic way on the one hand and grasping the situation by pointing out the dread of looming nuclear apocalypse he most definitely felt on the other.

So Kennedy did not take 'escalation control' to mean control over the deterrence standoff in the sense of escalation dominance. He simply longed for as little escalation as possible due to the acute anticipation of *either* losing control (see on that especially WHT, 2001b, pp. 33–35, 175, 346–348) and nuclear war erupting *or* his having to initiate it according to plan. He stalled for time.

Then, a letter by Chairman Khrushchev was received on the evening of October 26. It was not made public and seemed to convey Khrushchev's shared sense for preventing catastrophic escalation in emotional language. It stated that if the U.S. pledged not to invade Cuba, this 'would change everything' because 'the question of armaments would disappear, since, if there is no threat, then armaments are a burden for every people' (WHT, 2001b, p. 353). Kennedy and his advisers took from that letter that Khrushchev was clearly proposing the following deal: Soviet missiles would be withdrawn in exchange for a U.S. guarantee not to attack Cuba.

While drafting a response the next day, another and this time public and more formal letter arrived, retracting the earlier proposal, reminding the U.S. president that '[y]our rockets are stationed in Turkey', which 'lies next to us', and suggesting a missile swap by removing 'those weapons from Cuba' if the U.S. 'will evacuate its analogous weapons from Turkey' (WHT, 2001b, p. 373). This change of the deal caused confusion and frustration on the U.S. side and set the stage for the last, immensely tense day of the crisis.

During the October 27 marathon meeting of the ExComm, General Taylor presented a recommendation for an all-out air strike by the Chiefs of Staffs, to be implemented two days later, on Monday, October 29, 'unless there is irrefutable evidence in the meantime that offensive weapons are being dismantled and rendered inoperable' (WHT, 2001b, p. 437), a recommendation about which Bobby Kennedy quipped, 'Well, I'm surprised' (WHT, 2001b, p. 437) in an attempt to defuse the tense moment. With the laughter about the attorney general's remark subsiding, President Kennedy (WHT, 2001b, p. 438) tried to use the opportunity to deflect from further escalation once again, insisting against repeated interjections by Taylor and, eventually, having to finally cut him off brashly, as the audio recording (Kennedy, 1962a, time code 14:40) confirms:

President Kennedy: Well, that's where we need to go. But let's get this letter [to Khrushchev] –

Taylor: I think the Monday morning date now is just something to think about. It does look now, from a military point of view...

President Kennedy: What are the reasons why?
Robert Kennedy: Can you find out about that?
Taylor: They just feel that the longer we wait now...
President Kennedy: I know, OK. But there's no...? Right. OK.

However, Kennedy's conviction to stall for time was put to the test the same day again, when a U.S. U-2 spy plane over Cuba was shot down. He briefly toyed with the idea of 'just tak[ing] the reprisal without making any announcement' (WHT, 2001b, p. 449). But officially acknowledging that U.S. planes were being fired upon over Cuba would have created *zugzwang*, an overwhelming compulsion for the U.S. to react. One last time he decided to first wait for confirmation that the plane did not go down due to mechanical failure (WHT, 2001b, pp. 450–451).

In this situation of confusion and rapidly mounting pressure, the answer letter to Khrushchev had to be drafted. President Kennedy decided to accept the deal he and his team had interpreted as being contained in Khrushchev's first, unofficial letter. His answer thus emphasized the need for a cessation of work on the missiles and furthermore proposed a Soviet removal of 'these weapons systems from Cuba' for U.S. 'assurances against an invasion of Cuba' in turn (WHT, 2001b, p. 483). Robert Kennedy was told to deliver the answer letter to Soviet ambassador Anatoly Dobrynin in person, along with a stern oral message that left no more wiggle room.

So after days of carefully monitoring the situation and forcing himself as well as his team to wait, in the end and in light of the events of October 27, President Kennedy did risk that Khrushchev might refuse to make the deal 'no missiles, no invasion'. For the first time he maneuvered himself into a position from which he would have to significantly escalate in case his demands were not met. However, at the same time he knew the Jupiter missiles in Turkey, to which Khrushchev's second letter had referred, were obsolete due to the introduction of U.S. Polaris submarines in the Mediterranean. Also, they had been under discussion from as early as the first day of the crisis when Rusk pondered Khrushchev's motivation for putting missiles on Cuba and suggested that 'we don't really live under fear of his nuclear weapons to the extent that he has to live under fear of ours' (WHT, 2001c, p. 410). U.S. Ambassador to the United Nations Adlai Stevenson then had urged Kennedy as early as October 18 to consider U.S. nuclear missile bases negotiable if necessary to avoid escalation into nuclear war (WHT, 2001c, p. 512).[5] That same day, Kennedy himself had also spelled out the possibility of a trade for the first time in the transcripts, still skeptical, however, at this point due to the uncertainty about Khrushchev's reaction and the ever-looming involvement of Berlin (WHT, 2001c, p. 532). So now, even though President Kennedy would not allow the missiles to be removed under force of Soviet threats, he instructed his brother to orally convey the possibility of the Jupiters' removal *after* the Cuban Missile Crisis was resolved and under the strict condition of the arrangement being kept a secret (WHT, 2001b, pp. 483–485).[6]

In the evening of Saturday, October 27, in light of his unambiguous proposal in the answer to Khrushchev, and considering that U.S surveillance planes over Cuba were still being fired upon, Kennedy leaned toward ending his careful stance of military abstention. However, again he opted for waiting one more day, delaying the attack until Monday (WHT, 2001b, p. 492).

On the morning of Sunday, October 28, Kennedy learned that Khrushchev had accepted his proposal. President Kennedy said to Eisenhower on the phone, 'If they attempt to do any aggressive acts and so on, then all bets are off. In addition, my guess is that, by the end of next month, we're going to be toe to toe on Berlin, anyway' (WHT, 2001b, p. 520).

Ironically, Kennedy was about to be proven wrong about the *only* thing he felt he could be absolutely certain of during the entire time of the Cuban Missile Crisis: the crunch over Berlin. He knew it would come, and he dreaded the prospect of then having to initiate a nuclear confrontation. The Berlin problem was a crucial guiding element in his decision-making – in both a strategic and a moral regard – linking the taboo to his deterrence strategy in a Gordian knot Kennedy was unable and unwilling to smash. But the crunch did *not* come, and the Berlin problem never actually materialized. As the editors of the Kennedy volumes aptly put it, 'For reasons that then remained obscure to the Americans, the end of the missile crisis also became the end of the Berlin crisis. Khrushchev simply dropped, without comment, the ultimatum he had issued in September. The ominous clouds dissipated, bringing an uneasy calm' (WHT, 2001b, pp. 524–525).

4.2.3 Concluding remarks

What could be reconstructed with regard to how the causes of nuclear non-use were invoked in decision-making practices characterized by crisis, especially regarding their specific meaning and their stability and prevalence as beliefs? After having taken a look at these (three deductive codes) in isolation, I will explain in more depth what can be concluded from the Berlin problem regarding nuclear deterrence and the nuclear taboo and their interaction in practice, presenting this study's first main result. The goal in the subsequent paragraphs is to then draw attention to a less preconceived aspect in play, the important role of human emotion. Following this trail further allows us to foster our understanding of nuclear abstinence further.

The explanations of non-use

The deductive code *Tradition* for the tradition of non-use was coded only five times over the entire Kennedy material (and basically all of those passages were only tentatively attributed this code, with memos attached that suggest caveats). The weighing of benefits against political costs such as reputation loss or the setting of detrimental precedents to which the tradition of non-use points primarily as explanatory factors could, for example, be found in Bundy's statement that 'there is, I would think, a substantial political advantage in limiting the strike in surgical terms to the thing that is in fact the cause of action' (WHT, 2001c, p. 413). Bundy states this in a context in which the question arose of whether high explosives would even be able to destroy the targets in Cuba. Pointing to political costs, Bundy opts for a 'limited' strike to not have to weigh alternatives involving nuclear ordnance. But other than that, and despite the fact that in other contexts reputation concerning *World Opinion* (coded 29 times) factored in, the U.S. relationship to the Western *Alliance* and its cohesion (coded 36 times) was heavily under discussion, and *Prestige* (coded 49 times) was in play regularly, the central motifs of the tradition of non-use did not play a meaningful role in the material.

The deductive code *Taboo* (coded 11 times including sub-codes) yielded similarly few clear-cut results – at least at first glance. The discussion of a U.S. surprise attack on Cuba provides some of the few unambiguous examples, including the already cited 'mark of Cain' remark by Rusk (WHT, 2001c, p. 547). Pointing to national identity and what the U.S. 'just does not' or 'would never do' are pivotal elements of how the nuclear taboo explains nuclear non-use, and they are spelled out literally in these passages. That using nuclear weapons was not completely taboo – that is, unspeakable or even unthinkable – to *everybody* in the Kennedy administration is documented in General Taylor's attempt to float the idea of a nuclear attack against Cuba. However, the taboo certainly mattered for President Kennedy. He *did* regard the use of nuclear weapons as wrong, literally as *the final failure*. That passage was coded *Taboo* accordingly, too. Judging from the transcripts, using nuclear weapons was in fact a dreadful prospect for him due to moral concerns. Tannenwald's (2007, pp. 191–192, 200, 203–209) assessment of the overwhelming impact of the nuclear taboo on Kennedy is thus strongly underlined by my analysis, which focuses on the way it figured in as a belief ruling action. In addition, the heavy element of tabooness contained in the code *Berlin* and what I reconstructed as the Berlin problem shows that this deductively derived concept was anything but absent from the material. So the mere frequency of specific, isolated codes was of little analytic significance here. Instead, it was analyzing the relations between *Berlin* and *Taboo* and sub-codes of *Use* such as *Contingency Plans* (coded 100 times), *Consequences of Use* (coded 22 times) or *Last Resort* (coded 21 times) that allowed the meaning of the Berlin problem to be evaluated properly. To that I will turn separately in the next segment, after having briefly touched upon the third and final deductive code in isolation, deterrence.

Explicit, by which I mean *literal*, references to nuclear deterrence (*Deterrence* was coded 28 times) were few and far between in the material. Nevertheless, with comparably clear statements such as Kennedy's Poodle Blanket letter or the justification of his slow use of nuclear weapons in Europe due to his 'being against a nuclear force', it figured more prominently than the other two deductive codes. Again, coding frequencies were, at best, a guidepost. The context in which the code *Deterrence* was embedded, and what deterrence *meant* for the decision-makers at the time were the more important questions. Here, the Berlin problem and the reconstruction of Kennedy's dwindling confidence in deterrence as a strategy during the Cuban Missile Crisis point to how Kennedy was actually struggling with the deterrence paradox and how he hesitated to fully buy into believing in deterrence as a reliable guarantor for keeping conflicts from escalating into nuclear war. So thinking about deterrence and the nuclear taboo, and their role in combination was key for better understanding their role with respect to nuclear abstinence.

The Berlin problem and the taboo's interfering with deterrence in practice

At first glance, especially by pointing to Kennedy's televised October 22 speech, one might simply say that deterrence kept the Cuban Missile Crisis from derailing. After all, in that speech Kennedy famously stated as a signal of resolve, 'It shall be the policy of this nation to regard any nuclear missile launched from Cuba against any nation in the Western Hemisphere as an attack by the Soviet Union on the United States, requiring a full retaliatory response upon the Soviet Union' (WHT, 2001b, p. 94). The two codes identified as pivotal during my analysis – *Uncertainty* and *Escalatory Control* – also seem to neatly fit the picture of the deterrence frame of reference. After all, according to deterrence optimist Kenneth Waltz (2003b, p. 143), 'the effectiveness of nuclear deterrence rests on uncertainty [...] Uncertainty about controlling escalation is at the heart of deterrence'. So as close a call as the Cuban Missile Crisis was, deterrence – and in its wake the non-use of nuclear weapons – seems simply to have prevailed.

However, considering that even protagonists such as McNamara (2002, p. 2) eventually concluded that they merely 'lucked out', the Cuban Missile Crisis should not prematurely be declared a case of deterrence 'working' (Scott, 2012, p. 258). Obviously, a hindsight bias lurks (Blight, 1990, pp. 57–58, 128–130), one prone to be invoked, one might add, by a scholarly enterprise eager to subsume events under the notion of deterrence so that they can be 'explained' and a law-like social regularity can be declared 'discovered' (Lebow, 2010b, pp. 8, 13–14, 40). While evaluating the political effects of nuclear weapons and pointing to the Cuban Missile Crisis as an example, Robert Jervis (1988, pp. 87–88), for instance, sees Thomas Schelling's idea of risk escalation, that is, the 'threat that leaves something to chance', at work.[7] According to him, it induced caution in this case – on Kennedy's side. Quoting Arthur Schlesinger Jr., he explains that 'Kennedy's worry was "based on fear, not of Khrushchev's intention, but of human error, of something going terribly wrong down the line"' (Jervis, 1988, p. 88). In this line of thought, one might conclude that, generally speaking, 'a little nuclear deterrence went a long way' during the Cuban Missile Crisis (Blight et al., 1987, p. 187). And this is definitely plausible, especially in light of *Uncertainty* and *Escalatory Control*. Kennedy without a doubt was struggling for 'some degree of control'.

But 'a little deterrence going a long way' is not the entire story. Against the background of my reconstructive analysis, I argue that Kennedy did not wholly buy into the Realist narrative of international politics as the great drama of rational statesmen making tough choices – the intellectual biotope of deterrence believers. Clearly, examples such as his discussions with former president Eisenhower and, most importantly, the problematic role of Berlin demonstrate in a concrete instance that his relationship with deterrence was in fact a complicated, extremely uneasy one. It amplified the president's awareness of the inherent paradox: what he would *have* to be prepared to do for deterrence to work 'according to plan', was the same thing he considered to be the 'final failure'. In other words, a closer, reconstructive look at President Kennedy and the crises in Berlin and Cuba – with him fervently trying to *replace* the 'threat that leaves something to chance' with 'threat of what is yet to come', as Jervis seems to forget – allows an exploration of the ruptures in the seemingly regular relationship between deterrence and nuclear non-use.

Generally speaking, with respect to the role of nuclear weapons, the two crises around Berlin and Cuba appear to be two very different affairs. Berlin is an example of decision-makers carefully planning and considering a controlled *use* of nuclear weapons for the purpose of contingency planning. In contrast, Cuba is an example of decision-makers struggling desperately against miscalculation or misunderstanding, trying to retain control and ensure nuclear *non*-use. Berlin – or what Kennedy called the Berlin problem – connects those two settings in a crucial way.

First, as already mentioned, there is ample research on this period of history, including West Berlin's 'special relationship' (Daum) with the U.S. at the time (see e.g. Daum, 2008, pp. 2–3, 21–50; Gavin, 2012, pp. 30–74). Clearly, keeping the U.S. presence in West Berlin as well ensuring access to the city was 'essential' to Kennedy, even though it harbored the risk of conflict escalation (Daum, 2008, pp. 8–9, 27). In consequence, 'Berlin obliged Kennedy to address the fundamental questions of war and peace in the nuclear age' (Freedman, 2000, p. 92) – and it also was 'still much on the minds of Kennedy and his senior colleagues' (Freedman, 2000, p. 172; cf. Lebow/Gross Stein, 1994, p. 100; Blight, 1990, pp. 120–121) when the Cuban Missile Crisis began. Here, 'Berlin preyed on Kennedy's mind throughout the crisis, acting as a significant constraint' (Freedman, 2000, pp. 172, cf. p. 189). The following anecdote underlines Berlin's paramount importance formidably: 'Sander Vancour, who covered the White House for NBC, walked through the Cabinet Room after an Ex Comm meeting and observed that the president had written on his yellow legal pad: "Berlin... Berlin... Berlin... Berlin"' (O'Donnell et al., quoted in Lebow/Gross Stein, 1994, p. 100).

Second, however, despite the role of Berlin being well documented, by focusing specifically on the question of nuclear non-use, this study reveals something new, another layer of the political problem that Berlin represented. It explains systematically what Lawrence Freedman calls Berlin's function as a 'significant constraint'.

In essence, the Berlin problem was Kennedy's difficulty with practicing deterrence as a non-use-ensuring strategy. It emerged in the context of his administration's attempt to assure nuclear non-use via a flexible strategy, geared toward effectively deterring the Soviets by making them 'realize the great risks of escalation to nuclear war' with regard to a possible grab of Berlin, as Kennedy (1961c, p. 521) himself put it in his letter to Norstad.[8] The central notion of flexible response was to do away with the morbid conundrum of 'surrender-or-*Götterdämmerung*'

(Kull, 1988, p. 103) lurking behind the overly dramatic idea of massive retaliation, essentially generating two non-alternatives and no actual choice for the president. Using nuclear weapons in situations short of nuclear Armageddon, which was pretty much inconceivable anyway, meant creating a more flexible defense for Europe and at the same time promised to allow for pushing back the 'great risk', that is, for using nuclear weapons only as late as possible.

Yet, the clever new strategy necessitated a careful timing of the eventual, controlled escalatory transition from conventional to nuclear war fighting – with the U.S. in the role of the nuclear initiator (Freedman, 2000, p. 108). After all, the Poodle Blanket plan still required 'selective nuclear attacks'. Lacking a 'clean line' of fire, however, Kennedy actually was anxious about and perceived as morally forbidden – as taboo – the initiation of nuclear actions to keep West Berlin (eventually followed by West-Germany) from being cut off or overrun. He dreaded the controlled precipitation of an 'according-to-plan situation' over Berlin that would have confronted him with the contingency of having to order the first nuclear attacks in the European theater. Then again, raising the nuclear threshold higher and higher ran the risk of jeopardizing the credibility of the entire U.S. nuclear deterrence posture in Europe. This could invite the Soviets to attack and generate outright deterrence failure, with them reaching the conclusion that the U.S. president's threat is not credible and that he would buckle and not risk nuclear war. His adviser and expert on the Soviet Union Charles E. Bohlen warned the president of just this scenario, as seen above. So how high to raise a bar one must never go across but cannot raise *too* high, this was the conundrum Kennedy faced.

With Soviet action against Berlin looming during *both* crises, according to President Kennedy's interpretation of the Western struggle against communism, the Berlin problem came to light in even more glaring clarity during the Cuban Missile Crisis. Kennedy came to realize once more that the risk of nuclear war breaking out derived not *solely* from possible miscalculation or inadvertent use, resulting in unwanted war. This loss of control was only one side of the coin. In addition, despite his certainly not *wishing* for it, he was in a dreadful situation in which he would have to initiate nuclear war himself in a controlled fashion according to plan – because it was inextricably linked to his commitment to the defense of Europe. *He* would have to dismiss Soviet-deterring threats in order to 'save' West Germany. Kennedy thus realized that the failure of deterrence could result not only from accident but also from a conscious choice. After all, the Soviet grab for Berlin that Kennedy expected to come at any day would leave him 'only one alternative, which is to fire nuclear weapons' (WHT, 2001c, p. 581). In blatant betrayal of his own commitment, Kennedy would then have had to sacrifice the free city of West Berlin he had sworn to protect. As a belief ruling action and allowing to cope with problems, deterrence became, in turn, severely doubted by Kennedy as the Cuban Missile Crisis kept unfolding (Marfleet, 2000).

Even while the management of the Cuban Missile Crisis emerged from the deliberative process between him and the ExComm members and from a situation of pervasive uncertainty, the omnipresence of 'Berlin' in Kennedy's statements and his certainty about the coming 'crunch' over the city speaks volumes about the status the Berlin problem had for presidential decision-making. So in declaring a nuclear exchange the 'final failure' during the Cuban Missile Crisis *in light of the Berlin problem,* Kennedy revealed his deep, torturous and morally grounded worry about falling victim to his own deterrence strategy and the contingency planning for Berlin. Kennedy's moral sensitivity for the taboo-ness of nuclear weapon use made this much more than an intellectually tricky strategic challenge; rather, it meant days of anguish of despair.

Kennedy's Berlin problem can thus be summed up as a fundamentally conflictive interaction of moral limits with strategic requirements. Trying to conduct nuclear deterrence as a strategy while recognizing an obligation to the nuclear taboo and its prohibitions amounts to a problem in practice. To put the first main argument advanced in this study briefly, nuclear deterrence and the nuclear taboo, when understood as beliefs that rule action, are prone to developing an intricate interplay in which *the taboo interferes with deterrence in practice.*

In light of this, Kennedy's decision-making practice was more hesitant than the deterrence model he favored – violence escalation, rather than risk escalation – suggested he be. He did not act in accordance with it. To him, escalation control during the Cuban Missile Crisis came to mean not escalation dominance but the avoidance of any escalation whatsoever. Hence the study of Kennedy's decision-making also reinforces the third-wave deterrence critique that argued that state leaders do *not* wish to escalate risks by 'leaving something to chance', if in any way possible. In fact, one of the seven important lessons Robert Kennedy (1968 [1999], pp. 85–98) took from his brother's handling of the Cuban Missile Crisis was to 'not humiliate your opponent; leave him a way out' (Blight et al., 1987, p. 172). This 'leaving of a way out' is the opposite of what *both* deterrence models prescribe, one suggesting to stoically punish the opponent into surrender with escalating violence, the other dictating to corner the opponent in the ultimate dead-end of nightmarish risks. According to Robert Kennedy's (1968 [1999], pp. 98, emphasis added) *Thirteen Days*, the president reasoned, 'If anybody is around to write after this, they are going to understand that we made every effort to find peace and every effort to *give our adversary room to move*. I am not going to push the Russians an inch beyond what is necessary'.

So none of the two models of rational deterrence theory were applied in practice, at least not in an unambiguous fashion but rather one that can be called refracted at best. This takes us back to the caveats I raise about deterrence theory as a conclusive, satisfying ex post explanation and the all too convenient assessment of non-use as proof of its simply having 'worked' in practice. In addition, it demonstrates how deterrence as a belief relevant for decision-making in practice is a devilishly tricky thing and that the crisis had President Kennedy doubt it and seek more creative solutions instead, most importantly declaring the naval blockade a mere quarantine. Obviously there was no clear-cut, causal effect of deterrence for him to rely on. Instead, agency made all the difference.

Lastly, and to further underline the importance of agency, Kennedy and his team did not take signals of resolve as just plainly 'out there' and to be taken at face value, as suggested in deterrence models. Rather, decision-making meant fierce debates about language (*Communication*, coded 101 times) to be put into policy papers, speeches and especially the letters to Khrushchev. Also, how to make sense of the crisis was a great concern, that is, what meaning to attach to certain events such as, to give only three examples, the missiles themselves to start with (only a 'trading ploy' [WHT, 2001c, pp. 450–451]?), the two conflicting letters sent by Khrushchev or the shoot-down of the U-2 ('How do we interpret this', struck McNamara [WHT, 2001b, p. 446] as the key question in that last regard). And the accompanying question became how to convey their interpretation of events to the enemy without inadvertently escalating the conflict. None of this is simply covered by referring to deterrence as a guarantor of non-use during the Cuban Missile Crisis; rather, all of these situations were ripe with agency and involved genuinely creative decision-making. So even while Kennedy and his advisers might well have understood themselves to be acting within the 'laws' of the deterrence paradigm and within the confines of a deterrence strategy regulating the relationship between the superpowers at the time (including their making use of the pertinent deterrence vocabulary and trying to 'play by the rules' of the deterrence game, as Kennedy certainly did or at least tried to do), the results of the reconstruction suggest two main things with regard to the existing explanation provided by deterrence theory: one, the actions of the decision-makers did not correspond with any of the theoretically derived models prescribing how deterrence *ought* to be practiced successfully. Two, the decision-makers were extremely uncertain whether the 'laws' of deterrence would actually play out as the theory and models suggest, especially regarding the steps of escalation.

Lastly, what follows from all this with regard to the current state of the debate around nuclear deterrence and the nuclear taboo as well as their conceptual synthesis (cf. section 3.1.)? Obviously, at the end of both crises nuclear weapons had not been used. Judging this in hindsight and asking why non-use trumped use ex post, it practically suggests itself that the nerve-racking Cuban Missile Crisis 'reinforced the idea that nuclear weapons of any kind were unusable' (Tannenwald, 2007, pp. 253–254), and thus it can be concluded that the nuclear taboo went on to contribute to the practice of deterrence as a non-use-providing strategy. However, I have argued that a perspective focused on reconstructing fine-grained instances of presidential agency suggests a more complex and ambivalent picture. In light of the defensive plans for Berlin, it becomes clear that the taboo (Kennedy's voicing a moral obligation not to use nuclear weapons) did *not* strengthen deterrence (Kennedy's praxis of trying to issue the threat of using nuclear weapons credibly). Instead, the taboo strengthened self-deterrence, that is, the shying away from the 'unpredictability and enormity of nuclear weapons', as T.V. Paul (2009, p. 2) quite rightly describes it. But it did so not out of reputation or precedent-setting concerns as the tradition of non-use approach would have one expect, but out of moral concerns. It did so because Kennedy dreaded the use of nuclear weapons without a 'clean line' of fire, absolutely and fundamentally declaring nuclear weapon use a 'final failure'. So, the taboo actually magnified the *paradox* of deterrence with which Kennedy was faced, that is, having to resolutely facilitate that which he wanted desperately to avoid.

While in the reconstruction of Kennedy's decision-making practice nuclear deterrence and the nuclear taboo were shown to be present and as interacting with each other, the existing literature on non-use and the conceptual thoughts by Tannenwald and other scholars in the field would have one expect this interaction to be a 'stabilizing' or, simply put, a 'positive' one in practice. The results of this empirical study contradict this theoretically derived expectation, however. While deterrence and the taboo *were* indeed fused in Kennedy's decision-making process (because both were beliefs referred to in order to make sense of the world and act purposefully in it), the synthesis produced a *negative* result with respect to achieving the goal of nuclear weapons not being used. Kennedy's Berlin problem shows how, in practice, the nuclear taboo can come wrapped in the deterrence paradox – with the taboo yielding detrimental effects to the aspired successful application of deterrence as non-use-ensuring strategy.

In light of this result, a more cautious stance toward the possibility of synthesizing the two concepts for simply obtaining a more comprehensive, causal explanation of nuclear non-use seems warranted. As cautioned by William Walker and as seen in section 3.1, deterrence and the taboo can apparently not be synthesized seamlessly in the abstract, and while the two factors do of course shine more light on the empirical phenomenon than one alone could, scrutinizing how they unfold in practice shows that they do not simply 'stack up'. From a deterrer's perspective, the taboo as an 'internalized norm strengthening internalized deterrence' on the deterree's side is, of course, a welcome development. Yet, deterrence works both ways between nuclear adversaries such as the U.S. and the Soviet Union. In other words, *both opponents are deterrer and deterree at the same time*. And viewed from the bottom up, that is, from a deterrer's perspective on his *own* decision-making practice, as Kennedy's example demonstrates, the taboo presents a major detriment to trying to make deterrence work. In reconstructing the process that is considered necessary by decision-makers *themselves* for a deterrence strategy to be viable, we find the nuclear taboo putting a spoke into strategic thinking, and we are able to understand why the Berlin problem was so pivotal. This sheds doubt on Tannenwald's (2007, p. 19) proposition that '[t]he taboo has helped to stabilize, not undermine, mutual nuclear deterrence'. At the end of Chapter 4, I will evaluate this result again in somewhat broader terms.

The importance of human emotion

With decision-makers being confronted with a great deal of uncertainty and overwhelmed by worries, it became evident over the course of the first empirical analysis that *human emotion* was heavily in play. Against this background, it is not surprising that existing clear-cut concepts (codes) for explaining nuclear non-use played either a marginal (*Tradition*) or an important yet ambivalent role (*Deterrence* and *Taboo*) in the material. Real-life decision-making situations were simply way more muddled than these abstract concepts can account for. For scholars solely expecting non-use to be evoked by either the logic of consequentiality or the logic of appropriateness (or some synthesis of the two), the salience of emotion must come as somewhat unforeseen. After all, human emotion fits in with neither one (I will return to this).

Decision-makers turned out to be neither rational deterrence and precedence-setting calculators nor moral norm conformists. Rather, they appeared as *stressed* – and oftentimes *confused* – human beings. 'The transcripts reveal people searching for a way out of a dreadful quandary, displaying raw emotion as much as steely rationality, occasionally rambling, sometimes reflective, rarely systematic', as Freedman puts it (2000, p. 171; cf. Blight et al., 1987, pp. 180–184; Blight, 1990, pp. 37–38; Lebow/Gross Stein, 1994, pp. 331–338). 'At first angry, then by turns confused and finally deeply worried', is how James G. Blight (1990, p. 22) describes the emotional roller coaster during the Cuban Missile Crisis, putting the development into a vocabulary of *emotion*: anger, confusion, worry.

It is worth noting that Kennedy's decision-making process was influenced by a great many factors. For example, to ensure minimal escalation, he could have chosen not to confront the Soviets over the missiles and potentially risk being impeached. But *Domestic Politics* (coded 12 times) and the question of U.S. *Prestige* (coded 49 times) led him to choose otherwise.[9] Moreover, his experience with the Bay of Pigs fiasco had left him suspicious of premature military actions (Freedman, 2000, pp. 8–9, 123–146). Regarding the nuclear question, the taboo and deterrence figured in heavily, albeit in an intricate interplay and not in textbook fashion. And while Kennedy struggled with implementing rational deterrence theory in practice himself, the deterrence effect the Soviet missiles on Cuba and abroad had on him was not a manipulation of his rational strategic calculus, based on warhead numbers, flight time and a perception of the strategic balance. Rather, over the course of the meetings and especially during the discussion of different escalation scenarios, Kennedy seemed 'deterred' by the missiles in the sense of being *terrorized*. The possibility of nuclear weapons being used (beginning with Berlin) evoked the sheer horror of his being responsible for the destruction of not only his country but also maybe the world.

This is not to say that Kennedy appeared as shy or extremely hesitant in the transcripts. A quite drastic measure such as poisoning the Vietcong's food supply, for instance, he weighed rationally regarding its effectiveness, its potential detrimental effects on the U.S. reputation, precedents and possible effects on innocent third parties, eventually leaning toward it but wanting some more questions answered before making his final decision (WHT, 2001c, pp. 165–169). This is not the way an overly scrupulous or timid president would have dealt with such an option. Regarding the use of nuclear weapons, in stark contrast, President Kennedy appeared simply *fearful* regarding the potential consequences that might result.

Of course, this point is not entirely new. Jervis points to it casually, for example, when quoting Schlesinger's observation about how 'Kennedy's worry was "based on fear, not of Khrushchev's intention, but of human error"' (Jervis, 1988, pp. 88, emphasis added). But Kennedy's worry, I argue, was twofold because he feared accidental *and* deliberate nuclear war. Kennedy came to fear not Khrushchev's but *his own* intention, so to speak. Also, Freedman (2000, p. xi)[10] mentions fear when highlighting that, 'when it came to the fundamental issues of foreign policy [Kennedy's] strategy was dominated by a determination to avoid the nuclear cataclysm that he *feared* above all else without giving ground in the cold war' (Freedman, 2000, pp. xii, emphasis added; cf. Blight et al., 1987, p. 180). What is more, Richard Ned Lebow and Janice Gross Stein, in their analysis of the Cuban Missile Crisis, point out that 'Soviet accounts reveal that Khrushchev and his advisors suffered from similar angst [...] [W]hen Kennedy and Khrushchev were "eyeball to eyeball", *both* leaders blinked. They did so out of a wholly commendable fear of war and its consequences' (Lebow/Gross Stein, 1994, pp. 145, 144, emphasis added; cf. Blight, 1990, p. 6; Cohen, 2013, pp. 444–445).

So there are many indicators scattered in the existing literature that make it seem worthwhile to follow the trail of fear further and more systematically. To back this notion up, one of the statements by Vice President Lyndon Johnson in an ExComm meeting can serve as another, illustrative clue. When the ExComm discussion on October 27 touched upon the night surveillance flights over Cuba that were using flares to light up the sky, Johnson admitted, 'I've been afraid of those damned flares [for night reconnaissance] ever since they mentioned them [...] Imagine some crazy Russian captain doing it. The damn thing [the flare] goes "blooey" and lights up the skies. He might just pull a trigger. Looks like we're playing Fourth of July over there or something. I'm scared of that [...] Psychologically, you scare them [the Soviets]. Well, hell, it's always like the fellow telling me in Congress, "Go on and put the monkey on his back." Every time I tried to put a monkey on somebody else's back, I got one' (WHT, 2001b, pp. 467–477). It is worth keeping Johnson's metaphor of 'putting a monkey on somebody else's back' in mind.

4.3 Following the fear trail: conceptual reflections on atomic anxiety

To further flesh out the notion that fear is in play during nuclear decision-making, I will examine the Kennedy material more closely and systematically in that regard. With a clearer idea about how fear presented itself empirically, I will then interrogate the pertinent literature by, first, visiting the two explanations of nuclear non-use yet another time and, second, by including literature above and beyond that. More specifically, I will draw on historic, cultural and critical security studies, as well as on the recently burgeoning body of IR 'emotional turn' literature to develop the concept of atomic anxiety.

4.3.1 Revisiting empirical sources: the three faces of fear

In the Kennedy sources, fear presented itself in a threefold fashion. First, it was explicitly present in passages in which decision-makers admitted to being worried, scared or anxious themselves. President Kennedy was not only fearful of inadvertent or accidental war over Cuba (Blight et al., 1987, pp. 176–177, 179) but also dreaded a situation in which he would have maneuvered himself into a situation that necessitated his initiating nuclear escalation knowingly and according to plan over Berlin. It is also in light of this *emotional experience* that he did not choose a decision-making course with an optimal risk-benefit ratio but rather one with the absolute lowest possible risk. Dreading escalation and hasty steps into the unknown, President Kennedy was, for instance, 'most anxious that we not have to announce a state of war existing, because it would obviously be bad to have the word go out that we were having a war rather than that it was a limited blockade for a limited purpose' (WHT, 2001c, p. 577; Kennedy, 1962b, time code 4:04). This feeling was of course limited neither to only the president nor to the period of the blockade around Cuba. Right from the first day of the crisis, as this exchange between CIA Deputy Director Marshall S. Carter and Bundy, which took place on October 16, illustrates, similarly emotional expressions are present in the material (WHT, 2001c, p. 466):

Carter: It's a series of single, unrelated acts, not by surprise. This coming in there, on a Pearl Harbor [kind of surprise attack], just frightens the hell out of me as to what goes beyond. The Board of National Estimates have been working on this ever since...

Bundy: What goes beyond what?

Carter: What happens beyond that. You go in there with a surprise attack. You put out all the missiles. This isn't the end. This is the *beginning*, I think. There's a whole hell of a lot of things...

This is not the only passage in the material that suggests a strong connection between fear and uncertainty, how not knowing the consequences of actions evokes a powerful feeling of unease. The following exchange between Bundy and McNamara further underlines this (WHT, 2001c, p. 410):

Bundy: Are you absolutely clear on your premise that an air strike must go to the whole air complex?

McNamara: Well, we are, Mac, because we are fearful of these MiG-21s. We don't know where they are. We don't know what they're capable of. If there are nuclear warheads associated with the launchers, you must assume there will be nuclear warheads associated with aircraft [...].

In addition, in the first of Khrushchev's famous two letters, which was received on the evening of October 26 and contained a very personal message in emotional language, the chairman pondered the looming 'worldwide cruel and destructive war' (WHT, 2001b, p. 353) and wrote to Kennedy: 'I see, Mr. President, that you are not devoid of a sense of anxiety for the fate of the world, of understanding, and of what war entails' (WHT, 2001b, p. 349), which is why he, Khrushchev, would accept proposals pointing a way 'out of the situation [...] which would give the peoples the possibility of breathing calmly' (WHT, 2001b, p. 352). Similarly, in his radio message that effectively ended the crisis on October 28, Khrushchev referred to emotion again: 'I very well understand your anxiety and the anxiety of the United States people in connection with the fact that the weapons which you describe as "offensive" are, in fact, grim weapons. Both you and I understand what kind of weapon they are. [...] Therefore, you can imagine what kind of responsibilities you assume, especially now during the anxious times we are now experiencing' (WHT, 2001b, p. 512). Worry, fear, anxiety, it is safe to say, were all present in the material and could be reconstructed as relevant to the decision-makers struggling with the question of nuclear use or non-use at the time.

Second, however, the material also suggests that the decision-makers were worried that their fear would *show*. More precisely, appearing scared in the eyes of the enemy would be an intolerable weakness, some passages suggest. Charles E. Bohlen, for instance, worried that the U.S. could not look like it was 'back[ing] away' from nuclear first-use over Berlin due to 'the horrors of a nuclear war' (WHT, 2001c, p. 186). After all, it would mean the failure of extended deterrence and provide a window of opportunity for Khrushchev to invade Europe. During the height of the Cuban Missile Crisis, similar notions were invoked. For example, Douglas Dillon (WHT, 2001c, p. 442) insisted that the U.S. could not allow itself to look 'scared of the Cubans'. Similarly, Robert Kennedy was concerned with how the U.S. would appear in the eyes of the Soviets during the management of the quarantine line: 'The only weakness, in my judgment, is the idea to the Russians that we are backing off and that we're weak and' (WHT, 2001b, p. 276). Furthermore, while discussing how to deal with the press, especially regarding troop movements that could be interpreted as preparation for an invasion of Cuba, Rusk advised to keep a low profile, talk only about precautionary moves and that in a critical situation such as the one at that time, the public did not need to be concerned with each and every one of the administration's decisions. But Bundy quickly added, 'One slightly supplementary point. We don't want to look as if we got scared off from anything. [...] I think that's very important' (WHT, 2001b, p. 51).

So, interestingly, in addition to experiencing fear themselves, decision-makers had to manage it with respect to their public appearance, minding *both* the domestic audience to whom they had to communicate reassurance and the clear sense that the situation was under control *and* the opponent to whom they had to communicate steadfastness. The quarantine around Cuba serves to illustrate this. Kennedy preferred the quarantine because he was 'anxious' not to stumble into a state of war. Calling the limited blockade a 'quarantine' was thus a reasonable reaction to the fear of uncontrolled escalation. However, the quarantine carried other elements in need of consideration, too. A fine balance needed to be struck, because it had to avoid unnecessary escalation while sending a strong enough signal to the Soviets *and* at the same time soothe the worries of the domestic audience. Under Secretary of State George W. Ball reminded Kennedy of these delicate matters: 'I think this is one of the real problems of the blockade, is that it's a rather a slow agony and you build up all kinds of fears and doubts in the minds of people here' (WHT, 2001c, p. 543).

Third, the multifaceted presence of fear in the material can consequently be said to also involve fear being not only *endured* by decision-makers and *managed* in order for it not to show, but it also had to be *actively created* in the adversary, for deterrence purposes. Rusk points to the reciprocal characteristic of fear this way: '[O]ne thing Mr. Khrushchev may have in mind is that he knows that we have a substantial nuclear superiority, but he also knows that we don't really live under fear of his nuclear weapons to the extent that he has to live under fear of ours' (WHT, 2001c, p. 410).

This reciprocity of fear created by the superpower arsenal is clearly and intimately connected to the basic idea behind deterrence. President Johnson's monkey metaphor points the way: deterrence is about putting the monkey on someone else's back. But in doing so, one is bound to get the monkey oneself. Schelling (1966, pp. 121–122), while pondering the effect of threats involving loss of control, also realizes – albeit only in a footnote in *Arms and Influence* – that those threats can become '"external" to the participants; the threat becomes part of the environment rather than a test of will between the two adversaries'. Following this line of thought further, one might also point to the crucial assumption in deterrence theory that one is already threatened by an adversary's looming first-use of nuclear weapons. After all, this is why one adopts a deterrence posture. In other words, *being afraid* is the reason for turning to deterrence *in the first place* – as a quasi-tit-for-tat reaction. But as seen above, by scaring the opponent into non-use, deterrence disseminates fear – in this way threateners are eventually threatened by the situation created by their own threats (Blight, 1990, pp. 109, 162). The role that fear plays for deterrence (theory) clearly warrants a closer look.

4.3.2 Reviewing pertinent literature: is atomic anxiety old news?

Is the notion I put forward here, namely that nuclear non-use is somehow connected to fear (or what I will conceptualize as atomic anxiety below), entirely new? The short answer is no. Revisiting the explanations of nuclear non-use, especially deterrence literature, and looking for the element of fear with a fine-tooth comb, there is plenty to discover. This 'insight' must sound banal to either those just superficially contemplating the idea behind deterrence or those intimately familiar with the pertinent body of literature and its nuances.

This points toward the longer answer to the question of atomic anxiety's news value. And this longer answer holds my key argument: even though IR literature has not entirely ignored that human emotion (fear) is involved regarding nuclear abstinence (because it is quite commonsensical), this involvement remained conceptually underdeveloped and empirically understudied.

Consider in connection to this that the taboo-ness of nuclear weapons, too, has always been present in people's minds – ever since the dawn of the nuclear age (see e.g. Life, 1945, p. 32; cf. Boyer, 1994 [1985], pp. 8–10). But even though the notion would occasionally be touched upon by scholars in passing – such as Arnold Wolfers (1946, pp. 116–117) in *The Absolute Weapon,* Schelling (1979 [1960], pp. 257–266) in *The Strategy of Conflict,* Jervis in *The Illogic of American Nuclear Strategy* (1984, p. 35) or John Lewis Gaddis (1987, p. 142) in *The Long Peace* – it took more than half a century for it to be spelled out explicitly and systematically as a full-fledged analytic concept by Tannenwald. Morally agnostic, unemotional, Realist, rational deterrence theory was the non-use paradigm for so long and with such overshadowing preeminence in both academia and policy-making that not much breathing room existed for non-orthodox perspectives. This way, the nuclear taboo remained hidden in plain sight. And the case of atomic anxiety is quite similar in that regard. A final look at rational deterrence theory – focusing not on the 'theory' but on the 'rational' bit this time – is the best way to start demonstrating this and to develop the concept of atomic anxiety further from there.

Nuclear Deterrence

It bespeaks of my emphasis on the importance of language and the notion of deterrence as a belief that the English word 'deterrence' does not translate easily into other languages, meaning in fact quite different things in different languages and social contexts (Lupovici, 2010, p. 717; Lewis, 2008, p. 40; 2009). The concept of 'rational deterrence' thus does not simply mirror a pre-existing, law-like, 'cost-benefit-weighing mechanism in reaction to the world out there'. Nevertheless, I argue that there is something like a lowest – yet often neglected – common denominator.

It is not for nothing that nuclear weapons are often referred to as a 'terror weapon', and consequently feared as the ultimate weapon for a terrorist attack since the beginning of the nuclear age (Gavin, 2009).[11] After all, etymologically the word *terror* is at the root of the English word de-*terr*-ence. And the *Oxford English Dictionary* (quoted in Freedman, 2004, p. 27) defines deterrence accordingly as 'to discourage or turn aside or restrain by fear'. In addition, Spencer R. Weart (1988, p. 234) notes that the Soviets used to translate 'deterrence' as 'terrorization, which did not address the intellect at all'. No sophisticated calculations, no rational deductions, no chess analogies. In German, 'deterrence' translates into *Abschreckung,* meaning to fend someone off by scaring him. It is thus safe to say that, across the board, the element of *inducing fear* is inextricably linked to the basic idea of 'deterring someone'. So what has deterrence theory to offer in that regard?

Brodie (1946b, pp. 73, 77, 84), not yet dealing with the issue in the formalized vocabulary of rational deterrence theory but phrasing his ideas in more straightforward terms, postulated that an atomic aggressor weapon would lose its nimbus if 'that nation which proposes to launch the attack [...] must fear retaliation' Hence '[a]ll conceivable situations where the aggressor's fear of retaliation will be at a minimum' would have to eliminated to achieve security. '[M]utual fear of retaliation', as even a cursory reading of *The Absolute Weapon* shows, was pivotal for Brodie's basic idea at the time of deterrence theory's advent.[12] That this fear is a *mutual* one underlines that deterrence is not only about creating fear in the opponent but that it derives from being afraid in the first place, afraid of falling victim to a first strike if deterrence is not practiced.

However, even though fear was key to Brodie's thinking and writing, and even though it remained a central theme in deterrence literature, today it is usually only the adornment for a more 'serious' and scholarly discussion of deterrence theory and the way *rational* deterrence works. So while one reads about fear and the horror of a nuclear holocaust in deterrence literature here and there, feelings and emotion clearly do not seem to deserve explicit conceptualization. Their involvement is not fleshed out thoroughly and systematically. After all, to explain how deterrence works is what neat and tidy models of rational actors that cold-bloodedly weigh costs and benefits are for.

Even Jervis, who was always critical of strict rationality assumptions and susceptible to considering alternative views on deterrence, admits to that neglect. In an interview with Thierry Balzacq (2004, pp. 564–565, 567), who notes that 'many students of security dilemmas often overlook the emotion variable' and states that Jervis has in fact 'recognized that dynamics of misperception are also driven by emotions', Balzacq ends up asking why Jervis nevertheless 'devoted little time to the scrutiny of such pervasive factors'. Jervis answers, 'You are quite right: *Perception and Misperception* completely put aside emotions; indeed one chapter denies the importance of wishful thinking. This was a major blunder. Part of the reason for it was that the dominant psychology of the time was purely cognitive; part was my personal desire to conclude that what Herbert Simon called bounded rationality ruled the world. Had I been a bit older and more mature I probably would have realized that this was a foolish way to understand individuals and collectivities [...]. [A]s we learn more about the role of emotions, it becomes clear that we cannot even imagine life, let alone sensible life, without their playing a large role'.

So I am not saying that emotional notions – such as fear or the horror of nuclear war – have been *denied* by all deterrence scholars. Quite the contrary, they oftentimes were a seemingly taken-for-granted matter. But this way they also remained, at best, an implicit assumption or something merely mentioned in passing, definitely not a thing to be dealt with analytically and in its own right.

Schelling (1966, p. 99), for example, casually invokes fear in *Arms and Influence*: 'Any situation that scares one side will scare both sides with the danger of a war that neither wants, and both will have to pick their way carefully through the crisis, never quite sure that the other knows how to avoid stumbling over the brink'. The offhand use of 'scaring' in this passage, as well as the occasional mentioning of 'fear' and even a 'the balance of fear' in other works by Schelling (1975 [1961], p. 5), is noteworthy coming from a scholar who is famous for his ground-breaking work on game theoretic models of deterrence threats in which actors are assumed to be purely cost-benefit calculating 'rationalists'. Karl W. Deutsch (1963, p. 70, emphasis added) poked fun at this inconsistency in his critique of Schelling's *Strategy of Conflict* by pointing out how rational deterrence theory 'first proposes that we should frustrate our opponents by *frightening* them very badly and that we should then rely on their cool-headed rationality for survival' (see also Morgan, 1977, pp. 13, 21–23).

So deterrence theorists were not completely ignorant toward the idea that human emotion is – *somehow* – involved. However, the highly influential second wave of deterrence theorizing – during which 'developing the theoretical raiment with which to garb deterrence' (Morgan, 1977, p. 10) began as a scholarly enterprise that spoke of interaction processes and calculated bargaining – was unable to *systematically* include emotion into its models. Because it was ready at hand, deterrence scholars, quite a few of them economists by training – such as, most prominently, Schelling – employed actor models imported from microeconomics, models relying on an emotionless and individualistic *homo economicus* (Morgan, 1977, p. 10; 2011, pp. 147–148; Blight, 1990, pp. 43, 50; for the same argument regarding IR in general, see Crawford, 2000, p. 122; cf. Lebow, 2005; Mercer, 2005, pp. 80–86; Booth/Wheeler, 2008, pp. 63–64). And with this (as far as such a general statement about the massive and convoluted body of literature on deterrence theory is possible), the rational foundations were laid for what we (until today) take to be the (mainstream) theory of rational deterrence. Schelling can be cited once more to exemplarily demonstrate the result, that is, how rational deterrence was perceived of without having to include fear. He painted a picture about how humankind's dealing with the possibility of nuclear war equals people watching the traffic roar by while standing on the curb. Never would they step onto the road in this situation, Schelling (quoted in Blight, 1990, p. 42) argued, the reason being simple: 'They are absolutely deterred. But there is no fear. They just know better'. The character of Professor Groeteschele, played by Walter Matthau in *Fail-Safe* (Lumet, 1964, time code 00:54:58), brilliantly sums up rational deterrence theory's idea that U.S. theorists came to develop about the way rational – read *emotionless* – deterrence works to keep their Soviet enemy in check: 'They're not motivated by human emotion such as rage and pity. They are calculating machines. They will look at the balance sheet, and they will see they cannot win'.

Examining more closely how emotion and its involvement in decision-making ended up neglected in rational deterrence theory (Crawford, 2000, pp. 145–149), one finds that, insofar as it recognized emotion at all, deterrence literature tended to treat it as *mutually exclusive* with the assumption of rationality.[13] The inner contradiction resulting from this becomes clearer when reviewing the two flanks of critique that deterrence theory's assumption of rationality opened up.

One, the strictness of the rationality assumption was, of course, a constant bone of contention during the development of deterrence theory (cf. subsection 2.1.2). Rationality was eventually qualified with the introduction of rationality-constraining notions such as group think or standard operating procedures in connection to bureaucratic politics models. Christopher Achen and Duncan Snidal (1989, pp. 148, emphasis added) summed this up as follows: 'These studies are united by misgivings over the rational theory of deterrence [...]. In one popular approach, deterrence is seen as a fundamentally psychological process, in which cognition failures, *fear*, or simple time pressures disrupt the rational calculations assumed by deterrence theory'. In other words, an overly emotional, impulsive opponent might suffer cognition failures, might thus not be deterrable, his feelings being a reason for deterrence *not* to work. Or, an overly emotional decision-maker might inadvertently trigger the cocked deterrence apparatus and unleash accidental nuclear war. Invoking human emotion to point to mistakes, judgment errors and deterrence failure in general was especially characteristic for the critique raised by third-wave deterrence scholars.

Blight (1990, pp. 29–30, 44–48, 149–167) argues that the deterrence debate during the third wave indeed saw extremely radical renunciations of rationality. Jervis, Lebow and Gross Stein, to name only three prominent representatives of that body of literature, wrote extensively in that critical vein. Generally speaking, by introducing political psychology, their work aimed at recognizing decision-makers as emotional human beings rather than rational, essentially mindless, cost-benefit calculators, with all the implications of stress, misperception, miscalculation or cognitive biases involved. However, what was the role of emotion? Take Lebow and Gross Stein's study *We All Lost the Cold War* (Lebow/Gross Stein, 1994, pp. e.g. 291–300) as an example. While it points to fear explicitly and repeatedly, fear is only one among several moving parts the authors identify as influencing the way in which the crises under analysis developed and became resolved. It is not fleshed out further, and the notion of a cautioning 'fear of war and its consequences' (Lebow/Gross Stein, 1994, p. 144) regarding the non-use of nuclear weapons is not developed systematically. The reason – and this is crucial – is that this literature stayed within the confines of the rational deterrence paradigm because it was aimed primarily at an intrinsic critique of the strong rationality assumption in deterrence theory (not an analysis of the role of emotion at large). So while third-wave deterrence literature effectively 'rediscovered' human emotion, the fundamental dichotomy of 'rationality' (good for deterrence) versus 'irrationality/emotion' (bad for deterrence) remained encapsulated in – and even *entrenched* by its critique of – rational deterrence theory. Hence deterrence to be a rational concept – and infringed rationality as inimical to it – is still the common viewpoint today, especially in light of (and because of) the third wave, which drew on emotion to show how deterrence can fail, not how fear might actually make it tick.

Two, in addition to what has already been said about the deterrence paradox and weird simultaneous assumptions of rationality and irrationality, the rational deterrence framework at large ended up utterly incoherent regarding the role of emotion, despite the third-wave critique. This is the second flank of critique. Patrick Morgan (1977), for example, in a 'valiant attempt' (Freedman, 2004, p. 29; Jervis, 1988, p. 81) to salvage rational deterrence, famously proposed to drop the strict assumption of rational actors and assume 'sensible' actors in lieu thereof, thus trying to escape the trap of having to simultaneously assume rationality and irrationality (Powell, 1985, p. 80 fn. 13). Nevertheless, the assumption that rational (or at least sensible) decision-makers cannot have their judgment clouded by too much emotionality remained a central pillar of deterrence theory. So proponents of rational deterrence theory remain tangled up in a basic inner contradiction: in reaction to the first critique, many deterrence scholars came to state that total rationality is not necessary, that 'some' rationality or sensibility in decision-makers is sufficient for deterrence to work (seemingly an easy concession to make). With this, however, they in fact confirm the notion that 'too much' emotion is indeed *detrimental* to deterrence. In other words, they concede that emotion *can* be involved, but they insist that as long as 'enough' rationality or sensibility remains, deterrence functions. So the assumption that emotion and rationality are mutually exclusive remains intact again, with emotion responsible only for deviations from the rational workings of deterrence. This is the case up to this day. Consequently, when people nowadays worry about terrorists or so-called rogue states such as Iran or North Korea being 'undeterrable' (for a brief overview of these debates, see Lupovici, 2010, pp. 718–720; see also Knopf, 2010; Etzioni, 2010), the argument is not that these actors have no feelings or are utterly fearless (which might even be the case sometimes); rather, it is framed as their being *not rational* (enough) for deterrence to work (reliably) because their value system is so extremely different (i.e. especially with respect to terrorists, of whom it is said that to them, there exists nothing of value to 'hold at risk', no territory, no population, no military hardware, no will to survive even). And even those who oppose this view and argue, in contrast, that terrorists *can* be deterred, base their claim not on the possibility of inducing fear but on showing how the terrorists' political goals *can* be held at risk and how their cost-benefit ratio *can* be influenced nevertheless (see e.g. Trager/Zagorcheva, 2005/06). The common understanding behind both lines of argument is thus clearly that deterrence essentially rests on some form of utility maximization, about weighing costs and benefits, in theory and in practice. In other words, the debate is old wine in new skins, namely about the old question on 'how much rationality is enough'. Yet, at the same time, below the elaborate constructs of rational deterrence theory and the discussions about varying degrees of rationality and sensibility, there persists the initial, unspoken assumption that deterrence begins with human emotion, more specifically the primal feeling of fear. Fear is *necessary*, it is *obligatory* for deterrence (similar: Blight, 1990, p. 49; Crawford, 2000, p. 146). After all, the *conditio sine qua non* for deterrence was and is that the opponent, no matter if 'completely' or 'just enough' rational, has to *fear* retaliation, according to Brodie.

This central tenet – deterrence relying on fear – is frequently repeated throughout the entire body of deterrence literature. But without facing the conceptual consequences of this, that is, what that basic assumption of emotion being at the heart of the idea of deterrence implies for rationality in deterrence theory, and by trying to fence in such issues by stating that while rationality is required, even a good deal less than total rationality will do, rational deterrence theory ends up incoherent. By keeping 'emotionality' and 'rationality' fundamentally at odds with each other at the conceptual level, even gradually softening the rationality assumption cannot eliminate the theory's basic conceptual inconsistency.

Consequently, I argue that rational deterrence theory fundamentally relies on human emotion and utterly neglects it at the same time (just as deterrence theory claims to be 'scientific' while being impossible to 'prove'). The kernel of human emotion in deterrence was never adequately acknowledged and fleshed out systematically in 70 years of developing a theoretical framework for rational deterrence, not even during the critical third wave.

Against this background, the reason for why Waltz's writings are influential *for* and at the same time out of tune *with* rational deterrence theory becomes clearer. It is because his thinking is extremely consequent in that regard. Drawing on a quote by another famous movie character, yet in stark contrast to how Professor Groeteschele conceptualizes deterrence, I would describe Waltz as strictly endorsing a 'Strangelovian' notion of deterrence. After all, in Stanley Kubrick's 1964 movie *Dr. Strangelove or: How I Learned to Stop Worrying and Love the Bomb,* the ingenious Dr. Strangelove explains deterrence as 'the art of producing in the mind of the enemy... the *fear* to attack' (quoted in Lindley, 2001, p. 663, original emphasis). And indeed, unimpressed by the preponderance of sophisticated rational deterrence models, Waltz, too, simply and unequivocally states, 'Deterrence does not depend on rationality. It depends on fear' (Waltz, 2003b, p. 154).[14] Furthermore, he inimitably insists that '[d]eterrence is not a theory' (Waltz, 2003b, p. 154). Since 'rational deterrence theory' is neither a 'theory' nor 'rational', according to Waltz, it all boils down to the practice of instilling angst, terror, and fear in the adversary. Waltz thinks about deterrence along the same lines as the first-wave scholars such as Brodie did before the second wave had 'rationalized', 'formalized' and 'scientificated' deterrence: namely as a primarily practical enterprise. '[C]omplicated calculations are not needed, only a little common sense', Waltz (2003b, p. 154) argues, pointing out that the existential fear of being put out of existence is enough to create the result that is aspired to. So merely conceiving of deterrence as the art form of producing the feeling of fear required to keep the enemy in check, the assumption of rationality, as already touched upon in the passages about deterrence as a belief in Chapter 3, is *explicitly* exempt from Waltz's notion of deterrence. Moreover, along with it the conviction that the intellectual effort poured into 'theorizing deterrence' qualifies the result as a 'theory' is dropped. Waltz dials down rationality even more than concepts of bounded rationality or the sensible actor refinement do. The reason for Waltz's concept of rationality being so extremely thin is that even in his IR theory, it adds up to little more than the wish to survive, a notion he only later and most reluctantly accepted 'for convenience [to be] be called an assumption of rationality' (Waltz, 1986, p. 331). Regarding deterrence, however, this assumption becomes even more crucial for Waltz's thinking. After all, deterrence is about creating the fear of *death*; hence, the primal need for survival is at the core of deterrence.

Lastly, when following Waltz means endorsing the idea that deterrence as a social practice is indeed not the application of a rational theory with mathematical precision but probably better described as statecraft, as an art form, the art of producing a very powerful *feeling* in the mind of the enemy, the *fear* to attack, there is one last thing to consider. Waltz's take on the role of fear is irritating because he ends up so immensely 'optimistic that *the rationality instilled by nuclear fear* will ensure that deterrence continues to pass whatever future tests it faces' (Wheeler, 2009, p. 433, emphasis added). With utmost persistence Waltz sticks to his famous notion that 'more may be better', for example, recently arguing *Why Iran Should Get the Bomb* (Waltz, 2012). Thanks to Waltz's Strangelovian notion of deterrence (that takes rationality instilled by fear as literally nothing more than survival-instinct kicking in), he can brush aside the arguments of those who doubt that a deterrence relationship involving the 'irrational' Iranian regime could be stable. This sets him apart *again* from many scholars pondering such nuclear issues, many of them ending up more skeptical about the absolute and total stability of deterrence.

However, and this is where I decidedly part ways with Waltz, even in the early days of deterrence thinking, Deutsch remained unconvinced by this logic, that is, by deterrence *stably* coming to rest on fear. After all, 'frightened or overstrained men may react aggressively' or with a '"spiteful" response', Deutsch (1963, p. 70) suggested. Similarly, Brodie (1959, p. 397) mused toward the end of *Strategy in the Missile Age* quite skeptically, 'Deterrence after all depends on a subjective feeling which we are trying to create in the opponent's mind, a feeling compounded of respect and fear, and we have to ask ourselves whether it is not possible to overshoot the mark. It is possible to make him fear us too much, especially if what we make him fear is our over-readiness to react, whether or not he translates it into clear evidence of our aggressive intent'. In other words, why we should take fear to render deterrence reliable has never been systematically answered by Waltz (Cohen, 2013, p. 442). He merely assumes it or apparently takes history to suggest it so (critical on this is Müller, 2013, pp. 545–554). Yet, in light of the nuclear age's many close calls, it is impossible for me to share Waltz's peculiarly optimistic *belief* in atomic anxiety making nuclear deterrence reliable and nuclear weapon states in general behave cautiously and responsibly – a stance that also fits recent, quantitatively derived empirical findings on nuclear weapon state belligerence better (Bell/Miller, 2015). I will pick up the question of fear rendering deterrence reliable in the concluding chapter of this study.

To sum up, deterrence literature is upholding a dichotomy between rationality and emotionality. One can either ditch the notion of rationality completely (like Waltz does) or try to live with that conceptual inconsistency (as the majority of other deterrence scholars seem to). I consider this inconsistent and confused treatment of fear and emotion not very helpful in my endeavor of coming to grips with the involvement of fear conceptually. So maybe the second line of thought, the nuclear taboo – under which I sorted the tradition of non-use – yields a better account.

Nuclear taboo

In the works of Paul and Tannenwald, the reader is presented with a comparably clear-cut picture regarding the role of human emotion. In comparison to rational deterrence theory's all in all self-contradictory invocation of fear, the picture is clear cut insofar as human emotion plays no significant role at all.

This specifically applies to Paul's work on the tradition of non-use. A rereading of the conceptual passages in his book shows that human emotion simply does not figure in. Of course, aspects of nuclear weapons that are loosely tied to emotion find consideration, such as, for example, their 'awesome destructive power' or the 'great danger in the use of nuclear weapons with respect to casualties and aftereffects, in both psychological and physical terms' (Paul, 2009, pp. 12, see also 23–25). Also, most importantly, reputation plays a pivotal role. However, it does so strictly in a manner of 'calculation' (Paul, 2009, pp. 27–28) and not – as one might think about reputation just as well – in terms of affect. So, in short, the cogs and springs that make Paul's 'rationalist-normative' (Paul, 2009, p. 13) concept tick are just not connected to emotionality.

The nuclear taboo is a bit more complicated. Tannenwald (2007, p. ix), right on the first page of the preface of her book-length study, points out how she was appalled by the destructive power of nuclear weapons and the icy, sterile deterrence thinking. With her not being alone in this, of course, the shared 'sense of revulsion over nuclear weapons' plays the key role conceptually for the nuclear taboo (Tannenwald, 2007, p. 59). It is at the same time a motivation and a conceptual pivot point for Tannenwald's alternative perspective, one that takes the abhorrence evoked by nuclear weapons into consideration more coherently than the deterrence paradigm does. Hence it is in fact not too much of a stretch to read into the entire notion of the nuclear taboo a fair amount of sensitivity to emotion in general and the element of fear in particular. After all, deterrence theory's concern with 'credible threats of massive destruction' that Tannenwald (2007, p. ix) finds irritating are, as seen above, meant to create fear. And so the revulsion that has the taboo thrive in society is in part fed by the rejection of a practice that has the creation of fear via threats of mass death and vast destruction at its center. In addition, it stands to reason that emotional reactions and moral consideration can go hand in hand, with fearful things getting stigmatized and revolting things invoking fear in turn. Cannibalism, for instance, is seen not only as an unspeakable taboo but also a frightening, creepy scenario in most societies. Yet, despite this vague but noticeable proximity between taboo-ness, stigmatization and emotionality, rereading *The Nuclear Taboo* shows that the emotional groundings of morality – moral reasoning and 'moral *sentiments*' (Tannenwald, 2007, pp. 59, emphasis added) – in general and the nuclear taboo in particular are not plumbed further by Tannenwald.

To sum up, with moral reasoning and the logic of appropriateness as the nuclear taboo's springboard, conceptually speaking emotion and feelings are, again, merely a taken-for-granted background matter, not requiring substantive conceptualization. The same is at least as much the case regarding Paul's work.

To put my rereading of that literature in perspective: I am not *charging* these two concepts with carelessly or negligently overlooking emotion. This would be disingenuous because they never set out to include it in the first place. With the explanatory approach they employ to close in on nuclear of non-use, taking recourse to the realm of human emotion is not required – because the emphasis simply lies elsewhere, namely at the level of specific, isolatable factors affecting agency. However, I uphold the idea that a shift of perspective and a closer, systematic look at human emotion's involvement with nuclear non-use might be a worthwhile undertaking. But after having taking stock of the explanations of non-use one last time, it is clear that I need to look for inspiration elsewhere in that regard.

An alternative perspective

A book that offers an alternative view – criticizing rational deterrence sharply, but written before the nuclear taboo had been fleshed out as an analytic concept – is Blight's *The Shattered Crystal Ball.* Therein, inter alia drawing on earlier versions of ExComm transcripts, Blight focuses on 'fear and learning' during the Cuban Missile Crisis, trying to 'approach more closely the core of the human experience of nuclear danger' (Blight, 1990, p. x). When thinking about nuclear weapons and their possible use, fear 'has been discounted by many serious students of nuclear policy as the understandable but hyperbolic enervations of the powerless and ignorant, fed by a sensationalist media', Blight (1990, p. 6) argues, addressing the professional defense communities' supposedly serious, rational, cool-headed deterrence thinking. In contrast, he (1990, pp. 8, 29) states that U.S. decision-makers clearly were afraid during the Cuban Missile Crisis, not simply for their own life and limb – afraid of perishing in a nuclear conflagration with the rest of the country – but of becoming the ones responsible for that catastrophic result. Leaving behind the dichotomy of 'good rationality' versus 'bad irrationality' of the traditional deterrence paradigm, he points out how fear is *neither* irrelevant to nuclear non-use *nor* solely reducible to an impediment that paralyzes or maddens decision-makers (Blight, 1990, pp. 6–7, 149–167). Consequently, he sides with neither believers in rational deterrence theory nor with critical third-wave theorists such as Jervis, Lebow or Gross Stein who, Blight argues, drew on psychology solely for questioning deterrence by pointing to the detrimental effects of emotion. Instead, Blight (1990, pp. 7, 29–30) argues that the feeling of fear was in play adaptively and *productively* during the Cuban Missile Crisis, facilitating 'the learning required to escape the predicament without a war'. I will pick this notion up again when conceptualizing atomic anxiety more systematically myself.

The train of thought I present in this study shares important features with Blight's book, notably the focus on agency and meaning, and the methodological decision to heavily rely on reconstruction to better understand nuclear abstinence, as well as the importance of actors experiencing crises. However, apart from Blight's (1990, pp. 55–83) approaching the subject matter from the distinct perspective of a psychologist striving for a phenomenological description, whereas I couch my study in the disciplinary framework of IR and its pertinent vocabulary, there is a crucial difference to be noted, making Blight's book important and worthwhile but in itself no satisfying answer to the questions I have about atomic anxiety and nuclear abstinence. This requires a detailed explanation.

Blight is focused on the Cuban Missile Crisis, inquiring into what fear in this particular crisis 'was *like*, and what it was *about*' (Blight, 1990, pp. 8, original emphasis). Despite highlighting the sense of responsibility that weighed heavily on decision-makers' minds, he puts great emphasis on the *fear of inadvertent nuclear war* throughout his book. He deems this the 'ultimate fear', the fear 'of *fate*' (Blight, 1990, pp. 96, 152 original emphasis), of events spiraling out of control and an unwanted war erupting. Blight emphasizes that a shared and fundamental insight (deriving from the metaphorical 'crystal ball') was (and is) that nuclear war is not worth fighting and must never be fought. Decision-makers were thus struggling to not let events slip through their hands and into the nuclear abyss. Hence the 'fear of inadvertent nuclear war' is the key formula Blight repeats almost like a mantra over the course of his book. I agree with this part of the analysis. And as I argued above, 'chance' and the acute fear of uncontrolled escalation are key notions when analyzing the Cuban Missile Crisis, commonly and plausibly invoked, commonly so even by deterrence theorists who simply see 'the risk that leaves something to chance' at work.

But I have also argued that this represents only one side of the coin, its 'passive' side. The second facet of fear, intimately connected to the notion of 'inadvertence' but in need of differentiation from it, must not be ignored. In this study, I draw attention to the details of the decision-making dilemma Kennedy faced during the crisis, evoked by the dreaded moment in which he would have to actively, deliberately and in a controlled fashion initiate war. This is what gave the sense of responsibility its brisance in the first place. In other words, how to come to grips with the deterrence *paradox*, that is, having to actively facilitate that which Kennedy wanted to avoid at all costs, is what I emphasize as the source of the conundrum he faced. Kennedy feared both unintended and intended consequences of his decisions, more precisely their concatenation, both sides of the coin in any case. After all, fear did not only have to be endured by him passively (eventually with productive results, according to Blight) but he also had to actively create and uphold it in his opponent's mind at the same time because deterrence in practice *requires* facilitating a dangerous course of risk escalation or, in Kennedy's case, the initiation of an exchange of violence that also bears the risk of spiraling out of control. Blight barely, if at all, takes notice of this. But this is what conjured up Kennedy's Berlin problem. And only in its light did President Kennedy, originally determined to secure Berlin by deterring the Soviets with violence escalation, come to eventually act the way he did.

Furthermore, I argue that moral qualms were at the heart of the Berlin problem. Granted, at the time of writing in 1990, Blight could not yet refer to the nuclear taboo as a full-fledged analytic concept. But he (1990, p. 93) does consider the impact of morality, arguing that '[i]n the Cuban missile crisis, the sense of distress may have derived in large measure from moral anguish over not being able to envision a way around committing an act, that one take to be profoundly wrong, that is, immoral'. Yet, why did Kennedy have to ponder that 'profoundly wrong' act – what he himself called the final failure – in the first place? The answer is that he tried to practice deterrence in order to create fear. I am thus able to demonstrate more clearly the genesis of Kennedy's anguish by reconstructing how he found himself in the field of tension between 'moral forbiddances' on the one hand *and* deterrence requirements on the other hand (i.e. the taboo's interfering with deterrence in practice). By not taking the intricate interplay of morality and strategy on the *active* side, the side of *creating fear*, further in both conceptual and empirical terms, it is clear why Blight's focus had to stay squarely pointed to the fear of inadvertent nuclear war. Consequently, Blight's neglect for the pressures deriving from the deterrence paradigm and its inherent paradox – and thus a lack of insight into the actual genesis of the angst-ridden crisis – is my major point of critique regarding the otherwise splendid analysis in *The Shattered Crystal Ball*.

It stands to reason that the Cuban Missile Crisis was 'unique' (Blight, 1990, p. 9) in terms of the risks – and the level of anxiety – involved. But not only do I argue that the *paradox* encountered while practicing deterrence should not be one-sidedly reduced to the fear of inadvertent war, I will also argue further that atomic anxiety can be investigated above and beyond that one historic event as well as conceptualized systematically in reference to today's thinking in IR about non-use at large. This is what I will aim for in the remainder of this section. Hence, while a remarkable exception in terms of embracing the importance of human emotion in nuclear decision-making, I consider Blight's book not the last but rather the first word in terms of working toward conceptualizing atomic anxiety and how it connects to nuclear non-use.

4.3.3 Conceptualizing atomic anxiety: consequentiality, appropriateness and emotion

Human emotion falls through the cracks of the positivist research design with which the existing explanations of non-use are equipped. Not measurable with any sort of reliance, not straightforwardly causal at all, most certainly not arrow-diagrammable as in 'if atomic anxiety, then non-use', its influence must seem way too elusive and fuzzy from such a point of view (for the general argument, see Bleiker/Hutchison, 2008; cf. Bleiker/Hutchison, 2014, p. 490; Bially Mattern, 2011, p. 63; Ross, 2014, p. 3).

However, a growing body of 'emotional turn' literature seeks to answer how we can nevertheless acknowledge and theorize the influence of emotion when studying international politics – a challenging effort that is only at the beginning (Mattern, 2014, p. 589). Accordingly, this emerging literature is not consistent in terms of terminology (with terms like human emotion, emotions, feelings, affect etc. used varyingly) as well as regarding questions about how to think about emotion and feelings conceptually or how they can best be inquired into methodically.[15]

I will thus pick and choose pragmatically, taking my cue from this literature solely for the purpose at hand. The first task with regard to conceptualizing atomic anxiety is to sort my vocabulary. So far I have used the two terms 'fear' and 'atomic anxiety' more or less interchangeably. So to better organize things, a couple of questions need to be answered. First, what are feelings and what is human emotion within the context of my study? More precisely, what is the fear I pointed to regarding nuclear weapon use, and what is atomic anxiety conceptually speaking, that is, over and above the mere standard dictionary definition 'feeling of worry, nervousness, or unease about something with an uncertain outcome'? Also, how do those two relate to nuclear abstinence and how can they be studied empirically? How are they connected to existing explanations such as deterrence, the taboo and the tradition? Lastly, how do they relate to the impact of these concepts on agency?

Toward an 'emotional concept' of atomic anxiety

An entry point for my discussion of the questions raised above is provided by Neta C. Crawford (2000, p. 116), who seminally – and for my purposes very suitably – suggests that '[t]heories of international politics and security depend on assumptions about emotion that are rarely articulated and may not be correct'. And right off the bat she points to deterrence theory as the prime example, arguing that it 'may be fundamentally flawed because its assumptions and policy prescriptions do not fully acknowledge and take into account reasonable human responses to threat and fear'. As already touched upon during my own discussion of deterrence, she identifies the 'ubiquitous [...] assumption of rationality in international relations theory' as one reason for the widespread neglect of human emotion in IR (Crawford, 2000, p. 116; cf. Lebow, 2005, p. 304). In the resulting dichotomy between rationality and irrationality, emotion was filed under the latter – and hence ignored – as soon as the rational actor paradigm took hold (Crawford, 2000, p. 122).

Affect, feelings, emotion, all these concepts emerging from varying brain states of individuals are still objects of biological and psychological research (Crawford, 2000, pp. 127–130; McDermott, 2004, p. 692). There is no universal linguistic description to fix their meaning. They are, as is the language in which they are constructed, culturally and socially contextualized and contingent.

Conceptually speaking, especially human emotion *is immediately social* this way, while feelings as bodily experiences are less so. In other words, '[f]eelings are internally experienced, but the meaning attached to those feelings, the behaviors associated with them, and the recognition of emotions in others are cognitively and culturally construed and constructed' (Crawford, 2000, p. 125). I consequently define the *fear* of nuclear weapon use as a *feeling* (the individual, bodily experience), and I define *atomic anxiety* as *human emotion* (the socially shared experience of that particularly 'nuclear fear'). And what is key is that the meaning of human emotion is transmitted and learned socially, in this way rendering it political (Crawford, 2000, pp. 125, 132–133; Hutchison/Bleiker, 2014, pp. 499–500; see also Bourke, 2005, pp. 8, 73–76, 287–290; Bially Mattern, 2011, pp. 76–79; Ross, 2014, pp. 1–2, 15–38).

My working definition of emotion I thus borrow from Khaled Fattah and Karin Fierke (2009, pp. 70, emphasis added), who characterize emotion as 'inherently social and relational', '[finding] expression only in language', and hence define emotion as composed of '*socially meaningful expressions,* which depend on shared customs, uses and institutions'. In this vocabulary a decision-maker experiences (and maybe expresses) the feeling of fear in a social situation characterized by a wider sociocultural state, namely the intersubjectively shared emotional state of atomic anxiety.

Regarding, next, the question of how to study emotion, it is of course correct that it begins as a feeling, as an internal, individual experience. However, when 'expressed in relation to others, and in a language understandable to them' (Fattah/Fierke, 2009, p. 70), emotion extents from the realm of individual corporality and biology into the realm of society and politics, becoming accessible for analysis. All that is required is identifying sources in which emotion is expressed (Crawford, 2000, pp. 130–131; Bourke, 2005, p. 7; Bleiker/Hutchison, 2008, pp. 128–133). Reconstructing this empirically 'comes as close as possible to actually understanding emotions: it is the simple acknowledgment that representations matter' (Bleiker/Hutchison, 2008, p. 130). And just as it is neither possible nor particularly important whether a speaker 'really meant what he said', I am not aiming at any kind of declaration about whether he 'really felt what he expressed' since I was and still am primarily interested in the concatenation of situated and socially meaningful speech acts and decisions.

This answers what fear is, what atomic anxiety is, how the two relate, and how they can be studied. But how does all this connect to the existing explanations of non-use and my reconceptualization of them as beliefs that provide rules for action?

Here, Jonathan Mercer's (2005; 2010; 2014) work is helpful. He, while using the terms emotion and feeling synonymously, first re-emphasizes their point of origin, namely body-internal, subjective experiences (Mercer, 2010, p. 3). This helps in putting the focus back on individual, decision-making actors. The argument Mercer makes in this regard is that against the background of results from neuroscientific research, human emotion and rationality are *not* mutually exclusive (see also Fattah/Fierke, 2009, pp. 69–70).[16] On the contrary, not only are they indistinguishable in the brain with existing means of medical imaging, it stands to reason that rationality actually *depends* on feelings. Mercer (2005, p. 93; 2010, p. 5) points to documented patient cases to illustrate this. Having lost their emotional capacity due to brain damage, they became unable to make sensible 'rational' decisions, sometimes even unable to come to any kind of decision, stuck in an endless loop of cost-benefit calculations, despite memory, language and other cognitive functions remaining unimpaired. 'Emotion is necessary to rationality and intrinsic to choice'. It 'is part of reasoning and not a distraction upsetting a coldly rational process', Mercer concludes (2005, p. 94; 2010, p. 5). Like Blight (1990, p. 30), who demonstrated that fear was 'mortifying but adaptive' and eventually 'crisis-resolving' because it promoted learning during the Cuban Missile Crisis (rather than just creating mistakes and deterrence failure), Mercer (2005, p. 94; cf. Mercer, 2010, pp. 10–11) finds that '[e]motions can, of course, lead to mistakes, but so can cognition, and no one suggests that cognition is only a source of mistakes'.

Especially for the rational actor assumption in deterrence theory, these are very helpful considerations. They might apply in a similar fashion to the tradition of non-use, which also assumes rational, calculating decision-makers and the logic of consequences to be at work predominantly. As seen in my discussion of fear and deterrence above, if rationality and emotion are treated as mutually exclusive, there is little opportunity to fit emotion into the existing lines of thought as anything but a detrimental, upsetting effect on deterrence. But with this dichotomy left behind, it is possible to acknowledge deterrence's reliance on fear without having to conclude that rational deterrence theory cannot be called rational, the way Waltz does.

Second, Mercer's concept of emotion is also not devoid of a social dimension. He (2005, pp. 95–97) points to the importance of emotion to identity formation. Emotion provides building blocks for group identity (see also Bleiker/Hutchison, 2008, p. 123). This notion resonates with the definition of emotion as 'socially meaningful expressions which depend on shared customs, uses and institutions' that I draw on here. So it stands to reason that what a group considers acceptable, unacceptable or even taboo is intimately connected to emotion as well. Fattah and Fierke (2009, pp. 70, emphasis added) make that point when highlighting that emotion only 'finds expression [...] in language *and a culture which is linked to a moral order and a moral appraisal*'. So even while not putting a specific focus on it, Tannenwald of course points to emotion and feelings, for example when considering the 'revulsion' (Tannenwald, 2007, pp. ix, 8) nuclear weapons evoke in a society, a sentiment that fostered their stigmatization. Emotion is thus intimately involved with norm emergence.

In addition, emotion facilitates adherence to existing norms. After all, it is the larger framework of societal norms that allows the process of *shaming* actors into obeying certain norms, a widely accepted emotional notion in mainstream constructivist norm literature (Mercer, 2010, p. 19). Clearly, 'feelings are responsible for ethics because they provide the incentive to understand and evaluate our behavior' in the eyes of others (Lebow, 2005, pp. 298–299). For most people, being singled out as a taboo breaker is an unpleasant experience, while acting in line with prescriptions and reaping social approval tends to make people, generally speaking, feel good (Crawford, 2000, p. 154). Emotion is thus not only innate to rationality but also to socially acceptable behavior according to the logic of appropriateness, to reasoning in a social framework. This is why the emotionless patients already mentioned above not only fail benchmarks of rationality but also of sociality, of *normal* behavior: 'They violate norms because they do not care – they feel neither embarrassment nor pride – or because they cannot imagine how others will feel if they are treated in a way that violates a social norm such as fairness' (Mercer, 2010, p. 20).

A taboo conveys a very strict prohibition to protect people from the dangerous consequences of disobeying it. Because breaking a taboo poses such great risk to not only an individual but society as a whole, it goes along with threats of automatic and severe punishment in case of a violation. The emotional reaction connected to individual and societal consequences of breaking a taboo – the fear and the *felt* obligation to obey that rule, 'follow[ing] prescriptions for emotional reasons' (Crawford, 2000, p. 154), in other words – is where the reflections in this subsection tie in with the logic of appropriateness on which the nuclear taboo relies.

Against the background of the 'emotional turn' in IR, many signs thus point toward a close conceptual linkage between emotion and the logics underlying the two explanations of non-use. But since I reconceptualized these as beliefs to allow for an agency-focused study of how they play out in decision-making practice, the last question remaining is how emotion fits into that particular framework.

It is worth remembering that, to distance myself from positivist approaches fixated on causality and the accompanying notion of decision-makers as either billiard balls subdued to a law-like logic of mechanical consequentialism or norm-obedience automatons subdued to a somewhat softer logic of constant appropriateness, I defined agency as the ongoing interplay between routine and crisis situations experienced in the unending stream of decision-making practice. Therein, a system of beliefs provides the rules for action, resting on past interpretations to make sense of the world, on socially shared usable meanings and on established useful practices in a society. Clearly then, that system is subject to constantly evolving experience, and thus belief systems are remolded while coping with crises. Furthermore, I conceptualized the existing explanations of non-use as specific beliefs that rule action, allowing actors 'meaning-making' and meaningful agency in practice. The nuclear taboo provides rules for making sense of reality in light of one's identity and socially appropriate behavior; deterrence in terms of weighing material costs and benefits; the tradition in terms of reputational and precedent-setting considerations. But no matter if the ideationalist logic of appropriateness, the materialist logic of consequentiality or a mix of the two is emphasized, so far these concepts have been framed as beliefs with merely *cognitive* benchmarks.

But human beings are not reducible to 'pure mind' and cognitive states defined by a mere consideration of rational and moral motives. After all, human beings are also corporeal beings, capable of and subject to feelings and emotion. Against this background, I suggested above that emotion ('feeling about nuclear non-use') and the existing explanations of non-use ('reasoning about nuclear non-use') might be conceptually compatible, interdependent even (Ross, 2006, p. 209). And, to further elaborate on this point, the notion of agency as dependent on 'beliefs that rule action', which, at least prima vista, admittedly has quite a cognitive ring to it as well, does in fact provide a point of contact where the influx of emotion into belief constitution can, conceptually speaking, be located. So if 'a radical separation of thinking from feeling is descriptively inaccurate and provides a shaky foundation for normative (or rational choice) theories of decision' (Mercer, 2010, pp. 5–6), conceptually acknowledging this allows a better exploration of how 'emotion *and* cognition co-produce beliefs' by 'constituting' and 'strengthening' them (Mercer, 2005, pp. 6–8, emphasis added). The entry point of emotion into this process of belief constitution is *experience.*

Fear of death en masse as a collective experience

Because humankind learned about the fearful effect of using atomic bombs in 1945 and subsequently, *experiencing atomic anxiety is the emotional springboard of all beliefs that rule against using these weapons,* in short, atomic anxiety is the key underlying element of our thinking about nuclear weapons and their use. I argue that a collectively experienced feeling of fear, the 'Great Fear' (Boyer, 1994 [1985], p. 14) of *death en masse,* containing deeply and widely felt uncertainties and grueling worries about the survival of the entire human race – atomic anxiety for short – has been woven deeply into the cultural fabric of modern society in a process that began immediately with humankind's first steps into the nuclear age.

After all, what is unique about nuclear weapons is how they drenched modern civilization in a culture all their own, an 'atomic culture' (Zeman/Amundson, 2004; Szasz, 2012). Historic and cultural studies such as *By the Bomb's Early Light* by Paul Boyer (1994 [1985]), *Life Under A Cloud* by Allan M. Winkler (1993) or *Nuclear Fear* by Spencer Weart (1988) argue this forcefully, plausibly and in great detail. Numerous facets of atomic culture lend themselves to closer examination. Guy Oakes (1994), for instance, analyzes the role of civil defense in U.S. Cold War culture (see also Masco, 2008). Kenneth D. Rose (2001) focuses on the example of the fallout shelter. Peggy Rosenthal (1991) and Titus

Constandina (2004) analyze the mushroom cloud as a global icon. Anne Harrington de Santana (2009) suggests thinking about nuclear weapons in terms of 'fetish' and the 'fetishism of force' they represent in international politics, thus overriding the paradoxical problem that they produce immense amounts of security and insecurity at the same time. Vincent Pouliot (2010) goes as far as arguing that nuclear warheads have a symbolic life of their own. E.L. Doctorow (quoted in Gusterson, 1996, p. 1; 2004) summed it all up like this: 'The bomb first was our weapon. Then it became our diplomacy. Next it became our economy. Now it's become our culture. We've become the people of the bomb'.

The symbolic power and cultural status of nuclear weapons transcends the realm of military strategy. Reconsidering them in this wider context means unhinging them from the comparably narrow context of deterrence and also expanding on the notion of their being stigmatized devices garrisoned with a society taboo by society. The aforementioned studies demonstrate the wider impact of nuclear weapons by exposing the hope initially connected to them on the one hand, the hope for finally ending all wars and progressing toward the era of world government – the hope of the 'nuclear one worlders'. However, on the other hand this literature reveals '[h]ow *quickly* Americans began to articulate [fear], [...] bone-deep fear [...], primal fear of extinction' right at the dawn of the nuclear age (Boyer, 1994 [1985], pp. 15, original emphasis). As the famous American journalist and opinion molder Edward R. Murrow put it in his radio program on August 12, 1945, 'Seldom if ever has a war ended leaving victors with such a sense of uncertainty and fear, with such a realization that the future is obscure and the survival is not assured' (quoted in Hunner, 2004, p. 38). This is what I focus on here. And while there can probably be made a case for atomic anxiety pervading all societies, I will concentrate on the postwar U.S. to develop my argument about the experience of atomic anxiety further.

Specific knowledge in the U.S. about the gruesome effects on the populations of Hiroshima and Nagasaki was confined to a small circle of decision-makers and scientists at the beginning. And by 'carefully stage-managing' (Boyer, 1994 [1985], p. 187) the media coverage of Hiroshima and Nagasaki, the U.S. military went to great lengths immediately after the dropping of the bombs not to let accounts or images of destruction and suffering slip out into the general public (Weart, 1988, pp. 236–237; Gusterson, 2009; 2004, pp. 64, 68). However, with President Truman's public statement on August 6 about the bombing of Hiroshima, wide public awareness of the existence of the atomic bomb developed (I will return to this watershed moment). '"For all we know, we have created a

Frankenstein"', H.V. Kaltenborn (quoted in Weart, 1988, pp. 104–105), a famous NBC radio pundit, concluded that day, setting the tone for the public reaction and the upcoming avalanche of radio commentaries and editorials. In the days that followed, a 'dense cloud of fear' (Boyer, 1994 [1985], p. 29) sank on people's minds. Aptly, four days after the Japanese surrender, Norman Cousins (quoted in Boyer, 1994 [1985], p. 8; cf. Oakes, 1994, pp. 43–44) wrote, '"Whatever elation there is in the world today, it severely tempered by a primitive fear, the fear of the unknown, the fear of forces man can neither channel nor comprehend. This fear is not new; in its classical form it is the fear of irrational death. But overnight it has become intensified, magnified. It has burst out of the subconscious and into the conscious, filling the mind with primordial apprehension"'.

In terms of the speed of news spreading, the dropping of the atomic bomb was an 'event of almost unprecedented proportions' at the time, with 98 percent of the adult population knowing of it by 1946, according to a survey by the U.S. Social Science Research Council (Boyer, 1994 [1985], pp. 22, 105). But many had 'known' about the atomic bomb already. It had made an appearance in science fiction decades before. With H.G. Wells' fantastic novel *The World Set Free*, published in 1913, as merely the pinnacle and the most widely known, close to prophetic, example (also coining the term 'atomic bomb') of the bomb's prominence in fiction, the (mad) scientists developing a super weapon capable of destroying the earth and the notion that a single plane could wipe out an entire city had already had a well-established presence as fantastic and *frightful* products of the imagination in that segment of popular culture (Weart, 1988, pp. 24–26, 59–74; Franklin, 2008 [1988], p. 44, 132–133; Szasz, 2012, pp. 32–40). And also to those U.S. citizens less familiar with the formerly fictional bombs, '[f]rom August 1945 on, the whole tangle of fantastic nuclear imagery, mingled with the very few facts then available, was a significant part of the mental equipment of everyone within reach of a radio' (Weart, 1988, p. 106).

So the initial secrecy surrounding the bomb notwithstanding (Boyer, 1994 [1985], pp. 257–258; Szasz, 2012, pp. 29–32; Winkler, 1993, p. 7), *everyone* eventually learned about the bomb, the mushroom clouds, the obliterated cities, the rubble and flames, the wastelands populated by only a few shells of remaining buildings; the human silhouettes left on scorched walls, the people who had simply vanished in the explosion, the charcoaled human remains, the ugly, festering wounds on the survivors, the burn patterns branded onto their skin by their clothes. Reading descriptions and witness reports, trying to grasp the reality of it, thinking about it, talking about it was (and is) a disturbing, deeply emotional experience: '[A] set of horrifying images was burnt permanently into the public mind. These images became new emblems of nuclear energy, and at the same time new emblems of modern war – and death itself' (Weart, 1988, p. 108).

The emotional state evoked by this collective experience, one based on a shared, intensified, magnified fear of death, was the sociocultural background against which thinking about the future existence of the U.S. – indeed of all nation states – in the nuclear age took place in the months and years after the end of World War II (Boyer, 1994 [1985], p. 24): 'Physically untouched by the war, the United States at the moment of victory perceived itself as naked and vulnerable. Sole possessors and users of a devastating new instrument of mass destruction, Americans envisioned themselves not as a potential threat to other peoples, but as potential victims' (Boyer, 1994 [1985], p. 15; cf. Oakes, 1994, p. 23).

So, even while it would take four more years for the Soviet Union to end the U.S. nuclear monopoly, the initial fear of falling victim to this new and horrible weapon, the nightmare of being 'Pearl Harbored' (Kaplan, 1983, pp. 90–110) again, only in a 'nuclear Pearl Harbor' this time (Oakes, 1994, p. 44), fueled the immediate impetus that, with nothing less than extinction looming and survival at stake, something had to be done to escape that fearful situation. It was *the world at the crossroads* (Weart, 1988, p. 115).

The one path, which the 'nuclear one worlders' pressed for, was international control of nuclear energy and world government. Hope rested on it to function as the ultimate protector from nuclear war. The alternative was one that advocates of world government such as Cousins considered '"a tempting but dangerous one"', '"quasilogical"' since '"war is no respector of logic"' (quoted in Boyer, 1994 [1985], p. 39; see also Weart, 1988, pp. 114–116) – it was deterrence. And firmly embracing it was the other immediate reaction. The pioneers of this opposite path in world history deemed Cousin's 'call for world government as a substitution of "hysteria for history"' (quoted in Boyer, 1994 [1985], p. 51). They proposed to meet the new fear by relying on diplomacy, strategy and military posture, in short, on practicing deterrence for the prevention of nuclear war and thus – as spelled out in 1946 in Brodie's *The Absolute Weapon* – on fighting fear with fear *in response*. I already argued that the Realist *zeitgeist* benefitted that path. But the specific catalyst for this development was *fear*. Deterrence presented itself as a pragmatic, doable solution because it suggested a seemingly simple thing, the creation of fear *in turn*, in a tit-for-tat reaction to a threat that had not actually presented itself yet, but had to be prevented from materializing in the future (Boyer, 1994 [1985], pp. 29–45).

Of course, this early dispute already points to the fact that after its sudden emergence, atomic anxiety has not had the same freeze-frame quality since the beginning of the nuclear age. Nor do these passages mean to suggest that the public – in the U.S. as well as elsewhere – was undivided. Even during the most anxious time periods, atomic anxiety was thus not necessarily experienced by every member of society the same way, nor was there – as seen above – a consensus on how to react to it. For example, parts of the U.S. general population expected a nuclear exchange to promise victory over the enemy, even in concrete instances of widespread fear such as during the Cuban Missile Crisis (Blight, 1990, pp. 27–29; Weart, 1988, p. 259). '[P]assing through Armageddon to world rebirth' was certainly a perspective held by some (Weart, 1988, p. 139). This, however, merely underlines the argument I put forward here, namely that atomic anxiety is undeniably part of the collective memory. And because this emotional state is 'socially constructed' (Lebow, 2005, p. 295; cf. Ross, 2010, p. 111), atomic anxiety is always re-evoked and contested (by meeting it with confidence instead of despair, for example), re-memorized and reshaped. After all, it needs to be articulated in order to be remembered. Hence society is in a 'state' of anxiety, yet this is not to be mistaken for a static, fixed situation – rather, atomic anxiety is a lasting yet alterable sociocultural condition. Section 4.4 will reconstruct its development over time, backing up this proposition empirically.

Atomic anxiety holds the preeminent, shared ideas of what a use of nuclear weapons would mean. It means instant horror, vast destruction, total annihilation, dying a horrible *death* (Boyer, 1994 [1985], pp. 277–278) – death, that is, with a good chance of little to no warning, no time to run or prepare for. From perishing within the blink of an eye in a flash of light, to being ripped apart by a tremendous blast wave, to being set on fire and burned alive, to being buried under a ton of rubble. And while conventional bullets and bombs will kill or maim a person, with nuclear weapons, even surviving this initial onslaught could only mean dying an agonizing, slow death in the aftermath of a nuclear war, from acute radiation sickness, or starvation in a postapocalyptic wasteland, or from contracting cancer a couple of years down the road, or from being buried alive in some fallout shelter. Life itself, should a person survive, might no longer be worth living on the contaminated planet, with DNA damaged by radiation, bringing suffering to yet unborn generations. Hence the end of civilization is a preeminent motif invoked by the thought of nuclear weapon use and accompanying atomic anxiety, making it a strong emotional experience: 'The imagery of nuclear explosions is a cultural obsession unlike any other, because it ties in with so many deep images, mutant monsters, suicidal madmen, the apocalypse, etc. [...] At present, nuclear weapons have a unique status. [...] You say "nuclear bomb" and everybody immediately thinks of the end of the world' (Weart, 2008, p. 12).

Atomic anxiety is the painful and constant reminder that living in the nuclear age means living under the sword of Damocles. Works of nonfiction have been dealing with this intensively for decades, sometimes so brutally realistic that they ended up extremely hard to stomach. To give but one example, the British documentary *The War Game*, produced by the BBC in 1966 (and awarded with an Academy Award for Best Feature Documentary), was never aired – because it was found '"too horrifying"' at the time (quoted in Bourke, 2005, pp. 265–266). The same applies to works of fiction, with many interpreting atomic anxiety via the popular motif of the nuclear apocalypse. With nuclear weapons crossing over from the realm of the imagination into the real world in 1945, their appearance in fiction has since then evoked this motif again and again, effectively continuing where Wells left off, but in the knowledge that science fiction and reality can now become one and the same at any given moment. By way of illustration, I will name only a few of the countless examples: books such as *A Canticle for Leibowitz* or *On the Beach* (which later was made into a record-grossing movie), and motion pictures from *Them!* to *Godzilla* to *Fail-Safe* to *Dr. Strangelove* to *The Day After Tomorrow* to *The Terminator*, as well as, more recently, video games such as the *Fallout* or the *Metro* series. With the *Doomsday Clock*, atomic culture even found a way to symbolically measure the time to the apocalypse. '[T]...ogether with the mushroom-shaped cloud itself', the *Doomsday Clock* is 'one of the best-known visual symbols of the atomic age' and 'a remarkably apt representation of [...] fear and urgency' (Boyer, 1994 [1985], p. 64; see also Weart, 1988, pp. 217, 401–406; Winkler, 1993, pp. 40, 67–68; Vuori, 2010).

There are plenty of attempts to cope with or even fence in atomic anxiety. Civil defense is a good example of an 'emotion management' effort launched to counter the collective experience of despair and helplessness, 'to channel public anxieties about nuclear war into civil defense activities, convincing Americans that their fears of annihilation were groundless' (Oakes, 1994, p. 8). Some officials even hoped to '"inoculate" them against panic, getting them accustomed to horrid sights so they would not run around screaming when the bombs came'

(Weart, 1988, p. 130; see also Oakes, 1994, pp. 34–46; Bourke, 2005, pp. 267–276). Of course, on the one hand civil defense provides some protection. On the other hand rates and conditions of survival in an all-out nuclear exchange with thermonuclear weapons are surrounded by giant question marks, so it is not overly cynical to assume that U.S. civil defense policy served at least also another, additional purpose: namely to convince the American people that they could protect themselves in order for them to keep up the necessary support for a nuclear deterrence policy – the failure of which they would only tolerate if they remained convinced of their own survival (Oakes, 1994, pp. 6–7). Seen in this light, civil defense measures – from bomb shelters and nuclear exercises to 'duck and cover' slogans – can also be interpreted as an attempt at underpinning the practice of deterrence: by disentangling its reciprocity to manage one's own fear while keeping the opponent scared to death.

Consequently, at the beginning of the 1950s '[c]ivil defense theorists tried to replace [the] apocalyptic view of nuclear war [gained from the initial post-war coverage] with a very different conception designed to check American anxiety about the bomb', for instance, with booklets published by the Office of Civil Defense suggesting that a nuclear raid could easily be survived and, most importantly, that nuclear weapons 'were not fundamentally different from conventional arms' (Oakes, 1994, p. 52). Yet, the official booklet, *Fallout Protection: What to Know and Do About Nuclear Attack*, issued by the Department of Defense in 1961, states, for example, on its first page that '[i]n a major attack upon our country, millions of people would be killed' (DoD, 1961, p. 5). This was hardly reassuring. 'Civil defense would give the people the facts about nuclear weapons, but these facts would only substantiate some of their worst fears' (Oakes, 1994, p. 146). With national exercises and simulations such as 'Operation Alert', with classroom drills, courses, instructional films, radio programs, brochures, traveling exhibits, slide shows and lectures (Weart, 1988, pp. 130–134; Oakes, 1994, pp. 84–104), civil defense served to alert people over and over again to the possibility of a nuclear attack. Consequently, by continuously bringing the apocalypse to the forefront of their minds, it ended up scaring most of them even more. It is safe to say that 'inoculating' society against atomic anxiety for good, civil defense measures could not – the idea of surviving nuclear war never really caught on. Instead, in a famous saying 'duck and cover' ended up getting ridiculed as '"get down on the floor, put your head between your knees...and kiss your ass goodbye"' (quoted in Weart, 1988, p. 240).

Aside from responding with sarcasm, people's most common reaction was, as polls suggest, denial: suppressing anxiety and going on with normal life, resigning themselves to fate and hoping for the best (Weart, 1988, pp. 134–137, 257, 263–266, 379; Winkler, 1993, p. 5). Later, in the 1970s, U.S. psychologists found that nevertheless in many young people's minds – who had grown up during the era of civil defense – '[n]uclear weapons had become almost inseparable [...] from overwhelming death itself' (Weart, 1988, p. 134; see also Bourke, 2005, pp. 255–257). Civil defense had merely cemented atomic anxiety as an emotional undercurrent by passing it on to the next generation.

So the emotional foundation of atomic anxiety ended up reinforced, a foundation that bore – in alternation with intervals of relative indifference and silence (Weart, 1988, pp. 262–269), a numb 'atomic apathy' (Boyer, 1994 [1985], p. 352), if you will – further periods of acute fears, both in the U.S. as well as globally (Weart, 1988, pp. 375–388). In this ongoing process of ebb and flow, the specter of atomic death returned to the fore long after the civil defense efforts of the 1950s and 1960s had been abandoned, evoked by technological novelties and political developments during the arms race era of the Cold War as well as, more recently, by the increased fear of nuclear armed terrorists or so-called rogue states.

Trying to maintain an unemotional, sterile discourse on nuclear war is another, longer lasting attempt of emotion management. Deterrence theory's cold and steely logic is the prime example here. The real-life *Wizards of Armageddon* (Kaplan, 1983) 'at the RAND Corporation, devoted to rational analysis, such as calculations of how many millions of people might die in this or that eventuality' (Weart, 1988), along with their fictional *doppelgangers* such as Professor Groeteschele, embody it. Carol Cohn's (1987) work as a participant observer of what she calls the 'technostrategic' language among defense intellectuals points to why and how this sort of language functions in terms of emotion management: it 'can be used only to articulate the perspective of the users of nuclear weapons, not that of the victims', she notes (Cohn, 1987, p. 706). In other words, learning deterrence theory's technostrategic language not only yields the benefits I already noted in subsection 3.3.1, those granted to the elite caste of nuclear priests, for themselves it also works as an antidote against thinking about death and feeling victimized. 'In learning the language, one goes from being the passive, powerless victim to being the competent, wily powerful purveyor of nuclear threats and nuclear explosive power' (Cohn, 1987, p. 707). So the deterrence paradigm spawned a language without 'emotional fallout' (Cohn, 1987, p. 691), in which 'discussions are carefully and intricately reasoned, occurring seemingly without any sense of horror, urgency, or moral outrage' (Cohn, 1987, p. 690). This clean and sober language puts distance between a person and the source of that person's fear, here nuclear weapons and their possible use in war, with 'sanitized abstraction' reintroducing a sense of control or 'cognitive mastery' over the latter (Cohn, 1987, pp. 697, 704–707). In short, technostrategic discourse helps deterrence theory preserve the mental firewall between that blunt, intimidating, fear-inducing threat at its heart and the detached rationality that it in the same breath claims to be relying on instead.

U.S. society at large never adopted that cold and unemotional perspective, as the widespread public dismay and abhorrence surrounding nuclear weapons – the emotional sources nurturing the nuclear taboo – suggest. A metaphor used by Spencer R. Weart (1988, p. 127) to describe the early post–World War II discourse on atomic 'secrets, control, and security' characterizes the entire history of emotion management attempts perfectly: 'Nuclear fear was like a Chinese finger-trap: the harder people tried to pull out of it, the tighter it gripped them'.

More generally speaking, atomic anxiety carries characteristics of what I conceptualized as a crisis. It is an especially problematic one, because what can one do to deal with it? Since there is no way to run from nuclear Armageddon, most people chose to try to live in denial, as seen above. Collectively felt helplessness thus adds despair to the experience. But for a nuclear decision-maker, denial is not an option. And being responsible for the fate of entire peoples and maybe humankind as a whole is an immense burden that atomic anxiety brings with it. I have already fleshed out atomic anxiety's multifaceted characteristics when revisiting the Kennedy sources. That discussion showed how atomic anxiety is always in play on several levels: created by decision-makers, experienced by them in reciprocity, yet not only by them but 'resonating' (Ross, 2006, p. 204) back and forth between them and domestic and foreign audiences, thus pervading all levels of society. This takes us to the role of atomic anxiety with regard to nuclear abstinence.

Atomic anxiety's constitutive function

Reasoning and deciding on nuclear use or non-use is subject to the collective experience of atomic anxiety pervading society, characterized first and foremost by a shared fear of *death en masse*. Atomic anxiety, I thus argue, is *constitutive* for nuclear non-use. It does not *cause* nuclear non-use; rather, it provides a basic condition for the possibility of nuclear abstinence to repeatedly emerge from the ('emotional-cognitive') reasoning of decision-makers facing choices.[17] Not all decision-makers experience it the same way, obviously, but they are all made of flesh and blood and are members of society. In that sense, atomic anxiety as a fear of *death en masse* is hardwired into their reasoning about nuclear weapon use.

Atomic anxiety thus also underlies existing explanations of nuclear non-use. After all, the idea of nuclear deterrence, born out of fear, is to create a situation of reciprocal fear. Deterrence theory – in its most basic, unscientificated and unrationalized sense – is about figuring out how the fear of being attacked can be harnessed and turned against the enemy to forestall a first strike. Applied as a strategy, nuclear deterrence resorts to fear by actively using it against the enemy to scare him into submission with credible threats of retaliation. The nuclear taboo, in contrast, is the flip side of this, that is, the endured fear impacting collective identity formation and the resulting moral disgust and pangs of remorse that come along with the fearful and repulsive thought of actually using the angst-inducing terror weapon against others. Atomic anxiety, in both cases, is the emotional springboard.

However, atomic anxiety's relevance to the phenomenon of nuclear non-use is understudied empirically. This is in fact the more important point. Because next to conceptually pointing out the plausibility of atomic anxiety being worth a closer look, in what way it actually impacted the nuclear age and how it is in play with respect to nuclear abstinence remains a question that can only be answered empirically. This is what I turn to now.

4.3.4 Selecting new sources: presidents, fear and nuclear non-use

This being the first systematic empirical study dedicated to atomic anxiety and how it can serve to better understand (the causes of) nuclear abstinence, it has a comparably explorative character. The inquiry into the sociocultural state of atomic anxiety and the societal space in which it resonates required a wider perspective to arrive at the bigger picture of atomic anxiety's history and role vis-à-vis nuclear abstinence at large. In other words, in contrast to the fly-on-the-wall angle in the Kennedy study, broader brushstrokes and a longer period of investigation, spanning the entire nuclear age, were necessary.

But all the arguments regarding the nuclear monarchy still applied. So there was ample reason for keeping the presidency in the spotlight. After all, 'emotions [sic!] [...] are significantly affected by commemorations and discourses propagated by authorities' (Lebow, 2005, p. 295). So key for selecting sources was U.S. presidents as *the* authority of nuclear weapon use and how atomic anxiety is expressed in a 'socially meaningful' (Fierke, 2009, p. 70) way by them – in *public* discourse. This shift from private to public and from short term to long term is best described as one from the micro to the meso level, with the interest in mapping the macro level of discourse in its entirety – the *overall* horizon for what agents can know and say – as still only of secondary interest (since it would require a much larger material base and a significantly more comprehensive analysis).

The notion of crisis from which I developed my original train of thought about how creative agency unfolds in a constant experience stream and a crisis routine dialectic had a different significance at that level. I will return to this in light of empirical results. Suffice to say at this point that a president's public speech is obviously not the same as an ExComm discussion behind closed doors. The latter allows a glimpse into the instant-to-instant development of decision-makers attributing meaning, debating and making decisions. A president's public speech, in contrast, is developed in a comparably slow process, over time, drafted, rewritten, with multiple persons next to the president – speechwriters, advisers and so forth – involved. That, as my re-evaluation of the Kennedy sources suggested, decision-makers might not want to display fear thus required special consideration, because a prepared speech allows words to be selected more carefully, potentially concealing more than a spontaneous utterance could. I will critically reflect on this particular aspect again in section 4.5, especially by reviewing alternative perspectives on the issue. Yet, this point was neither a deal breaker nor even particularly problematic because I was not interested in *why* decision-makers invoke emotional language. Following the trail of atomic anxiety further throughout the nuclear age, I only cared about reconstructing *whether* and *how* they do. After all, the idea was to understand whether and how atomic anxiety is constituted and reproduced as a sociocultural state. Whether and how it is invoked – be it reiterated, denied or belittled – in a socially meaningful fashion in public discourse over time was the main focus. And, more particularly, I was of course interested in a better understanding of the constitutive relationship between this emotion and the relevant beliefs that rule action.

The baseline of material for the analysis thus consisted of all presidential inauguration and farewell addresses as well as all State of the Union addresses delivered before Congress since President Truman announced the bombing of Hiroshima on August 6, 1945 (up until the 2012 presidential election). These three types of public addresses served to create a continuous picture of what concerned presidents politically when they entered and left office as well as what they took to be the successes and important challenges as their term progressed and when they reported to Congress about the State of the Union and policies of national interest. Receiving the widest possible media attention, these public statements served to reconstruct whether and how atomic anxiety was invoked publicly by them and how this socially meaningful expression was formulated respectively at any given time throughout the period under investigation. In addition to that, I included all presidential debates up until (and including) the 2012 election. Furthermore, I included additional sources to focus more particularly on the possible use of nuclear weapons and issues surrounding them. Truman's statement about Hiroshima was an obvious candidate, for instance. I also chose to include – in brackets, so to speak, and as the one and only exception because it is not a presidential statement – the 'Baruch Plan' speech delivered to the United Nations Atomic Energy Commission (UNAEC). But, this being an open research process, I decided on which additional sources to include mostly by following clues within the material. So when President Richard Nixon announced in his State of the Union address a separate report on foreign policy in 1971, I would include that – and so on. Many announcements about arms control agreements – such as the Limited Test Ban Treaty (LTBT), the Strategic Arms Limitation Talks (SALT) or the Comprehensive Test Ban Treaty (CTBT) – were especially prone to suggest themselves because they, taking years to develop, negotiate and eventually sign, were oftentimes prominent fix points for raising and discussing questions surrounding nuclear weapons, and thus were also included. As with the Kennedy study, the MAXQDA project file holds the entire source material.[18]

Regarding the coding process, it is noteworthy that the small, initial deductive framework devised during the Kennedy study was applied again. The two head codes *Use* and *Non-Use* were naturally part of the code system. Also, the three main codes, *Deterrence, Taboo* and *Tradition,* remained in place. That applying these particular codes sometimes worked a tad differently with respect to public speeches than White House tapes is self-explanatory. For example, the code *Deterrence* was frequently used not for an explicit threat against an explicit opponent in the material but for passages in which the development of the deterrence apparatus – oftentimes in connection with progress in certain fields of technology such as ballistic missiles, for example – is described, with the purpose of the military apparatus declared as a deterrent to war. 'Deterrence' would often be used literally in such passages, but not always. To provide an example for the latter case, take this phrase taken from President Eisenhower's (1958) sixth State of the Union address: 'Military power serves the cause of security by making prohibitive the cost of any aggressive attack'. The notion of 'making the cost of an attack prohibitively high' allows for straightforwardly coding this phrase *Deterrence* in rational deterrence theory's sense.

However, the main idea was to learn more about atomic anxiety and how it is in play as the emotional springboard for the beliefs that rule action. I thus included the newly developed concept *Atomic Anxiety* as one, new, deductive head code. As coding progressed, naturally many more codes were inductively generated. Some of those inductive codes, such as *Civil Defense* or *Apocalypse/End of the World,* resonated with what I knew from the literature. Others, such as *Proliferation* or *Rogue States,* were comparably surprising in their salience, specific meaning or in their context with other codes such as *Nuclear Terrorism.*

A passage from the transcript of the presidential debate between President Jimmy Carter and Republican candidate Ronald Reagan, in which Carter (1980) paints the following picture (in a whole passage coded *Atomic Anxiety*), provides an example: 'Ultimately, the most serious terrorist threat is if one of those radical nations, who believe in terrorism as a policy, should have atomic weapons. Both I and all my predecessors have had a deep commitment to controlling the proliferation of nuclear weapons in countries like Libya or Iraq'. Three sentences later, Carter adds, 'This ultimate terrorist threat is the most fearsome of all, and it's part of a pattern where our country must stand firm to control terrorism of all kinds'. This passage is interesting for its strong language in terms of atomic anxiety alone (with the 'ultimate terrorist threat' being 'the most fearsome of all'). But it is particularly interesting for invoking *Proliferation, Rogue States* and *Nuclear Terrorism* in one breath, making it worthwhile to study up close how these concepts are intertwined. To illustrate what my analysis of *Atomic Anxiety* entails, compare Carter's statement with one by President Barack Obama (2010), taken from his second State of the Union address: '[A]t April's Nuclear Security Summit, we will bring 44 nations together here in Washington, DC, behind a clear goal: securing all vulnerable nuclear materials around the world in 4 years so that they never fall into the hands of terrorists. Now, these diplomatic efforts have also strengthened our hand in dealing with those nations that insist on violating international agreements in pursuit of nuclear weapons. That's why North Korea now faces increased isolation and stronger sanctions, sanctions that are being vigorously enforced. That's why the international community is more united and the Islamic Republic of Iran is more isolated'.

To illustrate how the results presented via the analytic narrative below were arrived at, it is instructive to focus on the slightly different meanings of 'terrorism' in that comparison. Obviously, contemporary *Nuclear Terrorism* as invoked by Obama primarily means non-state entities getting their hands on nuclear material or weapons. In Carter's statement, however, the connection between *Rogue States* and *Nuclear Terrorism* is a closer one, with terrorism coming very close to meaning terrorism aided or directly conducted by states. In short, the source of nuclear terror in the first statement is primarily states (who embrace 'terrorism as a policy', according to Carter), while it is primarily non-state entities (i.e. nuclear weapons 'fall[ing] into the hands of terrorists', according to Obama) in the other. It is important to be careful here, because none of this meant to say that the notion of states aiding and abetting terrorists has disappeared in the Obama era. On the contrary, 'Iran is a state sponsor of terrorism. And for them to be able to provide nuclear technology to non-state actors, that's unacceptable', President Obama (2012) reminded the American people in his debate with Republican challenger Mitt Romney. Instead, what this comparison exemplifies is that the relevance of (and emphasis on) non-state entities regarding nuclear terrorism has increased in the material under analysis when comparing the Carter and Obama presidencies. Already during the debate with Republican presidential nominee John McCain, soon-to-be President Obama (2008) summed up this shift like this: '[T]he biggest threat that we face right now is not a nuclear missile coming over the skies. It's in a suitcase'.

This touches exemplarily on *one* facet of what the analysis entailed. It illustrates how atomic anxiety seeped from the old world order of nation states into the new world order of new, non-state actor threats after the Cold War, and how the meaning of key concepts connected to it – threatening 'rogue states' and frightening 'terrorism' – slightly changed over time. Through analyzing presidential public addresses by developing and applying more inductive codes this way, the salience and development of atomic anxiety and what it meant at different stages of the nuclear age could be reconstructed.

4.4 Empirical inquiry #2: twelve U.S. presidents and the age of atomic anxiety

The following section aims to empirically substantiate and systematize further what I have established about atomic anxiety so far. After all, a critic might still argue that some cultural studies literature is not enough to vindicate atomic anxiety as a viable concept and a helpful lens to employ for analyzing nuclear non-use in IR. So a systematic and comprehensive empirical analysis of *whether and how* atomic anxiety is indeed propagated by the principal authority on the question of U.S. nuclear weapons use – the president of the United States – is required to decide whether it is possible to uphold my claim about atomic anxiety's importance and my proposal about how it conceptually connects to nuclear abstinence. I will reflect on this in the concluding remarks.

4.4.1 The long nuclear shadow

On August 6, 1945, President Harry S. Truman announced the dropping of an atomic bomb on Hiroshima. The president (1945c) conjured up the image of a new and incredibly powerful weapon, a weapon 'harnessing [...] the basic power of the universe' by taming and using '[t]he force from which the sun draws its power', derived from 'the greatest scientific gamble in history'.

Entering the nuclear age: anxiety and aspiration

With the atomic bomb presented as such an intimidating weapon, it was of course first and foremost supposed to frighten the opponents of the U.S. Yet, from the perspective of the American people, it was hard not to feel somewhat intimidated and scared as well. It was an inadvertent effect of presidential language invoking images of an unshackled 'basic power of the universe' (on this see also Truman, 1945b) when the broader public was brought in touch with the atomic bomb for the first time, which created an intense, collective feeling of bewilderment and worry about what humankind had begun toying with. Despite the U.S. holding a nuclear monopoly, a nuclear shadow was cast over the future, a shadow characterized by worried anticipation and uncertainty.

On September 1, 1945, Truman announced the surrender of Japan and with it the end of World War II, expressing both joy and uncertainty about the future. Though not explicitly mentioned in this speech, the atomic bomb thus overshadowed even V-J-Day. But the United Nations promised hope: '[W]e face the future and all its dangers with great confidence and great hope. [...] Together with the United Nations, it can build a world of peace rounded on justice, fair dealing, and tolerance' (Truman, 1945a).

Yet, the widely recognized, exceptionally strong language contained in the speech delivered by Bernard Baruch (1946) before the UNAEC cemented the prevalent impression that there was every reason to be scared, too, and, with fear as the speech's sounding board, an *urgent need to act* if the peace necessary for survival were to be achieved. 'Science has torn from nature a secret so vast in its potentialities that our minds cower from the terror it creates', as Baruch put it, again invoking anxiety. In this 'situation of gloom and hopelessness', the Baruch Plan offered the famous 'choice between the quick and the dead'. And it warned that '[i]f we fail, then we have damned every man to be the slave of Fear. Let us not deceive ourselves: We must elect World Peace or World Destruction'. Baruch conveyed all of this with extreme urgency: 'To delay may be to die'.

Fear of death, the nucleus of atomic anxiety, was the first cornerstone of Baruch's speech. The second one was hope. Truman (1945b) had summed up the mixture of hope and fear even before Baruch's speech, in his message to Congress on the atomic bomb: 'Never in history has society been confronted with a power so full of potential danger and at the same time so full of promise for the future of man and for the peace of the world'.

During the balancing act between 'anxiety and aspiration' (see e.g. Truman, 1948) in these early years of the nuclear age, Truman's State of the Union addresses, when dealing with what was then referred to as the issue of 'atomic energy', were largely concerned with establishing domestic and most importantly international control via the United Nations. But with hope for success regarding the latter dwindling, and with the Soviet Union conducting its first atomic test in 1949, the president in 1950 noted with renewed urgency that '[t]he human race has reached a turning point. Man has opened the secrets of nature and mastered new powers. If he uses them wisely, he can reach new heights of civilization. If he uses them foolishly, they may destroy him' (Truman, 1950).

With renewed anxiety due to the 'grim fact' of growing Soviet military power, civil defense was first mentioned two years later. It was accompanied by anxious apprehension about its inadequacy which would equal 'an open invitation to a surprise attack. Failure to provide adequate civilian defense has the same effect as adding to the enemy's supply of atomic bombs', President Truman (1952) warned in his State of the Union address. Deterrence received a stronger emphasis in that same address as well, this time not as in the 1947 formulation, as the general notion of upholding 'strength' in order not 'to become weak and invite attack' (Truman, 1947). Instead, Truman (1952) was determined 'to deter aggression and to inflict punishing losses on the enemy immediately if we should be attacked', adding, 'We had one Pearl Harbor – let's not get caught off guard again'.

In his final address to Congress, President Truman (1953a) reflected on 'the shadow of the atomic bomb', acknowledging that the tension between anxiety and aspiration still persisted and asking, 'Could there be built in the world a durable structure of security, a lasting peace for all the nations, or [will] we drift [...] toward another terrible disaster – a disaster which this time might be the holocaust of atomic war?'

If one were to capture these early years in the smallest of nutshells as the interplay of aspiration – for the UN or even world government, peace, and a bright, atomically powered future – versus anxiety – of being Pearl Harbored and with humankind doomed and on the verge of the abyss – anxiety clearly took the win. Eight years into the nuclear age and it became apparent that atomic anxiety was there to stay.

Facing anxiety: the Cold War

The bombastic and gloomy presidential language of the early nuclear age carried notions of an ultimate turning point and of an atomic holocaust drawing closer and closer. Yet, several years into the nuclear age the American people found themselves still in existence, alive and well. Did atomic anxiety start to wane at that point? It did not. Instead, around that time atomic anxiety's first gestalt change began.

Atomic anxiety and atomic aspiration had been as intense as they had been vague immediately after World War II. But with the U.S. monopoly ending, Cold War tensions intensifying and with a deterrence posture and civil defense as the U.S.'s chosen reactions, atomic anxiety – encompassing all kinds of diffuse fears after World War II, from 'sabotage' to 'terrorism' to any sort of surprise attack – got tied more directly to the Soviet Union. Associated with this specific enemy, atomic anxiety became tangible and concrete. The looming war with the ideological rival became its primary crystallization point, for in 'the atomic age [...] war [is] a very different thing from what it used to be', Truman (1953a) reminded Congress, adding that a '[w]ar today [...] might dig the grave not only of our Stalinist opponents, but of our own society, our world as well as theirs'.

The change of administration from Truman to Eisenhower embedded atomic anxiety more firmly in this overarching emotional architecture of the Cold War. In his first State of the Union address, the new president elaborated on what had to be done in light of the ongoing tension between hope and fear. He did so by confirming Truman's decisions on deterrence and civil defense on the one hand, and by stating that 'retaliatory power is one strong deterrent to a would-be aggressor' on the other. With these preparative measures the U.S. would prevail over the Soviet

Union, for '[t]here is but one sure way to avoid total war – and that is to win the cold war' (Eisenhower, 1953a). In this way, embracing hope and putting an end to fear became tied to *winning* the Cold War, and the Soviet Union became the key referent object for atomic anxiety.[19]

However, in that same year, 1953, Joseph Stalin died. Eisenhower saw a window of opportunity opening, reinvigorating the hope of 1945, because under Stalin's rule of the Soviet Union, '[t]he 8 years that have passed have seen that hope waver, grow dim, and almost die. And the shadow of fear again has darkly lengthened across the world'. Against this background, Eisenhower's 'Chance for Peace' speech contained another attempt at establishing '[i]nternational control of atomic energy to promote its use for peaceful purposes only and to insure the prohibition of atomic weapons' (Eisenhower, 1953c). At the end of this same year, Eisenhower's UN initiative 'Atoms for Peace' attempted to drive this point home with even more vigor in another effort to tie atomic power to peaceful use and hope rather than to weapons of mass destruction and fear within the framework of the U.S.-Soviet rivalry.[20] In this speech, Eisenhower fired a barrage of strong language about the amazing power of nuclear weapons. Deterrence, early warning, civil defense, all this was well and good, he mused, but the 'awful arithmetic of the atomic bomb does not permit of any such easy solution[s]', Eisenhower admitted. But turning anxiety into hope again through cooperation with the Soviet Union, via a bank of fissile material for the advancement of the peaceful uses of atomic power under the auspices of the International Atomic Energy Agency, was Eisenhower's proposal for how '[t]o hasten the day when fear of the atom will begin to disappear from the minds of people', so that the world can 'shake off the inertia imposed by fear, and [...] make positive progress toward peace' (Eisenhower, 1953b). However, this would be the last grand attempt to decouple atomic power from anxiety and tie it to the hope for 'world peace'.

In the upcoming years, atomic anxiety would stay firmly wed to the deadlocked Cold War framework – and to deterrence: 'If Communist rulers understand that America's response to aggression will be swift and decisive [...] they will be powerfully deterred' (Eisenhower, 1955). In the Eisenhower statements, facing and enduring atomic anxiety became part of persevering in the Cold War, of remaining strong and steadfast while upholding 'our own defense [...] to deter aggression' (Eisenhower, 1954). Along the way, the strife for world peace would be complemented and watered down with alternative formulas such as a lasting or a durable peace, a 'quest for a confident peace in this atomic age' (Eisenhower, 1957).[21] Economic rivalry (Eisenhower, 1958) grew in importance, and peace would be no longer connected to the nuclear question alone. In short, with the Cold War in full swing and the U.S.-Soviet rivalry now spanning across various dimensions, the world was no longer depicted as immediately standing at the crossroads.

A crystallization point of this development, that is, of atomic anxiety becoming embedded in the Cold War and tied to the Soviet Union, presents itself with the term 'disarmament'. The development surrounding it sets in with Eisenhower leaving office. Already for Truman (1947) with his striving for 'collective disarmament' and attempts at 'a concrete, practical proposal for disarmament' (Truman, 1952), disappointment had eventually set in. After all, 'until the Soviet Union accepts a sound disarmament proposal, and joins in peaceful settlements, we have no choice except to build up our defenses', was the situation he had deplored (Truman, 1952). But still, 'disarmament' was a standing term for Truman as well as his predecessor Eisenhower and to some extent Kennedy. Yet, eventually it started to fade away from presidential language. In its place, the new concept 'arms control' – non-existent in *all* the texts by Truman and Eisenhower under analysis (with the latter aiming to 'control and to reduce armaments' [Eisenhower, 1953c] but never using 'arms control' as a standing, meaningful term) takes over. Arms control made its first appearance with President Kennedy's first State of the Union address (Kennedy, 1961a; see also the American University commencement speech, Kennedy 1963b). And by the time of Johnson, the concept of disarmament had disappeared. None of the Johnson material contains it as an isolated term. If disarmament was mentioned at all, it was done so in the new formula 'arms control and disarmament' (Johnson, 1967; 1968). What is the significance of this change and how can it be interpreted with atomic anxiety in mind?

Adjusting to anxiety: arms control

Arms control is of course pursued for a number of reasons.[22] But nuclear arms control during the era of the superpower confrontation can be understood particularly well by analyzing it through the lens of atomic anxiety.

Arms control provided the welcome effect of breaking down the enormity of the atomic threat into a subset of political, technical and legal problems that were workable and manageable. No matter how tedious and politically unnerving, arms control removed the overwhelming and intense urgency of having either to choose 'disarmament' or face 'doom'. Also, arms control curbed atomic anxiety by enclosing it in the existing, down-to-earth and pragmatic framework of diplomacy and

Realpolitik. After all, from the perspective of arms control proponents, the initial, revolutionary attempts of breaking free and leaving the existing international framework behind via some sort of world government – presented as the only viable solution to the nuclear question by the 'nuclear one worlders' back in the day – had ended in deadlock, paralysis and only more frightful superpower clashes. Hence the honorable but fruitless hope for ultimate world peace was buried, settling for second-best instead, allowing for the diffuse and ominous nuclear shadow to be broken down into separate issues that specialists could then tend to.

Arms control measures aim to regulate and stabilize the balanced deterrence relationship,[23] curbing arms races and dangerous excesses by creating transparency, implementing verification measures and ultimately, maybe, even infusing a level of trust and relaxation into the conflict. In comparison to the early calls for either creating a world state or at least a nuclear monopoly at the UN or facing disaster, arms control is a comparably sober enterprise. Interpreted as a type of emotion management, arms control, with its manifold details and requirements for specialized knowledge and expertise, is striking because it is fairly technical and arid. It engages experts in idiosyncratic debates over counting rules and verification regimes, numbers of warheads and launchers, targeting doctrines and so on, but, most importantly, it does so in professional language *free of emotion*.

In this way arms control helped put an end to deadlock and paralysis. Instead of opponents helplessly having to endure an overwhelming anxiety, they were kept busy with compartmentalized technical, legal and political aspects of the issue. From an emotional perspective this helped manage anxiety because the scary problem was not only broken down into manageable parts but as a whole it also seemed a little less frightening with every agreement reached, every verifiable treaty entering into force. Consequently, arms control exchanged the grand but futile hope for utopia for the small yet graspable hope of slowly but surely exerting more and more *control* over the atomic specter step-by-step. In short, after the elusive atomic anxiety had been given a recognizable face in the form of the Soviet Union, deterrence complemented by arms control offered a way for *dealing with it* through the known means of diplomacy. It was the attempt to assert control over anxiety via the control of arms. By introducing the metaphor of a 'step-by-step' process, the Kennedy presidency represented a sea change in this development.

In his inauguration address, Kennedy (1961b) proclaimed, 'Let both sides, for the first time, formulate serious and precise proposals for the inspection and control of arms – and bring the absolute power to destroy other nations under the absolute control of all nations'. And he, most interestingly when his words are viewed through the lens of atomic anxiety, also stated, 'Let us never negotiate out of fear. But let us never fear to negotiate'.

But negotiation out of fear was exactly what arms control was about. After all, at that time the widespread worries generated by the fallout from nuclear testing had refreshed atomic anxiety in the mind of the public. And there were great worries about the further spread of nuclear weapons – proliferation, an issue Kennedy was especially pessimistic about. And looking forward only one and a half years, after the U.S. and the rest of humankind would have collectively experienced the intense jolt of fear that was the Cuban Missile Crisis, it is even more obvious that negotiating out of fear started during that era.

Invoking 'world peace' anew, 'the most important topic on earth', as Kennedy (1963b) argued during his American University commencement ceremony speech,[24] his political reaction to the Cuban Missile Crisis can be interpreted as an attempt to reformulate the old notion of world peace by tying it to the new approach of arms control: 'I am not referring to the absolute, infinite concept of universal peace and good will of which some fantasies and fanatics dream'. Instead, '[l]et us focus instead on a more practical, more attainable peace – based not on a sudden revolution in human nature but on a gradual evolution in human institutions – on a series of concrete actions and effective agreements', on 'first-step measures of arms control, designed to limit the intensity of the arms race and to reduce the risks of accidental war'. Kennedy's commencement ceremony speech provides the prime example for emotion management via arms control. To cut atomic anxiety down to size, he insisted 'Our problems are manmade – therefore, they can be solved by man'.

Another old motif, hope, could now be revived as well. And it no longer had to be the distant, utopian aspiration for world government; instead, reason for hope could be found in smaller things, in reaching agreements, in signing and ratifying treaties and building institutions, in humankind thus making visible progress, one step at a time. On occasion of the agreement reached about the Limited Nuclear Test Ban Treaty, President Kennedy (1963a) described this hope with words of light and darkness, signaling the hope that it was possible eventually to crawl out from under the nuclear shadow and regain control: 'I speak to you tonight in a spirit of hope. [A]ll mankind has been struggling to escape from the darkening prospect of mass destruction on earth. [...] Yesterday a shaft of light cut into the darkness. [...] For the first time, an agreement has been reached on bringing the forces of nuclear destruction under international control'. Of course, the Limited Test Ban Treaty was only one step. But that was the beauty of arms control: where there was a first step, others could – and had to – follow.

Kennedy's successors, Johnson, Nixon and Gerald Ford, by and large continued on that path (see e.g. Johnson, 1964) In Johnson's (1965) second State of the Union address, for instance, the characteristic 'steps' metaphor was used once again: 'In this period we have taken more steps toward peace – including the test ban treaty – than at any time since the cold war began'. Signing the Treaty on the Non-Proliferation of Nuclear Weapons (NPT) five years later, Johnson (1968) remarked, 'After nearly a quarter century of danger and fear – reason and sanity have prevailed to reduce the danger and to greatly lessen the fear'. President Nixon (1972), in his third State of the Union address, also pointed to incremental steps and hope for the future, yet the necessity of stable deterrence as the taken-for-granted underpinning. The speech demonstrates how far the initial, urgent post–World War II impetus of *disarmament now or never* had receded and how arms control and deterrence had settled comfortably side by side. President Ford's (1975) almost laconic remarks on occasion of the Conference on Security and Cooperation in Europe, which he made in Helsinki, underline this adjustment process: 'I have not come across the Atlantic to say what all of us already know – that nations now have the capacity to destroy civilization and, therefore, all our foreign policies must have as their one supreme objective the prevention of a thermonuclear war'. Presidential reference to atomic anxiety had come a long way since Truman. By the time President Ford took office, the possibility of nuclear war ending civilization was old news. It was certainly nothing to be indifferent about, and it was still scary and worrisome, but it was not the same atomic anxiety of the post–World War II era. Anxiety had by now been broken down, and it had also been processed to an extent, step by step, in an effort that had not been fruitless in terms of giving rise to real hope, according to Ford: 'Our people want a better future. Their expectations have been raised by the very real steps that have already been taken [...] in arms control. Our presence here offers them further hope' (Ford, 1975).

Interestingly, with Jimmy Carter's inauguration (1977) and his first and second State of the Union addresses (1978; 1979), some of the old notions of urgency regarding world peace returned, and Carter also dared to point to greater hopes again, to point explicitly to the *end* of the taken-for-granted stepwise process of arms control: '[w]e will move this year a step toward ultimate goal – the elimination of all nuclear weapons from this Earth. [...] [S]uccess can mean life instead of death' (Carter, 1977). President Carter summed up the reason for this attempt concisely in hindsight in his farewell address four years later, pointing out what having lived under the nuclear shadow for so long and adjusting to it by managing anxiety in incremental steps meant, namely that *atomic anxiety had still not gone away*: 'The great majority of the world's people cannot remember a time when the nuclear shadow did not hang over the Earth. Our minds have adjusted to it, as after a time our eyes adjust to the dark. Yet the risk of a nuclear conflagration has not lessened' (Carter, 1981). For President Carter, merely managing anxiety via arms control within the framework of a foe kept in check via deterrence ran the risk of falling short of the ultimate goal. In fact, he was convinced that '[t]he danger is becoming greater' because of the still ongoing arms race and of proliferation. Upon leaving office, he felt the need to re-emphasize and envision the ultimate goal and of underlining the need for taking bolder and more decisive steps toward it. For only by first getting rid of the weapons could the age of atomic anxiety finally be brought to an end – with anxiety pictured drastically as fear of gruesome *death en masse,* 'an all-out nuclear war [with] more destructive power than in all of World War II [...] unleashed every second during the long afternoon it would take for all the missiles and bombs to fall. A World War II every second – more people killed in the first few hours than in all the wars of history put together. The survivors, if any, would live in despair amid the poisoned ruins of a civilization that had committed suicide'. President Carter's successor had the same ultimate goal, but had an entirely different plan for how to reach it.

Curing anxiety: missile defense

Just as Carter had, Ronald Reagan (1984) described his ultimate goal as what today trades under the name of Global Zero: '[M]y ultimate goal, my ultimate dream, [is] the elimination of nuclear weapons in the world'. However, President Reagan turned conventional wisdom upside down. He wanted to end atomic anxiety *first* by 'rid[ding] the world of the threat of nuclear destruction' (Reagan, 1985). With that threat gone, getting rid of the weapons would follow naturally, he proposed.

President Reagan (1983) described the status quo as follows: '[W]e've sought to reduce the risk of war by maintaining a strong deterrent and by seeking genuine arms control'. His address on national security, which contained the proposal for the Strategic Defense Initiative, however, advanced the notion that due to the continuing, massive Soviet military buildup, the slow crawl toward the light and out from under the shadow was no longer sufficient, another interesting parallel to Carter. Consequently, on the one hand, Reagan argued that modernizing and expanding U.S. armaments was required. Yet, since 'deterrence of aggression through the promise of retaliation' (Reagan, 1983) accompanied by arms control might no longer suffice, he, on the other hand, floated a radical idea. This idea was that the traditional management attempts might not even be required any longer. For now, Reagan suggested, there was not only 'the necessity to break out of a future that relies solely on offensive retaliation for our security' but the possibility to do so for the first time in history, yielding 'a vision of the future which offers hope'. This hope Reagan invoked was the *old* kind of hope: the hope for a revolutionary solution and ultimate redemption. And the way to achieve this was to devise a system for defending against incoming ballistic missiles. Unlike arms control, it offered hope not in small, incremental doses. In contrast, it offered the chance for ending atomic anxiety with a single stroke and for good.

So rather than merely adjusting to atomic anxiety and managing it, missile defense promised a solution for *ending* anxiety. It was a technical, scientific solution for an emotional problem, and it went like this: nuclear weapons are used for issuing frightening threats, as a deterrent. In fact, that is the only thing they are useful for. But missile defense destroys them in flight and thus renders 'nuclear weapons impotent and obsolete' (Reagan, 1983). Impotent weapons no longer scare anybody. And since that was the only thing they were good for in the first place, they are obsolete as the soon as both opponents have missile defense. Hence, part of Reagan's idea was in fact to *share* the technology with the Soviet Union, or so he said at least. 'Why not?', he rhetorically asked in his debate with Walter Mondale (Reagan, 1984).

For proponents of missile defense, its potential for emotion management lies in rendering deterrence superfluous in the long run and promising to defuse the paradox of deterrence in the short run, that is, as long as the ultimate goal of total disarmament is not yet achieved. Missile defense allows the terribly frightening threat of nuclear destruction to be upheld without having to live under the same sword of Damocles. In other words, it allows one to keep the opponent scared, while effectively curing one's own anxiety at the same time. And should deterrence fail, missile defense effectively prevents a 'use them or lose them' situation in which a decision-maker has to quickly unleash his nuclear arsenal so that it does not get destroyed in the disarming first strike – thereby facing the choice of a second strike that is meaningless within the rational deterrence framework because it no longer serves a rational cause, but merely represents a by then pointless revenge. Also, missile defense creates more leeway for using nuclear weapons first, which is the most important counterargument made by skeptics (many of them members of the arms control community, who deem the effect of missile defense – the shield to hide behind after making the first blow with the sword – a dangerously destabilizing one, as President Reagan [1984] knew). But from a presidential perspective, all of this clearly adds up to an extremely enticing notion because it would be highly beneficial to be able to add missile defense to the equation. After all, given a hypothetical, perfectly functioning missile defense system, one would be able to escalate deterrence threats without (or at least with much less) gut-wrenching worry about deterrence failing. From an atomic anxiety perspective, missile defense and deterrence thus go very well together (at least as long as the latter is still required) because missile defense dissolves the reciprocity of fear that normally is the emotional price to pay for practicing deterrence.

There are still threats in the new world order: proliferation to rogue states and terrorists

Atomic anxiety had a face in the form of the Soviet Union. So with the abrupt end of the Cold War, the specter should have vanished. And indeed, 'the long, drawn-out dread is over', President George H.W. Bush (1992a) remarked in his second State of the Union address. However, '[t]here are still threats', he reminded his audience. The proliferation of nuclear weapons, an additional source for anxiety since at least the days of the Kennedy administration (see e.g. Carter, 1980), would be the vector with which atomic anxiety carried over from the old into the new world order. Nothing new in itself, it merely fostered the return of some old fears that had been sidelined by the Cold War emotional architecture.

In two presidential debates in October 1992, President Bush emphasized how much the risk of nuclear weapons being used had diminished and thus 'the fear of nuclear war is down' (Bush, 1992b), elaborating on what that meant: '[T]he parents of these young people around here go to bed at night without the same fear of nuclear war. We've made dramatic progress'. So 'less afraid of nuclear war', there is 'less worry that [...] kids are going to be faced with nuclear holocaust. All this is good' (Bush, 1992b).

His successor, Bill Clinton, agreed (Clinton, 1996a; 1996b; see also Clinton, 1994), invoking a similar image during his second inaugural address by picturing children 'sleep[ing] free from the threat of nuclear [...] weapons' (Clinton, 1997). However, President Clinton also cautioned, 'We've come so far so fast in this post-cold-war world that it's easy to take the decline of the nuclear threat for granted. But it's still there [...]' (Clinton, 1995). So he, too, felt 'there are still dangers in the world, [namely] rampant arms proliferation [...] and fanatics who seek to cripple the world's cities with terror' (Clinton, 1994).

Iraq is the prime example for this because the general notion of nuclear threats that still remained had gained further traction with the Persian Gulf War. George H.W. Bush (1991) was thus 'determined to knock out Saddam Hussein's nuclear bomb potential', an idea that would be echoed by his son roughly 11 years later (Bush, 2002).

In addition to more nuclear armed states, the notion made a return that non-state entities might possess and unhesitatingly use nuclear weapons, with nothing to stop them from doing so (for they were assumed to have nothing that a deterrence threat targeting a rational opponent could hold at risk). It had been contemplated since the beginning of the nuclear age. But 9/11 lent renewed credence and an immense feeling of urgency to this notion. George W. Bush (2002; see also Bush, 2003; 2004a) connected the fear of rogue states and the fear of terrorism in his first State of the Union address after 9/11, for '[s]tates like these and their terrorist allies constitute an axis of evil, arming to threaten the peace of the world. By seeking weapons of mass destruction, [Iraq, Iran and North Korea] pose a grave and growing danger. They could provide these arms to terrorists, giving them the means to match their hatred. [...] In any of these cases, the price of indifference would be catastrophic'. This connection made for renewed urgency, in President Bush's (2002) words: 'I will not stand by as peril draws closer and closer'.

During President Bush's (2004b) debate with Democratic challenger John Kerry, there could not have been more agreement between the two with respect to the threat of proliferation enabling nuclear terrorists:

Jim Lehrer: If you are elected president, what will you take to that office thinking is the single most serious threat to the national security to the United States?

John Kerry: Nuclear proliferation. Nuclear proliferation. [...] There's some 600-plus tons of unsecured material still in the former Soviet Union and Russia. At the rate that the president is currently securing it, it'll take 13 years to get it. [...] Now, there are terrorists trying to get their hands on that stuff today.

George W.Bush: [W]ell, first of all, I agree with my opponent that the biggest threat facing this country is weapons of mass destruction in the hands of a terrorist network.

President Bush was determined to meet the anxiety emanating from the possibility of the 'axis of evil' obtaining nuclear weapons, using them or passing them on to terrorists with resolute defiance: 'We refuse to live in the shadow of this ultimate danger', he swore (2004a). The Cold War was long over. But the nuclear shadow was not gone after all.

Four years later, in the debate between Republican candidate John McCain and Democratic candidate Barack Obama, the latter summed up the by now taken-for-granted change of state that atomic anxiety had undergone while passing through the Cold War era and on to the new world order: 'And the biggest threat that we face right now is not a nuclear missile coming over the skies. It's in a suitcase. [T]he biggest threat to the United States is a terrorist getting their [sic!] hands on nuclear weapons' (Obama, 2008).

The proliferation of nuclear weapons to so-called rogue states and terrorists became the biggest worry after the Cold War. It is the current gestalt of atomic anxiety. Rogue states and terrorists – and the assumed connections between the two – are the key referent objects of atomic anxiety today.

President Obama (2009) emphasized the development of atomic anxiety and the fact that there are still threats in especially strong terms in his Global Zero speech in Prague, summing it all up as follows: 'Today, the Cold War has disappeared but thousands of those weapons have not. In a strange turn of history, the threat of global nuclear war has gone down, but the risk of a nuclear attack has gone up'. This 'strange turn of history' can be interpreted as atomic anxiety surviving the end of the Cold War largely unscathed. Clearly, the scenario President Obama painted echoed the world-at-the-crossroads imagery of the early nuclear age, conveying a strong sense of urgency, with the danger resulting from nuclear weapons once again having presented humankind with a 'turning point', as Truman (1950) had once put it. President Obama (2009) feared that '[A]s more people and nations break the rules, we could reach the point where the center cannot hold'.

In Prague, then, President Obama invoked atomic anxiety in the old and colorful terms, touching explicitly and repeatedly on the *fear of death*, the nucleus of atomic anxiety: 'Now, understand, this matters to people everywhere. One nuclear weapon exploded in one city [...] could kill hundreds of thousands of people. And no matter where it happens, there is no end to what the consequences might be – for our global safety, our security, our society, our economy, to our ultimate survival'. The U.S.'s and its president's challenge? '[W]e must stand together for the right of people everywhere to live free from fear in the 21st century' (Obama, 2009).

4.4.2 Anxiety and abstinence

Reconstructing the alterable yet persistent sociocultural condition of atomic anxiety by analyzing its salience in presidential public remarks throughout the nuclear age, atomic anxiety's persistence could be firmly established. But how can its connection to nuclear abstinence be grasped? Fleshing out the answer and empirically illustrating it allows for bringing together much of what this study has so far developed. So the following argument draws on, first, deterrence and the taboo, and what I have established about them, especially harking back to the insight into how they interact in practice, namely that they work at cross-purposes. Second, the vocabulary developed in Chapter 3 – the concepts of crisis and routine, as well as the importance of agency – is drawn on again. Third, the salience of fear in the Kennedy material and especially its reciprocity is brought back into the argument.

Judging from what I reconstructed above, I argue that there are two types of reactions to (not to be mistaken for effects of) atomic anxiety discernible throughout the nuclear age. In light of the early divide between 'nuclear one worlders' and 'deterrers' after World War II, a historical marker to which I have referred numerous times over the course of this study and to which I want to return one last time here, I distinguish between a *transformative* and a *transitory* reaction type. Both should be understood as reactions in the sense of agents trying to cope with the ongoing crisis that is atomic anxiety. That is, both emerge from creative agency and a recombination of practices to deal with a problematic breakdown of routine.

The transitory reaction is characterized by attempts to somehow deal with atomic anxiety pragmatically by managing it in a step-by-step process, inter alia, via arms control and, crucially, while also making good use of it for deterrence purposes along the way. In terms of the metaphoric nuclear shadow, the transitory reaction reflects the small hope for slowly transitioning toward a less angst-ridden future and into the light. In short, it corresponds with the pragmatic, problem-solving reaction of the 'deterrers', the reaction of those who have accepted being in for the long haul.

The transformative reaction, in contrast, is characterized by impulses to make anxiety go away for good by radically breaking out of the status quo that gave rise to the anxiety in the first place. It reflects a greater hope for a path-breaking transformation, a prompt and lasting redemption from the nuclear shadow. In short, it corresponds to the revolutionary, world-at-the-crossroads urgent reaction of the 'nuclear one worlders'.

The reason *why* the taboo interferes with deterrence in practice, I argue, is because they are dissimilar in terms of the respective reaction type to which they belong. Understood as beliefs that provide the rules for action, deterrence comes to rest within the transitory, while the nuclear taboo comes to rest within the transformative type of reaction to atomic anxiety.

No decision-maker feels and reasons purely along only one of these two lines. So when I refer to presidential statements below, this should be kept in mind, for they serve not primarily to characterize this particular president but merely serve as illustration for the differences between a transitory and a transformative reaction to atomic anxiety.

That said, overarching trends can be identified when surveying the nuclear age as a whole. In other words, while the pendulum swung to a more transitory reaction during one era or presidency, it swung back more toward the transformative side at other times in the material under analysis. And morality, or more precisely, the salience and importance of moral imperatives, empirically indicates where on the spectrum the pendulum stands at any given time.

Abstinence and the transitory reaction to anxiety

I described deterrence as the belief that mutually credible threats of nuclear retaliation work to prevent the use of nuclear weapons. Accordingly, decision-makers who practice deterrence try to make use of the fear they themselves experience as a result of the ever-looming first strike they suspect from the enemy – by turning fear against the enemy, tit for tat, in short. In that sense, every deterrent threat is already a counterthreat. However, this condition of reciprocal deterrence fear is, of course, an uncomfortable, paradox-ridden and potentially extremely dangerous one. This is where arms control comes in as the attempt to slowly transition out of this situation.

I showed in light of empirical material above that, from an arms control perspective, the early, revolutionary attempts by the 'nuclear one worlders' ended only in deadlock and more frightful brushes with disaster, such as the Cuban Missile Crisis, characterizing arms control as an attempt to ditch utopian hopes and settle for second best instead. The nuclear shadow remained in place as a consequence of practicing deterrence, but arms control at least broke it down into political, technical and legal bits and pieces, thus allowing for anxiety to be managed and for its perpetuation to be dealt with through established fora and long-known diplomatic and military practices and mechanisms. I identified the use of the step-by-step metaphor as key in this regard. As a consequence of all this, that is, the necessity of temporarily holding on to nuclear weapons for survival, of relying on scary threats of unleashing nuclear holocaust and of introducing of arms control as an attempt at emotion management, the transitional reaction also strips away the *moral imperative* that the earlier, transformative call for total and obligatory disarmament and a revolution of the international system had conveyed.

Consequently, in the era of Truman and Eisenhower, the main challenge was still perceived as overcoming a 'problem more of ethics than physics' (Baruch, 1946). A framework of 'international law and morality' (Truman, 1950) established via the United Nations was aspired to. And humankind was supposed to stand the test of wielding 'the power to erase human life from this planet' by renewing 'faith in [...] eternal moral laws and natural laws' (Eisenhower, 1953d). 'Man must create the *moral and legal framework* for the world which will insure that his new powers are used *for good and not for evil*', President Truman (1950, emphasis added) stated in his fifth State of the Union address. Interestingly, this sort of language would be dialed down or disappear completely from the material under analysis with the rise of arms control. So the transitory character of dealing with atomic anxiety by means of deterrence and arms control is reflected in the way the morally charged urgency dissipates. The reason for this, I argue, is that deterrence and arms control take the weapons, the conflict and its potentially catastrophic escalation as a given.

Reciprocally upheld, 'institutionalized' fear (Crawford, 2014, p. 548) assures nuclear non-use due to the prospect of nuclear war's horrible consequences (the 'costs', as rationalized deterrence theory would put it). So upholding the fear that atomic anxiety brings along with it is required for deterrence. Hence nuclear weapons cannot be a problem per se with this reaction to atomic anxiety. They need to be taken as merely a symptom of the existing conflict, and their unique capability for producing deterrence actually makes them a (regrettable but necessary) requirement for regulating enmity, making them essential for survival even. Arms control builds on that logic, merely contending that the symptoms can be controlled and regulated in a pragmatic fashion. Anxiety can be 'medicated' with arms control via a treatment plan of stoic diplomacy, tough negotiations and the signing and ratifying of treaties – without ever questioning the existing framework of deterrence and *Realpolitik*. In short, that one might take a nuclear weapon to be 'an evil thing [...] by all the standards of the world we grew up in' (Oppenheimer, quoted in Brodie, 1946b, p. 73), a widespread notion during the era of 'Great Fear' immediately after World War II, ceases to be relevant from an arms control perspective. To manage atomic anxiety in a transitory fashion via deterrence and arms control, the dimension of moral responsibility *has* to be stripped away because it gets in the way of accepting nuclear weapons and the threat of their use as a necessary evil for the time being.

In sum, the first type of reaction to atomic anxiety that is observable in the nuclear age is transitory because it does not fundamentally question the status quo. Nuclear weapons are frightening but useful for deterring the enemy at the same time; arms control can curb scary, escalatory excesses and an unstable arms race; and in the long run, step by step, provided a stably upheld system of deterrence is kept in place, a slow crawl from out under the nuclear shadow and into the light is conceivable.

In terms of juxtaposing a transitory and a transformative reaction type to anxiety, emotion management via missile defense is of course especially interesting because it displays an intriguing mix of both, falling square in the middle of the juxtaposition I propose here. On the one hand, it is compatible with the pragmatic and sober framework of deterrence, even providing most welcome benefits in this regard by disentangling the reciprocity of fear that deterrence produces as a side effect. On the other hand, missile defense renders the tedious, transitory process of arms control superfluous because it holds transformative potential by promising to render nuclear weapons obsolete, continued reliance on them and especially their use pointless, thus *ending* anxiety once and for all. Missile defense, to stick with the metaphor of medical treatment, is the equivalent of a Xanax pill – the quick and easy way to alleviate the symptoms of atomic anxiety disorder. It allows for dropping the lengthy and arduous treatment sessions of arms control and reintroduces the hope for a utopian miracle healing, the one aimed for by the 'nuclear one worlders' with a radical cut through the political landscape. But rather than actually requiring this bold cut, it allows for keeping the familiar system of deterrence in place at the same time for as long as it is required.

The transformative characteristics of missile defense become observable in the resurfacing of moral categories. Largely lost in the technicalities of arms control, a moral impetus could be rediscovered at its heels. With the moral high ground regained, even distancing oneself somewhat from the unsavory practices of deterrence became possible. Having to 'rely on the specter of retaliation, on mutual threat [is] a sad commentary on the human condition', President Reagan (1983) mused. 'Wouldn't it be better to save lives than to avenge them? Are we not capable of demonstrating our peaceful intentions by applying all our abilities and our ingenuity to achieving a truly lasting stability? I think we are. Indeed, we must'. In that same vein, the president (1984) asked in his debate with Democratic challenger Mondale, '[W]ouldn't it be far more humanitarian to say that now we can defend against a nuclear war by destroying missiles instead of slaughtering millions of people?' Furthermore, '[i]s there either logic or morality in believing that if one side threatens to kill tens of millions of our people our only recourse is to threaten killing tens of millions of theirs?', he added in his second inaugural address (Reagan, 1985). Missile defense, in contrast, 'wouldn't kill people; it would destroy weapons', President Reagan impressed on his audience.

Abstinence and the transformative reaction to anxiety

A transitory reaction to atomic anxiety goes along with an attempt to employ fear for deterrence purposes and manage it by means of arms control. However, the fear of nuclear weapons being used in a deterrence relationship is a reciprocal one. As the first main argument of this study, I pointed out that the taboo is hindering the practice of deterrence because moral qualms make struggling with the deterrence paradox only more tantalizing for a decision-maker, amplifying self-deterrence and thus undermining the necessary practice of signaling grim resolve and issuing credible threats of nuclear weapon use.

Reanalyzing this through the lens of atomic anxiety and in terms of the juxtaposition between a transitory and a transformative reaction to atomic anxiety adds complexity to this train of thought: atomic anxiety underlies the nuclear taboo by providing its emotional springboard, the emotional dimension of the cognitively anticipated individual and societal consequences that would result from breaking the taboo. Atomic anxiety is thus a key emotional component of the social obligation to obey the rule never to use nuclear weapons. In other words, it adds fear to the moral revulsion that the thought of nuclear weapon use evokes. This way the nuclear taboo – in terms of its being a reaction to atomic anxiety – is characterized by a 'forbidding fear'. And that is exactly, I can now argue more specifically, what hinders the practice of deterrence.

So the conceptually derived and empirically substantiated insight that 'inhibitions on the use of nuclear weapons [...] [are] inimical to nuclear deterrence', as Walker (2010, p. 875) put it, can be understood at an even deeper level. Viewed through the lens of atomic anxiety, the practical interference the nuclear taboo creates for nuclear deterrence when their intricate interplay unfolds can be grasped as the forbidding fear getting in the way of the intention to create fear in the adversary, fear that is bound to come back in turn.

This is why the nuclear taboo is part of a transformative rather than a transitory reaction to atomic anxiety. From a nuclear taboo perspective, nuclear weapons are frightening and repulsive. And the remorse created by the thought of their use makes them a problem per se. Consequently, disarmament sooner rather than later is favored over the slow process of arms control, a transformative impulse, which, as I already argued above, is framed as a *moral* obligation in the material under analysis.

The clearest examples for illustrating this can of course be gained from the immediate period after World War II in which the challenge to old routines was most acutely felt, atomic anxiety was in full swing and no transitory means of emotion management had been put in place yet. 'We promptly advanced proposals in the United Nations to take this new source of energy out of the arena of national rivalries, to make it impossible to use it as a weapon of war', is how President Truman (1953a) looked back during his last State of the Union address on the transformative attempt to, for the first time in history, remove a weapon from the international landscape and make its use impossible. And in his farewell address he stated that a use of weapons against the Soviet Union was out of the question for moral reasons, that is, that it was taboo: 'Now, once in a while, I get a letter from some impatient person asking, why don't we get it over with? Why don't we issue an ultimatum, make all-out war, drop the atomic bomb? For most Americans, the answer is quite simple: We are not made that way. We are a moral people' (Truman, 1953b). That '[s]tarting an atomic war is totally unthinkable for rational men', as Truman affirmed in that same speech, points to the soon-to-be more vexing problem that a transformative reaction to anxiety posits for pursuing a more transitory one instead, for if 'rational men' want to successfully practice deterrence, starting an atomic war *must not be* 'totally unthinkable'.

Truman's predecessor, Eisenhower, is representative of a period of the nuclear age in which transformative and transitory reactions coexisted and intermingled even more obviously. On the one hand, as I reconstructed above, President Eisenhower was clearly leaning toward a pragmatic reaction to anxiety. He displayed the strong conviction that deterrence worked and that the Soviets could be bluffed and kept in check by displaying the necessary retaliatory capabilities and intentions (cf. in that regard also his conversation with Kennedy cited in subsection 4.2.2). This is why the statements and policy decisions in *all* of the Eisenhower speeches under analysis clearly represent the decision to beef up deterrence against the Soviet Union. To give but one example, in his first State of the Union address, President Eisenhower (1953a), combining deterrence notions of risk escalation (punishment) and violence escalation (denial), stated the following, 'While retaliatory power is one strong deterrent to a would-be aggressor, another powerful deterrent is defensive power. No enemy is likely to attempt an attack foredoomed to failure'. This statement also hints at how in Eisenhower's vocabulary the opponent is a sensibly planning actor whose expectations can be manipulated.

On the other hand, however, Eisenhower was deeply sensitive to the fearful global situation deterrence created: 'The worst to be feared and the best to be expected can be simply stated. The worst is atomic war. The best would be this: a life of perpetual fear and tension [...] This is not a way of life at all, in any true sense. Under the cloud of threatening war, it is humanity hanging from a cross of iron. [I]s there no other way the world may live?' (Eisenhower, 1953b). In his 'Atoms for Peace' speech (Eisenhower, 1953b), the ongoing and simultaneous relevance of a more transformative reaction is obvious: '[E]ven a vast superiority in numbers of weapons, and a consequent capability of devastating retaliation, is no preventive, of itself, against the fearful material damage and toll of human lives that would be inflicted by surprise aggression', Eisenhower worried. He continued in the ambivalent fashion that resulted from the transitory reaction not having displaced a transformative one quite yet (hence greater hopes are still possible): 'Should [...] an atomic attack be launched against the United States, our reactions would be swift and resolute. But for me to say that the defense capabilities of the United States are such that they could inflict terrible losses upon an aggressor – for me to say that the retaliation capabilities of the United States are so great that such an aggressor's land would be laid waste – all this, while fact, is not the true expression of the purpose and the hope of the United States'. A military man himself, who had seen the devastation during World War II, Eisenhower had no illusions about what a nuclear war would mean. Hence he 'sought persistently for some avenue, some formula, for reaching an agreement with the Soviet rulers that would place this new form of power under effective restraints – that would guarantee no nation would use it in war' (Eisenhower, 1953a), and the 'Atoms for Peace' program aimed at such a disentanglement of nuclear energy from the military and its rebranding for peaceful use. Accordingly, Eisenhower (1953b) continued in his speech by simply refusing 'to confirm the hopeless finality of a belief that two atomic colossi are doomed malevolently to eye each other indefinitely across a trembling world. To stop there would be to accept helplessly the probability of civilization destroyed – the annihilation of the irreplaceable heritage of mankind handed down to us generation from generation'. Eisenhower linked the immense costs that render victory forlorn and meaningless (deterrence) with moral (taboo) and reputational and precedent-setting (tradition) motives (foreshadowing Rusk's metaphor of the 'mark of Cain' worn by the user of nuclear weapons for generations to come) in another statement in that speech that is exemplary for the interim phase that his presidency represents. Pondering the 'probability of civilization destroyed', Eisenhower noted, 'Surely no sane member of the human race could discover victory in such desolation. Could anyone wish his name to be coupled by history with such human degradation and destruction'? Leaving office five years later, President Eisenhower (1958) reminded the American people that '[W]e could make no more tragic mistake than merely to concentrate on military strength. For if we did only this, the future would hold nothing for the world but an Age of Terror'.

In short, Eisenhower clearly identified the Soviet Union as the source of atomic anxiety and wanted to 'win the Cold War', yet he wanted to win while (or rather: by) never having to fight the Soviets, most definitely not with nuclear weapons. But with both pragmatic-transitory and utopian-transformative efforts running their course for a while and no transformative clearance reached in the end, the pendulum eventually swung more toward the pragmatic reaction to atomic anxiety, with arms control providing an answer to how to manage anxiety in a transitory fashion.

This development was expedited by President Eisenhower's predecessor Kennedy. As I said, presidential decision-making reality is made up of a mix of both reactions. And Kennedy clearly displayed a strong sensitivity to the nuclear taboo and the moral dimension of nuclear weapon use, as the Berlin problem demonstrates. Nevertheless, it is equally clear from the material under analysis that he invigorated the turn to pragmatic steps of arms control in an effort to adjust to – and manage, thereby regaining some degree of control over – the situation that had confronted him with an intense jolt of atomic anxiety during the Cuban Missile Crisis.

Consequently, with the advent of arms control and during the presidencies of Johnson, Nixon, Ford and to some extent Carter, the moral dimension got stripped away from presidential language in the material under analysis. After all, the transitional reaction would only work as an emotion management tool for atomic anxiety while staying firmly embedded in the framework of deterrence and arms control in which a morally framed obligation to disarm or revolutionize how nuclear weapons are handled internationally could no longer be viewed as urgent a task as before. Only President Reagan, by promising to overcome nuclear deterrence with missile defense, framed the issue of atomic anxiety in strong moral terms again, as seen above.

The pendulum began to swing back faster toward a slightly more transformative reaction after the end of the Cold War, however. 'Undeterrable' actors became the new referent objects of atomic anxiety, and with that a crisis emerged, a situation characterized by renewed doubt about the established, transitory routine in which atomic anxiety had been coped with so far. Not unlike the post–World War II period, there was now a renewed sense of vulnerability, an unease prevailing over the relief the end of the Cold War brought, evoked by the fact that 'there are still threats' from ominous sources.

It is possible to reconstruct in President Obama's (2009) speech in Prague the reconnection between atomic anxiety and moral obligations and a renewed pledge for disarmament to counter atomic anxiety: '[A]s a nuclear power, as the only nuclear power to have used a nuclear weapon, [the U.S.] has a moral responsibility to act', the president emphasized, thus seeking the goal of total disarmament with new vigor and injecting considerable transformative zest into the routine transitory process. This meant re-emphasizing the need to remove nuclear weapons from the international sphere once and for all. In short, it meant pointing explicitly to – and reminding everyone one of – the stated goal of Global Zero, a drastic reaction that clearly runs cross with the requirements of deterrence and (though to a lesser extent), by comparison, the leisurely pace of arms control. Clearly, this pendulum swing is still a far cry from the urgency of the transformational reactions during the period after World War II, and Global Zero remains presented mostly as a long-term vision. But what it demonstrates is how the resurgence of morally framed obligations and anxiety go hand in hand. It seems that with 'new' sources of anxiety – 'undeterrable' so-called rogue states as well as nuclear-armed terrorists – welling up in a president's mind, increasingly bolder steps have to be taken to put an end to atomic anxiety, to 'live free from fear in the 21st century', as President Obama (2009) put it in Prague. And the bolder, rather than just transitory, the steps toward this eventually transformative point in time, Global Zero, need to be, the more the moral dimension of the obligation reappears in the material.

4.4.3 Concluding remarks

The first main result of this study's second empirical inquiry is that atomic anxiety never went away. In addition, it demonstrated the gestalt change of atomic anxiety, reconstructing how it got tied closely to the Cold War but also outlasted it, seeping into the new world order after 1990. So while I have called atomic anxiety a sociocultural 'state', it did not have a freeze-frame quality. Furthermore, I reconstructed the efforts to manage atomic anxiety in addition to the example of civil defense that are found in the existing literature. Especially arms control and missile defense can be viewed through the lens of atomic anxiety in an unusual and novel way.

Only in the limited sense of attempting to manage it in a transitory fashion did presidents ever 'get used' to atomic anxiety, adjusting to it only to the extent that the early, transformative world-state-or-doom scenarios took a back seat over time. And, interestingly, a whiff of renewed transformative vigor can be observed in President Obama's push for Global Zero, the reasons arguably being new sources for anxiety that elude the old framework of dealing with a possible *death en masse* by nuclear weapons via deterrence and arms control.

The two reactions to atomic anxiety reconstructed above – trying to make use of fear by creating it in the opponent with threats of nuclear weapon use for deterrence purposes on the one hand, and being unable to continuously endure the fear evoked by exactly this on the other hand – can serve to help us understand the 'taboo's interfering with deterrence in practice' at an even deeper level. So the taboo, the second *main argument* of my study goes, hampers the practice of deterrence not only by adding a moral but also by intensifying the emotional dimension of the already paradoxical problem with which deterrence presents decision-makers, that of having to resolutely facilitate that which they want to avoid at all costs.

Lastly, the salience of atomic anxiety and the oftentimes strong language in which it is conveyed by presidents in the material under analysis is especially remarkable – surprising even – in light of the fact that the revisited Kennedy sources suggested that decision-makers might not want to display fear. After all, showing fear rather than resolve could undermine a deterrence posture. Judging from the sources under analysis, however, it is clear that U.S. presidents, while speaking directly and primarily to the American people, invoked atomic anxiety again and again. I will reflect some more on this in the next section.

4.5 Reflecting on results

The empirical inquiry into President Kennedy's decision-making process during the two crises in Berlin and Cuba demonstrated not only how those two geopolitical hotspots were intertwined in the Berlin problem. The Berlin problem also yielded an in-depth insight into the 'taboo's interfering with deterrence in practice', that is, the fateful entanglement of beliefs ruling action in which the taboo-ness of using nuclear weapons hindered Kennedy in his practicing deterrence as a strategy. Walker (2010, p. 875) already pointed out in the abstract that too successfully pursuing the goal to inhibit nuclear weapons use 'is inimical to nuclear deterrence'. And my reconstructive perspective that focuses on presidential decision-making underlines that the perception of nuclear weapon use as taboo can in fact be detrimental to the practice of deterrence, substantiating Walker's notion empirically.

While deterrence and the taboo are said to produce the same result – nuclear abstinence – at the conceptual level, an analysis of practice reveals that 'deterrence plus taboo' does not add up to 'more non-use'. Conceptually speaking again, the two causes of non-use suggest that the same goal can be achieved in different ways. But these different ways actually create a tension between them that is observable at the level of practice. Since a decision-maker's sensitivity to the taboo's coming in touch with the practicing of deterrence as a strategy inevitably means that the taboo-ness interacts with the inherent paradox of deterrence, which forces decision-makers to constantly ponder and act upon using nuclear weapons while actually aspiring not having to use them, the taboo does not add anything to a deterrence practice's capability to generate non-use. Instead, by amplifying the deterrence paradox, a strongly perceived taboo carries the danger of hampering a decision-maker's attempt to practice deterrence, undermining the belief in it. Focusing on agency, as my argument goes, more generally speaking reveals that in situations in which both deterrence and the taboo figure into a decision-making process as beliefs, the relationship between the two can be more complex and ambivalent than literature on nuclear non-use has acknowledged so far. An easy and straightforward synthesis that takes the two established concepts of nuclear deterrence and the nuclear taboo as mutually stabilizing to explain nuclear non-use more comprehensively is thus, considering that specific but considerable tension between the two concepts, unlikely to be achieved (cf. section 3.1.)

What is the possible scope of this first *main argument*? In light of empirical results, I feel safe to argue that it can be assumed to have plausibility beyond only this one, empirically reconstructed example. Clearly, a study like the present one does not claim any form of generalizability in the positivist sense of revealing covering laws. And the analysis presented here also does not and cannot claim to feature the only possible way of coding the material to 'make sense of abstinence'. In other words, this study is of course not fulfilling positivist criteria of 'reliability'. I am not insinuating that 'applying [my] procedure in the same way will always produce the same measure' (King et al., 1994, p. 25), and deliberately so. After all, the idea behind relying on a method mix that involves a heavy amount of inductive coding is to dispense with a specific predetermined scale for a replicable 'measurement' to a large degree, in order to allow a comparably more open research process. To be able to conduct this analysis in a more inductive way, my approach made 'it impossible to allow a precise and invariable definition of codes and concepts before the analysis', because that 'contradicts the aim of a flexible and open research strategy' (Herschinger, 2011, p. 152). However, the study not only laid out the compelling arguments for why 'inhibitions' due to the nuclear taboo are 'inimical to nuclear deterrence' (Walker, 2010, p. 875) at the conceptual level. Taken together with the empirically derived Berlin problem, it seems warranted to suggest that their intricate interplay is the case more often than not. While no sweeping generalization, it seems not unreasonable to at least argue that the ball is now in the court of those who (keep) claim(ing) the opposite.

At this point, an important first possible line of critique needs to be discussed because one might say that I failed to make an absolutely crucial distinction, namely between first strike and second strike. Deterrence, a critic might say, is about credibly threatening retaliation in kind. So practicing a nuclear deterrence strategy only requires thinking about the nuclear retaliatory strike, that is, about the second use of nuclear weapons. The nuclear taboo, however, morally prohibits only the first use of nuclear weapons. So from this point of view, by conflating the distinction between first and second strike, my taboo-interferes-with-deterrence argument is implausible. With strategic requirements only applying to threatening the second strike, and the moral limits applying to a first strike, there is no conflictive interaction between deterrence strategy and a sensitivity to the taboo-ness of nuclear weapon use at all.

In defense of my line of argument, I would respond to this critique that it – while compelling at the conceptual level and at first glance – simply (and conveniently) remains too much in the abstract. Thereby it ignores what Chapter 2 showed to be the clash between the nomothetically strong deterrence theory and checkered strategic practices, as well as, more importantly, the paramount importance of the paradox of deterrence.

What does the Kennedy study tell us about deterrence threats in practice? Kennedy's plan for Berlin was to deter a Soviet invasion in Europe while hedging more options than only the one, massive, all-out nuclear retaliation. And while the U.S. initiation of nuclear strikes according to the Poodle Blanket plan would 'only' have been a *first* use of nuclear weapons against conventional Soviet forces, it *was* a threat within the framework of deterrence nevertheless. So, in short, my first argument would be that the overly simple textbook definition of deterrence as retaliation in kind does not match strategic realities of the time. In a sense, Kennedy aimed at deterring a Soviet 'conventional first strike' with U.S. nuclear weapons. After all, flexible response was supposed to be about the escalation of violence, not nuclear risks, both of which are nevertheless established models of nuclear deterrence.

At this point, a critic might reply that it was simply Kennedy's folly to rely on deterrence via the escalation of violence. Stick firmly to the escalation of risks – the risk of nuclear conflagration because any *nuclear* first strike will be answered with a *nuclear* second strike – and everything is fine. Deterrence works – and the nuclear taboo does not figure in. Ergo there is no interplay. Since I claim that the insight into the 'taboo's interfering with deterrence in practice' can be assumed to be plausible beyond only my study, which takes me back to considerations about scope, I have to react to this as well.

One, the two deterrence models are theoretically derived ideal types. In practice, there is no neat and definite separation between *either* the escalation of violence *or* the escalation of risks. Two, in this study I have developed the argument that, by definition, every deterrence threat is a counterthreat. Unless a country feels threatened (and scared), there is no reason to practice deterrence. Hence the distinction between 'first threat' and 'second threat' is also blurred in practice. Looking at the unfolding Cuban Missile Crisis, Kennedy's threats of nuclear weapon use (for the defense of Berlin and to curb communist expansion in general) can thus be interpreted as threats *in retaliation* to the placing of Soviet missiles on Cuba, *in reaction* to his country being acutely threatened by Soviet nuclear weapons. Three, in connection to this Kennedy struggled with the paradox of deterrence, namely that, for nuclear weapons not to be used he constantly had to think about using them (for the defense of Berlin). Moreover, in practice, with the threats of nuclear weapon use going back and forth this way, the fact that *only* the second, retaliatory use of nuclear weapon needs to be thought through according to deterrence theory seems to have offered little consolation to Kennedy. In practice, the reciprocity of deterrence creates an infinite back and forth of (counter)threats of nuclear weapon use, all of which need to be *credible* and prepared and declared with utmost dedication and resolve, according to the deterrence paradigm, for nuclear weapons not to be used. And in this – strategically necessary – constant exchange of threats, moral inhibitions against using nuclear weapons are prone to creep in and manifest themselves in the detrimental fashion I reconstructed here.

I discuss all these empirically derived insights in terms of nuclear *threats* only, of course. This is – last but not least – why a critique pointing to the difference between first and second strike ultimately does not catch on here. After all, first and second nuclear strikes are theoretical constructs. Nuclear weapons actually *being* used – in a first strike by *any* one of the two opponents – is what a deterrence framework is supposed to prevent. In short, all this talk of first and second strikes is the counterfactual world against the background of which deterrence is theoretically developed. Critically interjecting from a theoretical perspective that the nuclear taboo applies only to considerations of first use, while deterrence applies to considerations of use in retaliation, that is, second use, means ignoring the deterrence paradox and what it means to decision-makers in practice, namely that the hypothetical situation of a second strike having to be executed *may never be allowed to arise anyway because it would mean that deterrence has failed.* In short, decision-makers do not have the luxury of neatly distinguishing between scenarios in which a first use of nuclear weapons might be inhibited by moral limits, and scenarios in which these limits do not apply because a second strike is then a bare strategic necessity only. After all, in the political practice of constant reciprocal nuclear threats this second scenario *does not and may never exist.* So with all decision-making taking place in, first, non-hypothetical, real-life scenarios, considerations of using nuclear weapons are necessarily subject to *both* strategic and moral beliefs all the time, and hence the intricate interplay of deterrence and the nuclear taboo in which the latter interferes with the first does in fact take place, as demonstrated via the analysis of Kennedy's decision-making above.

Finally, and in addition, we actually do not know what the nuclear taboo would mean in a hypothetical post-first-strike world. The nuclear taboo is perceived as a 'bright line norm' separating two worlds. Since the 'post-first-strike world' is counterfactual, one might also, quite plausibly, speculate that a once-broken nuclear taboo could be *stronger* in it, with the belief in the moral obligation that nuclear weapons may not be used (by anyone ever again) applying to second-strike considerations just as well or maybe even more so.

Taking this discussion a step further also allows reflecting on the second focal point of this study, the importance of human emotion, more particularly atomic anxiety. I argue that acknowledging the importance of human emotion for decision-making processes makes strictly distinguishing between strategic requirements that apply to only one scenario of use and moral limits that apply to only a different one even more questionable. In this line of thought, nuclear deterrence, applied as a strategy, resorts to fear by actively using it against the enemy to scare him into submission with credible threats of retaliation. The nuclear taboo, in contrast, is the flip side of this drawing on fear, the fear that one is forced to endure in turn and that is evoked by the repulsive thought of actually using this angst-inducing terror weapon against other human beings. This way, even more plausibility can be added to the notion that the taboo is interfering with deterrence in practice. This is my second *main argument*.

Particularly in that last regard, this study also raises new questions. The most obvious one is this: if there are indeed larger trends observable throughout the nuclear age with the mix of transitory and transformative reactions to atomic anxiety changing over time, and the presence of explicitly morally framed obligations being indicative of this, how does all this fit in with what we know about the development of the nuclear taboo? If nuclear weapons and threats of their use were not necessarily taken to be a problem per se and became framed *less* in moral terms during the era of the Cold War in which deterrence and arms control were at their all-time high, how does this correspond with what we know about the prevalence of the nuclear taboo during this period of time? For example, Tannenwald's work provides us with a picture of President Nixon as less perceptive to the taboo, which fits my broad brushstroke picture. His predecessor, Johnson, however, felt strongly about the taboo during the same era of deterrence and arms control, which would not fit the picture. This raises valid questions. But it is too early to decide whether these considerations are making or breaking what I have proposed so far. Rather, I take them to be a challenge for further, more fine-grained inquiries into the connection between nuclear abstinence and atomic anxiety. I will pick this up in the overall conclusion.

A number of more specific counterarguments could be advanced at this stage, arguments that shed an alternative light on what I have proposed with respect to atomic anxiety. First, an alternative view on atomic anxiety might stress that I am simply making too much of it. In *Atomic Obsession,* John Mueller (2010), extending his thesis about the 'irrelevance of nuclear weapons', critically reviews public discourse on nuclear weapons, their proliferation, their effects when exploded and the accompanying fears, in short, many aspects of what I summed up in the concept of atomic anxiety in this study. Mueller suggests that this anxiety, while understandable, derives from a largely unfounded, hyperbolic and excessive alarmism (resulting in false spending priorities and other counterproductive policies).

However, my argument is not about how justified by actual dangers atomic anxiety really is. I am not asking whether it is a warranted emotional reaction or rather a societal phobia. Overblown or not, I argue instead, atomic anxiety is a defining part of humankind's collective experience throughout the last some 70 years, as Mueller himself underlines by dissecting its various manifestations over time. Hence it will also be invoked – always to varying degrees, of course – by nuclear decision-makers. In that sense, Mueller's and my arguments simply reside at different levels and can peacefully coexist.

Second, one might ask *why* nuclear discourse is (still) the way it is. This alternative perspective on atomic anxiety would emphasize the *instrumental* thinking and speech acting of decision-makers, for example, by their using and fostering atomic anxiety only as a political ploy. Decision-makers might invoke emotional language only for a specific, political purpose, such as persuasion of the public. Maybe presidents even just 'feign emotion to advance their interest' (Mercer, 2010, p. 19). Schelling's 'risk that leaves something to chance' might be understood as outright requiring this from time to time. Furthermore, Jervis (1970) touched upon this notion very early on once, when studying signaling and deception in *The Logic of Images in International Relations* (see also Balzacq/Jervis, 2004) and before thinking about emotion in IR got superseded by the rationalization of the discipline. And more recently, Corey Robin (2004) also suggested an instrumental use of emotion in his historic study on fear as a political idea and its capabilities as a tool of repression. So, say a president wants to see a test ban treaty ratified, scoring a political goal with his constituency in terms of his foreign policy agenda. Stirring up people's fear of nuclear weapons might gather support for this and help push the treaty through Congress. Similar arguments could be made for speeding up a movement toward Global

Zero or for invading a 'rogue state' that is suspected to develop nuclear weapons. A figure of speech used widely by members of the Bush administration during the run-up to the Iraq war in 2003, the 'smoking gun' proof for Saddam Hussein's nuclear weapons program arriving in the 'shape of a mushroom cloud', comes to mind. Last but not least, today's fear of (nuclear) terrorism – that Mueller aims to debunk as exaggerated – is another case in point for how fear can be strategically used. After all, fear from terrorist attacks created the possibility for decision-makers to implement counterterrorism policies that infringe on civil liberties more than would have been possible otherwise.

My point here is obviously not to deny any of this. An instrumental use of language and the feigning of emotion can happen. It *does* in fact happen. And emotion, too, can be – and is oftentimes – instrumentalized. As a matter of fact, it explicitly was so in the early days of the nuclear age with the stated intention of flaming atomic anxiety. This was done by nuclear scientists, some feeling intense guilt and seeking atonement (Boyer, 1994 [1985], p. 49; Winkler, 1993, p. 36), when they formed the Federation of Atomic (today American) Scientists (FAS), the 'League of Frightened Men' (Oakes, 1994, p. 44). Harold Urey (ghost-written by Michael Amrine, quoted in Boyer, 1994 [1985], pp. 68, original emphasis) provides an excellent remark to illustrate this: 'I write this to frighten you. I'm a frightened man, myself. All the scientists I know are frightened – frightened for their lives – and frightened for your life... [We] who have lived for years in the shadow of the atomic bomb are well acquainted with fear, and it is a fear you should share if we are intelligently to meet our problems'. Others, including prominent figures such as Robert J. Oppenheimer or Albert Einstein, were counted as part of this group of 'nuclear one worlders' as well. So while the early atomic anxiety after World War II reconstructed above, 'was in no sense a creation of activists or the media' but a 'spontaneous and authentic response to the horror of Hiroshima and Nagasaki' (Boyer, 1994 [1985], p. 66), the 'nuclear one worlders' made no secret of their intention to *capitalize on atomic anxiety* by 'sustaining and intensifying' (Boyer, 1994 [1985], p. 68) it. They worked for the general and worldwide abolishment of war and world government and thought that instrumentalizing and stirring up fear would help their cause. The best-selling edited volume *One World or None* (Masters/Way, 2007 [1946]), published by the FAS in 1946, is an example of their spreading the message of 'world state or world doom' (Boyer, 1994 [1985], pp. 33–59, 70, 76–81 quote on page 34) – in short, 'scare tactics' (Weart, 1988, pp. 111–118) were used for the purpose of shocking people into political action. The Nuclear Freeze Movement in the 1980s (Gusterson, 1996, pp. 168–175, 191–218), which fostered a 'culture of terror' (Gusterson, 1996, pp. 197–198), utilizing imagery of Hiroshima and Nagasaki in regard to nuclear weapons, can also be seen in this light.

However, focusing on emotion as a mere instrument, while an interesting take on the issue in its own right, is at odds with the analytic perspective I chose for this study (developed in Chapter 3), more specifically two key assumptions: one, the impossibility of 'really knowing' the intentions of the speakers under analysis and, two, the performative, rather than instrumental, role that I attributed to language. So even if I were to pick up these arguments about emotion being 'used', my study points out that the issue is still more complicated and that there is in fact more to it than just that – because emotion is not simply a given but instead socially constructed.

Take deterrence, for example. A U.S. president issuing a threat with nuclear weapons means to scare his adversary into submission, into not using nuclear weapons. After all, this instrumental use of displaying and creating feelings is what deterrence is all about. However, not only is it impossible for – even – an authority as influential as the U.S. president to 'steer' an entire discourse, unintended and detrimental consequences can – and will, frequently – also occur over the course of the events set in motion. For instance, this threat could at the same time create fear and unrest in the domestic audience. And a worried or even panicking constituency is nothing any president wants if he plans to keep relying on deterrence, as for example civil defense efforts demonstrate. After all, the paradoxical nature of deterrence might make decision-makers 'inwardly [...] cautious' due to the fear they *endure*, yet in 'their public posturing [they are, they need to be] aggressive, risk-prone, and even irrational' (Lebow/Gross Stein, 1994, p. 367) to *create* fear. This is why the instrumental use of language for deterrence purposes is always an ambiguous endeavor. Since 'in the nuclear era, security means not fighting wars, and winning wars means no security', it comes as no surprise that the U.S. presidents of the nuclear era appear 'Janus-faced', according to Daniel Deudney (1995, pp. 108, 111) because they have to 'appeal simultaneously to opposing constituencies', attempting to 'constrain the military's appetite while soothing the fears of the citizenry'. Kennedy, I argued, was more than Janus-faced. In fact, he had to manage fear across several dimensions: regarding the Soviets, his divided group of advisers, the NATO allies, his domestic audience and last but not least himself. While he had to make the Soviets afraid, the fears of others needed to be soothed, all while dealing with his own fear as well. From a president's perspective, this clearly is a conundrum with regard to using language instrumentally: he has to communicate to the opponent, 'be scared, because you will be fired at'. In contrast, the citizenry needs to be reassured, 'don't be scared, I'm doing everything in my power not to have the enemy firing at us'. All the while, he himself is scared, too, and he has to make sure that his military really fires only when he tells them to. Atomic anxiety is in play on all these fields, and nowhere is it merely a passive instrument.

In short, the point I make about emotion in this study is one with a very different emphasis. I argue that invoking fearful notions, be it in connection to deterrence threats or by referring to the moral dilemma accompanying nuclear war or something else, *no matter with which intention these expressions are issued*, constitutes and reproduces a larger, sociocultural state, namely the persisting societal experience of anxiety accompanying nuclear weapons. So even if, for a minute, we were to take decision-makers as only 'instrumentally' issuing a deterrence threat – trying to use fear to prevail in a standoff –, this still contributes to the larger picture I am interested in here, namely, the continuation of atomic anxiety, the collectively experienced fear deriving from living under the long shadow of nuclear weapons that might get used, and how this is a constitutive element of the phenomenon of nuclear abstinence.

5
Conclusion

Unlike any other weapon in the history of mankind, nuclear weapons were used in war twice – against Hiroshima and Nagasaki – and never again since then. Against this background, this book aimed to contribute to the literature in IR that analyzes this puzzling 'nuclear non-use'. The goal was to both deepen and widen our knowledge about it by answering the following question: what can explain the persistent non-use of nuclear weapons after 1945, and how can we better understand (the causes of) this abstinence?

In answer to the first part of that question, two explanations of nuclear non-use were identified: nuclear deterrence and the nuclear taboo. They were presented and critically discussed in Chapter 2, touching on both deterrence as a 'scientific', 'rational' theory as well as a strategy, and discussing the plausibility of the nuclear taboo in contrast to a mere tradition of non-use.

Subsequently, in Chapter 3, both explanations were reviewed again, this time, however, solely in terms of the way these explanatory concepts approach the phenomenon. I described the research gap identified in connection to this as a lack of fine-grained understanding about how nuclear non-use – an elusive non-event – comes about in practice. I argued in this regard that the complexities, intricacies and ambiguities of practice largely fall into the existing approaches' blind spots due to their emphasis on general explanation, causal chains and effects.

To provide an in-depth look at the phenomenon with the aim of understanding nuclear non-use and also to cross-fertilize the existing explanatory concepts, I presented an alternative approach in Chapter 3 to study nuclear non-use up close and inquire into what the choice not to use nuclear weapons – nuclear abstinence – means and how it comes about. This approach aimed at reconstructing decision-making practices (defined as critical situations characterized by challenged beliefs and creative agency) with an open mind to deepen our knowledge about already established concepts as well as to widen our access to the phenomenon by picking up on so far understudied facets.

In Chapter 4, I subsequently presented the empirical research process, revisiting nuclear non-use, which focused on the U.S. president due to his unique authority in nuclear decision-making, and looking for answers to the second part of my research question. The chapter first presented an empirical inquiry analyzing the crises in Berlin and Cuba during the administration of John F. Kennedy, providing insights into how the causal factors invoked by existing explanations of non-use – which were reconceptualized as beliefs that rule action and subsumptively used as codes in my analysis – play out and interact in a decision-making practice. In a subsequent section, I followed a trail that I had discovered during this first inquiry and shed light on a facet of nuclear abstinence that has so far not been systematically been taken into account: atomic anxiety. After defining atomic anxiety as the collectively experienced fear of *death en masse* resulting from the notion of nuclear weapons use, I also proposed a way to conceptualize how atomic anxiety exercises a constitutive role with regard to the beliefs that rule action. In a second empirical inquiry, I then explored whether and how the sociocultural state of atomic anxiety played a role in presidential statements throughout the nuclear age, arriving, lastly, at an argument about how nuclear abstinence might be better understood when viewed through the lens of atomic anxiety.

More specifically, the study produced two major, empirically derived results. Both are to be seen in regard to the second part of the research question, that is, how we can better understand (the causes of) nuclear abstinence.

The first result is about nuclear deterrence applied as a strategy, about the nuclear taboo and how the two play out in practice as beliefs that rule action. Their interaction, and along with it the notion of their 'synthesis', was scrutinized for the first time not on an abstract, conceptual level but by means of an in-depth empirical inquiry. The result strongly suggests that nuclear deterrence strategy and the nuclear taboo are in an intricate interplay in which *conducting a nuclear deterrence strategy while recognizing an obligation to the nuclear taboo and its prohibitions results in a conflict, with strategic requirements and moral limits working at cross-purposes from a deterrer's perspective*, or, in short, *with the taboo interfering with deterrence in practice.*

So my *first main argument* is that the taboo cannot simply be said to amplify the 'effect of deterrence' (i.e. nuclear non-use); rather, from the perspective of decision-makers, the taboo amplifies the paradox evoked by every deterrence relationship. Deterrence literature has of course always been familiar with the paradox in the logic of deterrence, that is, having to resolutely facilitate that which one wants to avoid at all costs in order for deterrence to work. But by making unbearable due to moral qualms that which deterrence forces a decision-maker to threaten, the taboo becomes a detriment to the practice of deterrence, as I was able to demonstrate. This revealed the complex and problematic interplay between the nuclear taboo and deterrence at the level of practice, empirically substantiating a skeptical stance toward a simple, explanatory synthesis – at least in the sense of their combined 'effects' yielding more nuclear non-use, with the taboo 'helping to stabilize the practice of deterrence itself' and 'illuminating the normative and institutional bases of deterrence' (Tannenwald, 2007, p. 71). Since deterrence is always a two-way street, opponents are always deterrer and deterree at the same time. And while we now know more about 'how norms are part of the practice of deterrence itself' from a deterrer's perspective, the 'complex interrelationship' and interplay of the two concepts *does* seem to be '"norms" *vs.* "deterrence"' rather than 'norms *and* deterrence' (Tannenwald, 2007, pp. 19, original emphasis). Generally speaking, this first result *deepens* our knowledge about non-use by *adding complexity* to the overall thinking about the phenomenon, specifically in terms of deterrence and the nuclear taboo interacting in the practice of international politics.

The second result requires a bit more explanation. If one were to sum up the gist of the existing explanations for nuclear non-use in the smallest of nutshells, it would go like this: rational deterrence theory states that you *cannot* use nuclear weapons because it is too costly. The nuclear taboo states that you *must not* use nuclear weapons because it is morally unacceptable (while the tradition of non-use states that you *should not* use nuclear weapons because it is detrimental for your reputation). The proposal I developed in this book is, in contrast, about how nuclear non-use can be fruitfully reflected on by thinking about it in terms of human emotion. In short, I suggest an angle that largely escapes the others because it is more fundamental and precedes them. It states, you are *afraid* to use nuclear weapons anyway – due to the primal fear of death they evoke. Put this way, the argument seems obvious and bordering on the trivial. And what I call atomic anxiety is in fact not entirely new because deterrence literature has always casually touched upon the involvement of fear.

However, the role of human emotion has never systematically been accounted for in IR literature on the use or non-use of nuclear weapons, never been fully conceptualized nor empirically studied. Hence, against the background of the currently emerging literature on the impact of emotion on world politics in IR, I characterized atomic anxiety as hard-wired into nuclear decision-making, as the emotional springboard for the reasoning and experience processes in which existing concepts of non-use such as deterrence or the nuclear taboo are developed theoretically and upheld as beliefs that rule action in practice. I argued that it is the fear of *death en masse* evoked by nuclear weapons that makes the repeating non-use of nuclear weapons possible. The bomb's terror provides the fertile, underlying ground on which reasoning about nuclear abstinence – including all existing lines of thought from rational deterrence to social tabooization – takes place (in a constitutive sense).

Inquiring into these notions empirically, the question of whether atomic anxiety has persisted through the nuclear age and unto this day can be answered with a resounding yes. Additionally, I suggested an answer to how atomic anxiety connects to nuclear abstinence at the conceptual level. I arrived at a juxtaposition of two different types of reactions to atomic anxiety. What I called the *transitory* reaction is characterized by attempts to deal with atomic anxiety pragmatically and manage it in a step-by-step process, inter alia, via arms control and, crucially, while also making good use of it for deterrence purposes along the way. This reaction reflects the small hope for slowly transitioning toward a less angst-ridden future. It is the pragmatic, problem-solving reaction of the 'deterrers' who are in for the long haul. In contrast, what I called the *transformative* reaction is characterized by impulses to make anxiety go away for good by radically breaking out of the status quo from which it results. This reaction reflects the great hope for a revolutionary transformation, a prompt and lasting salvation. It is the world-at-the-crossroads-urgent reaction of the 'nuclear one worlders' who abhor nuclear weapons. This particular aspect of the second empirical inquiry, sorting through the nuclear age at large with these two reaction types to atomic anxiety in mind, offers a new possibility of *reducing complexity* when studying nuclear abstinence.

At the same time and more importantly, however, this train of thought can serve to help us understand at an even deeper and more complex level the first result. In other words, thinking further about atomic anxiety and how beliefs rule action systematically and from a conceptual perspective, I developed my *second main argument*, shedding even more light on why the nuclear taboo's moral limits hamper the practice of nuclear deterrence.

Tapping into literature about the link between human emotion and the logic of consequences as well as the logic appropriateness, I pointed to atomic anxiety's constitutive function, conceptualizing it as the emotional springboard for beliefs that provide the rules for nuclear abstinence. In this line of thought, atomic anxiety is a basic social *condition* for the *possibility* of nuclear abstinence to repeatedly emerge from what I have called the 'emotional-cognitive' reasoning of decision-makers. Regarding the nuclear taboo in particular, atomic anxiety provides a key emotional component of the social obligation to obey the rule never to use nuclear weapons. It adds the dimension of feeling, of fear, to the moral revulsion that the thought of nuclear weapon use evokes. As a reaction to atomic anxiety, the taboo evokes a 'forbidding fear'. Having to resolutely facilitate that which they want to desperately avoid is thus an ordeal for decision-makers not *only* due to the logical inconsistency and the moral revulsion that accompanies the thought of using nuclear weapons, that is, not only because they *know* it to be illogical, inappropriate or even unthinkable at a cognitive level. Rather, this ordeal is intensified by the fear that the thought of nuclear use induces. So the paradox of deterrence is not only a cognitive *and* morally amplified one. It is an *emotional paradox* first and foremost. Simply put, the deterrence paradox makes no sense because it also *feels* wrong. After all, even if the supposedly 'rational' deterrence strategy succeeds, creating a situation laden with apocalyptic potential makes the rational 'utility' it carries feel like an empty victory (Mercer, 2010, pp. 11–12). It serves only to perpetuate a reciprocal situation in which *oneself necessarily remains trapped in mortal fear, too* (a situation that would only be escapable through a desperate and revolutionary transformation). This is how the concept of atomic anxiety allows learning more in a systematic and conceptually grounded fashion about why the fear perpetuated by deterrence while leveraging it for transitory purposes must seem nearly inescapable for decision-makers who face the choice of using or not using nuclear weapons. They try to put a monkey on someone else's back, and they get one too, as President Lyndon Johnson aptly put it. In that sense, my study on atomic anxiety allows us to better understand what Hans Morgenthau (1964, p. 23) merely alluded to in passing when he once wrote that the deterrence paradox means creating fear through 'the commitment to the use of force [while simultaneously] paralyzed by the fear of having to use it'.

All in all, by substantiating the notion of atomic anxiety empirically and by offering it as an additional concept with which nuclear abstinence can be analytically approached, the present study thus also *widened* our knowledge about the subject matter.

5.1 Implications for future research: cross-fertilizing understanding and explaining

I left the trodden paths of positivism and of solely subsuming material under preformed, deductive concepts to inquire into nuclear non-use in this book. However, while I described positivist analyses of a non-event as a methodological misfit, I have also clearly stated my appreciation of the rich knowledge provided by deterrence and taboo literature, as well as that my goal here was dialectics, not dualism. I not only aimed at employing the existing knowledge but also hope for my research to inform explanatory thinking in the field. I am confident that causally thinking scholars working on both deterrence and the taboo will find my results about the 'taboo's interfering with deterrence in practice' both challenging and useful for further explanatory research and that this will inform the ongoing thought process about explanatory synthesis. Aside from these general remarks, in my mind the number one candidate for further possible cross-fertilization is rational deterrence theory.

Nuclear deterrence occupies a large space in this study because it represents a rich and diverse tradition of thinking, and there is simply no way around it when it comes to pondering nuclear non-use. Deterrence – with the creation of fear indisputably at its core – presents itself as especially compatible with what I have developed along the lines of atomic anxiety having a constitutive or underlying function for reasoning about abstinence. In that regard, I stated in subsection 4.3.3 that, were the dichotomy of *either* rational *or* emotional actors to be overcome, it would finally become possible to think through the reliance of deterrence on fear without having necessarily to conclude that rational deterrence theory cannot be rational.

So, first, developing an 'emotional-cognitive theory of deterrence' could be a fruitful way to overcome the problematic reliance on a rationality derived from an outdated *homo oeconomicus* actor model. This would fill such contentious concepts as 'rationality', 'threats' and 'credibility' with fresh meaning by taking their emotional dimension into account and introduce an innovation to deterrence theory building.

Kenneth Waltz was referred to again and again, first to capture the core idea of deterrence at the beginning of Chapter 2, then to contextualize and reflect on the strange process of the scientification of deterrence in Chapter 3, and, lastly, to cite him in Chapter 4 as an extreme thinker who explains deterrence by solely pointing to the fear created by threats with nuclear weapons, categorically rejecting the idea of a rational deterrence theory. Hence it would be a worthwhile endeavor, in my mind, for deterrence theorists to pick up the gauntlet and demonstrate that deterrence *can* be theorized, and that it can be rational theory, too, given that rationality does not mean the exclusion but rather the explicit embrace of emotion that conceptually rests at deterrence's core.

Second, gently unhinging deterrence theory from its current framework of Realism, positivism and social 'science' could point the way to more systematically recognizing and subsequently reflecting on deterrence's characteristics as a perpetually reproduced belief due to its ongoing theory-practice oscillation. In short, it would allow the theory's performativity to be embedded in the theory itself in a reflective manner, thus rendering the theory a more sophisticated and consistent one.

Thinking along the lines of the tradition of non-use – a notion resting somewhat uneasily between the logic of consequences and the logic of appropriateness at the moment – could also be enriched by explicitly informing the concepts on which the tradition relies with an emotional perspective. I have placed this line of thought under my discussion of the nuclear taboo, for practical reasons such as brevity of argument but also because Nina Tannenwald's nuclear taboo provides the comparably more consistent, full-fledged alternative to deterrence. Yet, the tradition of non-use could emancipate itself and overcome its current, meager 'not-quite-a-taboo-yet quality' by decidedly embracing one of its key concepts first and foremost: reputation. Similarly to deterrence, instead of dealing with reputation in a rational manner of pure calculation by *homo oeconomicus*, the reputation concept could be enriched by including the dimension of *affect*. In short, thinking about reputation loss could be conceptualized as an 'emotional-cognitive' process rather than just a computational problem.

There remain the questions raised by what we know about the nuclear taboo's development over time and my reconstruction of slowly shifting reactions to atomic anxiety in either a transitory or a transformative fashion. At this point, as I already discussed in section 4.5, it is simply too early to decide whether some form of contradiction will arise here or whether studying atomic anxiety further might rather lend additional credibility to the existing, explanatory accounts about the nuclear taboo in U.S. nuclear decision-making. The conceptual and initial empirical work I have provided here could be helpful for identifying additional sites and for digging deeper in future research. Revisiting the conceptual level and further tightening the links between agency, practice and emotion (as proposed by Bially Mattern, 2011) could allow for fruitful endeavors and for redeploying the concept of atomic anxiety in an inquiry directed at other materials and shorter periods of investigation. Approaches of this sort should hopefully be capable of yielding more detailed and fine-grained insights into what role atomic anxiety plays in the reasoning of decision-makers. More particularly, they could shed more light on the decline of moral obligations in presidential statements when deterrence and arms control are pursued, as I have established here, and the role and relevance of the nuclear taboo during the same period of time. So further research is needed, arguably inquiries not unlike the first one on Kennedy's two crises conducted for this study, that is, research focusing on specific political events, drawing on suitable types of materials such as diaries, memoirs or even interviews with decision-makers.

Lastly, and with regard to what I can contribute to the field of methodologically reflected and methodically sophisticated qualitative studies in IR, I believe that this study has demonstrated how studying micro practices and language up close can yield new insights and innovative trails to systematically follow further at a meso level later on. So qualitative approaches, such as the one in this book, offer not only the opportunity to enrich, refine and question existing concepts in IR in a transparent and intersubjectively comprehensible manner but also pioneering opportunities for generating a new and different sort of knowledge. All this promises further prospects for cross-fertilization between understanding and explaining, an especially enticing vista for the currently burgeoning literature on human emotion and the question of how it can be systematically accounted for when studying world politics.

5.2 Implications for policymaking: beware of complacency

The beauty of explanations is that they claim to reveal why regularities are the way they are. The amazing and peculiar can be made normal this way. But there is a danger to this, too, especially regarding nuclear non-use.

I stated in the introduction that two big explanatory lines of thought about the same phenomenon seem plenty, potentially convincing people that we have figured nuclear non-use pretty much out by now. However, Chapter 2 has argued that nuclear deterrence and the nuclear taboo alone are not enough for us to feel at ease, leaving too many questions unanswered. And their interplay offers no reassurance either. On the contrary, even if we were to assume a deterrence strategy to regularly and reliably produce non-use, the taboo can, rather than stabilizing it, put a spoke into the wheels of deterrence, as President Kennedy had to experience. With nuclear deterrence as widely employed a strategy as it is, this insight gives reason for renewed concern because deterrence theory and strategy derive from a decade-spanning, rich history of scholarly works with numerous authors introducing seminal notions (only to retract some or all of them later). And what I warned about is the alluring temptation to rely on what we allegedly know about deterrence from a luxurious hindsight position. After all, one can almost effortlessly point to the vast body of deterrence literature (even though it is riddled with disputes and contradictions) and suggest that some factor or model or blend of models worked in bringing about non-use in this or that crisis in the past. However, this study interjected that an in-depth reconstructive look brings to light the inconsistencies and ambivalences that come along with decision-makers trying to successfully practice deterrence, suggesting that events were not as necessary as references to deterrence theory make them out to be in retrospect. Glossing over those ruptures risks creating an illusion of posterity according to which 'deterrence worked', as demonstrated in the example of Robert Jervis' not implausible – but nevertheless imprecise and one-dimensional – evaluation of deterrence working during the Cuban Missile Crisis due to the worry of 'something going terribly wrong'. The danger in the long run is that similar deterrence-based simplifications of complex and inconsistent decision-making processes get locked in further and passed on until they turn into conventional wisdom about, for instance, how deterrence – narrowly – triumphed in averting World War III during the Cuban Missile Crisis. Deterrence's curious belief characteristics worsen this mentality, and some might thus say that this development has already run its path, that is, that rational deterrence theory is by now regularly used only as a rationalization after the fact. In stark contrast to this stance, this book suggests that we need to remind ourselves again and again of the near misses and failures surrounding deterrence. With agency making all the difference, and assuming for a moment that the nuclear taboo will gain even more weight in the future, the unfortunate scenario of a morally grounded, all-around good intention never to use nuclear weapons paradoxically ending up destabilizing an already delicate balance comes into view.

Furthermore, I have argued that atomic anxiety is not a 'non-use-producing thing' and that the reactions to it are not law-like effects but derive from agency. There is no causal arrow from anxiety to the explanations of non-use and further on to nuclear abstinence. So simply relying on the primal fear created by deterrence, as Waltz fervently does, seems equally misleading from a policymaking point of view, especially since '[p]roliferation fatalism and deterrence optimism interact in a particularly diabolical manner' (Sagan et al., 2007, p. 138), with one fueling the other and vice versa. Also, emotional upheavals can, as Neta Crawford (2000, pp. 146–148) points out, just as well have dangerous rather than stabilizing consequences. The fear created to deter might have perverse, war-provoking effects, leading to aggression instead of acquiescence, *fight* instead of *flight*. And Thucydides' Peloponnesian War provides probably the earliest cautionary tale for what results if fear takes over as a 'dominant motive' with 'its behavioral consequences [making] the expectations that aroused it self-fulfilling' (Lebow, 2005, p. 303) – a chilling perspective in a world in which the strategic use of fear, of all things, is relied on to prevent a nuclear war. Even though it is a very basic fear, the fear of death can be – and is in fact regularly – overcome through 'a higher sense of purpose or by a belief in an exalted afterlife', such as on the battlefield, for instance (Bourke, 2005, pp. 3–4). Hence, ongoing speculations about 'undeterrable' actors potentially wielding nuclear weapons are off the mark by identifying the problem to be a lack of rationality. Rather, fearlessness could be the actual crux here. And there is absolutely no reason to assume that fearlessness could never occur. In short, clinging to cherished assumptions and a settled belief in deterrence working, and explaining non-use either through simple fear or calculation as well as the nuclear taboo rendering the use of nuclear weapons unthinkable threatens to blind us to recognitions of this uncomfortable yet important sort.

Consequently, pondering what we can learn from this study above and beyond the case of U.S. nuclear abstinence, this is what I suggest: if decision-makers are to take anything from all the insights that academics studying the phenomenon of nuclear non-use over decades have produced, including this book, it is that they should beware of complacency and warily keep their eyes focused on the real possibility of nuclear weapons being used in the future – deterrence, taboos, traditions, fear and atomic anxiety notwithstanding. Nuclear abstinence is not a necessarily repeating pattern, an effect caused by law-like international forces. 'Use or non-use' remains a *choice*, and since *crises* are inevitable, decision-makers should not nurture the hope of nuclear abstinence having become (or ever becoming) a stable *routine* on which they can rely for good.

'[C]an we really expect this record of nonuse to continue indefinitely? Are we not riding our luck?', Lawrence Freedman (2009, p. 15) asks.

I would re-emphasize that I do not think that a sheer lucky streak kept nuclear weapons from being used; instead, atomic anxiety is at the heart of the phenomenon, with us using it for deterrence while at the same time dreading it due to the taboo. The cruel joke humanity plays on itself by keeping nuclear weapons around is thus not that we are 'riding our luck'. It is that deterrence fools us into thinking that, in order to survive, we *have* to keep living in fear.

Notes

2 Explaining Nuclear Non-Use

1. Thomas Schelling's *Strategy of Conflict* (1979 [1960]) and Herman Kahn's *On Thermonuclear War* (1960) are the cornerstones of systems analysis. See also Morgan (2011, pp. 147–148). See Klein (1994, pp. 113–114) for a critical assessment of systems analysis.
2. See Lupovici (2010, p. 708) for an overview over the literature dealing with this specific problem.
3. Kissinger's key contribution in this regard is his book *Nuclear Weapons and Foreign Policy* (1957). Brodie picked up the notion of limited war in *Strategy in the Missile Age* (1959) and *Escalation and the Nuclear Option* (1966). Osgood was also among the early thinkers about limited war, but later critically reviewed the concept in his *Limited War Revisited* (1979). In the 1980s, Robert Jervis took a pointed critical stance as well in *The Illogic of American Nuclear Strategy* (1984).
4. For more on the original notion, see Kaufmann (1956a; 1956b; 1956c).
5. To preclude a misunderstanding, this model is explicitly devised for sending signals of resolve and restraint and raising the opponent's costs. It does not – at least not primarily – aim at stripping him of his retaliatory capabilities (Powell, 1985, p. 83). So this model (being framed as primarily one of nuclear non-use here) should not be confused with the nuclear war-fighting school's string of thought of 'damage limitation' (for the nuances in nuclear war-fighting doctrine, see Lebovic, 1990).
6. The chess game analogy can, for example, be found in Schelling (1966, pp. 100–105) or, critically rejected, in Morgenthau (1977, pp. 257–258; 1964, pp. 26–27).
7. On this conclusion, see first and foremost Jervis (1984; see also Osgood, 1979, p. 8; Morgan, 2005, p. 754; Powell, 1985, pp. 80–83; Lee, 1996, pp. 14–15; Morgenthau, 1964; 1977, p. 258; Lebovic, 1990, pp. 160–164).
8. See also Gaddis (1987, pp. 105, 237), Wolfers (1946, pp. 116–117), Betts (1986), Rosenberg/Moore (1981).
9. 'Glory in possession, shame in use', is how William Walker (2012, p. 16) sums up his argument on why there is no taboo on the acquisition and display of nuclear weapons but only on their use.

3 Understanding Nuclear Non-Use

1. See Wight (1996) for a review and rejection of the incommensurability thesis. For more on the notion of synthesis in IR theory, see Jeffrey W. Legro's and Andrew Moravcsik's article 'Is Anybody Still a Realist?' (1999) and the subsequent *Correspondence* in International Security 25 (1), 2000.

2. Patrick Morgan's (2011) contribution *The practice of deterrence* bespeaks of the need to study deterrence from a practice perspective. It offers little in that respect, however, providing mostly a general historical survey of deterrence from 1945 to the present.
3. See Schmidt (2002) for a critical view on the narrative of the discipline progressing through 'great debates' such as Idealists vs. Realists vs. Behavioralists and so on.
4. In 1993, Waltz described nuclear weapons as on a par with bipolarity, i.e. as one of the two 'pillars' on which the long peace of the Cold War had rested (Waltz, 1993, p. 44). For more on that, see Waltz (1986, pp. 327–328; 1990).
5. See Achen/Snidal (1989) for a defense of this approach against the critical case study analysis of their third-wave colleagues and, to name only a few examples, Huth/Russett (1984; 1990) as well as, more recently, Signorino/Tarar (2006) for typical examples of such 'rigorous empirical testing' of deterrence theory propositions. Huth et al. (1993) is an interesting example for testing deterrence theory *against* hypotheses derived from structural realism (with results supporting deterrence theory over structural realism). This merely underlines my main point here, namely that the relationship between Waltz's seminal reformulation of Realism as a theory and deterrence research was actually quite muddled, while the overall paradigm in scholarly thinking about deterrence nevertheless became one of Realism *and* rationalism *and* positivism.
6. I am indebted to Carlo Masala for initially pointing me in this direction.
7. Richard Rorty's *Philosophy and the Mirror of Nature* (1979, pp. 315–322, 389–394) serves as a pertinent anchor in the literature and a general point of orientation for reading more about the scholarly mentality on which I draw.
8. The MAXQDA project file is available here: https://www.unibw.de/internationalepolitik/professur/team/Sauer/maxqda-kennedy.mx5/at_download/file.

4 Revisiting Nuclear Non-Use

1. It is important to note that NSC-30 does only recommend this after carefully considering public and foreign opinion, the situation in Western Europe, the UN's role regarding possible international control of atomic energy and the role of the military establishment in planning, preparing and executing the decision. NSC-30's recommendation is thus geared toward 'blending a political with a military responsibility' (NSC-30, 1948, p. 628), reserving the final decision for the president, however.
2. Note that any emphasis in the WHT quotes used here is always the original emphasis contained in the transcripts.
3. Note that time codes may vary slightly, depending on the software used to play the file.
4. Although there were both strategic and tactical nuclear weapons on the island, as the Cuba conferences after the end of the Cold War later revealed.
5. A recently declassified set of records suggests that Deputy Secretary of Defense Roswell Gilpatric, too, had pondered the option of a missile swap right from the start of the crisis (Burr, 2012).

6. The passages about Robert Kennedy's instruction contained in the Kennedy volume stem from McGeorge Bundy's *Danger and Survival* since the conversations were not taped (WHT, 2001b, p. 485 fn. 43). In connection with this, the editors discuss the possibility that President Kennedy had prepared another diplomatic, face-saving contingency plan with Dean Rusk (see also Lebow/ Gross Stein, 1994, pp. 127–129). The idea, according to Rusk, was to establish a backchannel to UN Secretary General U Thant so that in case Khrushchev rejected the missile swap, U Thant could propose the trade. The editors are unsure whether Rusk's account can be accurate. They conclude that it is more plausible that Kennedy did in fact commit to move toward an air strike in case Khrushchev did not accept the deal proposed in Kennedy's October 27 letter. Interestingly, and also in connection with this, Robert Kennedy later documented the covertly reached deal with Anatoly Dobrynin about the missile swap in his draft manuscript of *Thirteen Days*. But because he was assassinated before the book was published, Theodore Sorensen was able to edit this tightly kept secret out before the book went into print (Lebow/Gross Stein, 1994, p. 11; Munton, 2012, p. 314).
7. In *Arms and Influence,* Schelling (1966, p. 166) characterizes the Cuban Missile Crisis as a 'competition in risk-taking' and a 'manipulation of risk'.
8. See Freedman (2000, pp. 45–111) for more historical background on the evolution of flexible response and the Berlin developments leading up to and surrounding 'Poodle Blanket'. See Gavin (2012, pp. 30–74) for the argument that the actual strategic shift from massive retaliation to flexible response has been overstated.
9. Lebow and Gross Stein (1994, p. 97), who provide an in-depth analysis of the domestic aspects, caution to not take the worries of impeachment that the president confides to Robert Kennedy at face value. 'They might also represent a post-decisional rationalization', they suggest.
10. Freedman here and there also draws on transcripts of White House recordings, yet for his book published in 2000 he could only make use of the 1997 volume *The Kennedy Tapes: Inside the White House during the Cuban Missile Crisis* by Philip Zelikow and Ernest May. As they self-critically admit in the newly published transcript volumes, this first attempt to transcribe the tapes was not without its flaws (WHT, 2001a, pp. xiii–xvi).
11. Brodie (1946c, pp. 49–52) already contemplated such a notion when thinking about nuclear 'sabotage', as did E.U. Condon (2007 [1946]). See also Rosenbaum (1977) and Schelling (1982).
12. Classical Realists in general – oftentimes by pointing to the importance of fear in Thucydides' Peloponnesian War and Thomas Hobbes' Leviathan – were (and are) still susceptive to the role of emotion in international politics, without ever developing clear and systematic concepts in this regard, however. Fear is thus commonly referred to in connection with the uncertainty of the 'security dilemma' or as a 'cause of war (Crawford, 2000, pp. 120–121; see also Gray, 1999a, p. 196; Lebow, 2007, pp. 171–172; Booth/ Wheeler, 2008, pp. 1–18, 62–80). In contrast to classical Realist thinking, the entire notion of emotion is of lesser significance in Kenneth Waltz's Neo-Realism. It stands to reasons that this is to some degree because the 'first image' – individuals, where Neo-Realists would most probably locate human emotion – is removed from the theoretical perspective. Consequently, Waltz

(1979, p. 118; cf. Crawford, 2000, p. 121) refers to fear merely in passing and colloquially in *Theory of International Politics* when discussing the fear of the consequences resulting for units from improperly adjusting to the demands of the international self-help system. I mention this because Waltz, interestingly, thinks differently and way more explicitly about the role of fear with regard to deterrence, as I will discuss.

13. See Jonathan Mercer (2005) on the general argument about the dichotomy of rationality and psychology, the latter including emotion, in IR.
14. Waltz is, of course, not alone in this perspective on deterrence. In his critical assessment of U.S. strategic thinking in general, Lebovic (1990, p. 193) similarly concludes that in decision-making practice, deterrence 'acquires its power from the nonrational world of fear, psychological bias, and uncertainty and not from the world of deduction and mathematical precision'. But Waltz is cited here as clearly the most prominent author representing this view, criticized by some deterrence theorists as suffering from an 'existential bias' (Narang 2013).
15. See Bially Mattern (2011, pp. 63–70) for such an overview. For recent entries in the debate around the emotional turn, see the *Forum* on 'Emotions and World Politics' in *International Theory* 6 (3), 2014.
16. See Mercer (2010, p. 9) for the disagreements on this particular point of his argument.
17. Bleiker and Hutchison (2008, pp. 115–116) make a similar point about the political reactions to 9/11.
18. The MAXQDA project file is available here: https://www.unibw.de/internationalepolitik/professur/team/Sauer/maxqda-presidents.mx5/at_download/file.
19. See also Boyer (1994 [1985], p. 339).
20. See also Weart (1988, pp. 156–158).
21. World Peace via the United Nations had basically been a standing formula throughout Truman's entire presidency. See Truman (1945a; 1945b; 1945c; 1946; 1948; 1949; 1950; 1951; 1953a).
22. See the groundbreaking work by Thomas Schelling and Thomas Halperin (1975 [1961]). For a brief introduction into the basic concepts of arms control as well as a comprehensive historical overview, see Goldblat (2002). See also Burns (1993) and – for a brief historic overview that offers a perspective on nuclear arms control quite different from the one I develop through the lens of atomic anxiety here – Freedman (2009). Arms control literature does not need to concern me further here (and in fact it cannot due to space restrictions). The idea here is to focus on reinterpreting the rise of nuclear arms control distinctly from an emotion management perspective.
23. This close relationship between nuclear deterrence and arms control is well documented in arms control literature and needs no further elaboration here (see e.g. Morgan, 2011, p. 158). I focus instead on how they are linked in an emotion management perspective.
24. See also Blight (1990, pp. 144–145) and Winkler (1993, pp. 179–180).

References

C.H. Achen and D. Snidal (1989) 'Rational Deterrence Theory and Comparative Case Studies', *World Politics*, 41 (2), 143–169.

E. Adler (1992) 'The Emergence of Cooperation: National Epistemic Communities and the International Evolution of the Idea of Nuclear Arms Control', *International Organization*, 46 (1), 101–145.

E. Adler (1997) 'Seizing the Middle Ground: Constructivism in World Politics', *European Journal of International Relations*, 3 (3), 319–363.

G. Allison and P. Zelikow (1999) *Essence of Decision: Explaining the Cuban Missile Crisis*, 2nd Edition (New York, NY: Longman).

C. Atkinson (2010) 'Using Nuclear Weapons', *Review of International Studies*, 36 (4), 839–851.

J.L. Austin (1962) *How To Do Things with Words* (Cambridge: Harvard University Press).

P. Baert (2005) *Philosophy of the Social Sciences* (Cambridge: Polity Press).

T. Balzacq and R. Jervis (2004) 'Logics of Mind and International System: A Journey with Robert Jervis', *Review of International Studies*, 30 (4), 559–582.

B. Baruch (1946) 'The Baruch Plan', June 14, 1946, http://www.atomicarchive.com/Docs/Deterrence/BaruchPlan.shtml, date accessed October 4, 2012.

M.S. Bell and N.L. Miller (2015) 'Questioning the Effect of Nuclear Weapons on Conflict', *Journal of Conflict Resolution*, 59 (1), 74–92.

B.J. Bernstein (1991) 'Eclipsed by Hiroshima and Nagasaki: Early Thinking about Tactical Nuclear Weapons', *International Security*, 15 (4), 149–173.

R.K. Betts (1986) 'A Nuclear Golden Age? The Balance before Parity', *International Security*, 11 (3), 3–32.

R.K. Betts (2000) 'Universal Deterrence or Conceptual Collapse? Liberal Pessimism and Utopian Realism' in V.A. Utgoff (ed.) *The Coming Crisis: Nuclear Proliferation, U.S. Interests, and World Order* (Cambridge, MA: MIT Press), 51–85.

M. Bevir (2006) 'How Narratives Explain' in D. Yanow and P. Schwartz-Shea (eds.) *Interpretation and Method: Empirical Research Methods and the Interpretive Turn* (Armonk, NY: M.E. Sharpe), 281–290.

J. Bially Mattern (2011) 'A Practice Theory of Emotion for International Relations' in E. Adler and V. Pouliot (eds.) *International Practices* (Cambridge, MA: Cambridge University Press), 63–86.

B.G. Blair (1993) *The Logic of Accidental Nuclear War* (Washington, DC: The Brookings Institution).

B.G. Blair (2004) Keeping Presidents in the Nuclear Dark (Episode #1: The Case of the Missing 'Permissive Action Links'). Bruce Blair's Nuclear Column, Center for Defense Information,http://www.cdi.org/blair/permissive-action-links.cfm, date accessed May 25, 2009.

R. Bleiker and E. Hutchison (2008) 'Fear No More: Emotions and World Politics', *Review of International Studies*, 34 (S1), 115–135.

R. Bleiker and E. Hutchison (2014) 'Introduction: Emotions and World Politics', *International Theory*, 6 (3), 490–491.

J.G. Blight (1990) *The Shattered Crystal Ball: Fear and Learning in the Cuban Missile Crisis* (Savage, MA: Rowman & Littlefield Publishers, Inc.).

J.G. Blight and J.S. Nye and D.A. Welch (1987) 'The Cuban Missile Crisis Revisited', *Foreign Affairs*, 66 (1), 170–188.

K. Booth and N.J. Wheeler (2008) *The Security Dilemma: Fear, Cooperation and Trust in World Politics* (Houndmills: Palgrave).

J. Bourke (2005) *Fear: A Cultural History* (London: Virago Press).

P. Boyer (1994 [1985]) *By the Bomb's Early Light: American Thought and Culture at the Dawn of the Atomic Age* (New York, NY: Pantheon).

P. Brians (1987) *Nuclear Holocausts: Atomic War in Fiction, 1895–1984* (Kent, OH: Kent State University Press).

B. Brodie (ed.) (1946a) 'The Absolute Weapon: Atomic Power and World Order' (New York, NY: Harcourt, Brace & Co.).

B. Brodie (1946b) 'Implications for Military Policy' in B. Brodie (ed.) *The Absolute Weapon: Atomic Power and World Order* (New York, NY: Harcourt, Brace & Co.), 70–107.

B. Brodie (1946c) 'War in the Atomic Age' in B. Brodie (ed.) *The Absolute Weapon: Atomic Power and World Order* (New York, NY: Harcourt, Brace & Co.), 22–69.

B. Brodie (1959) *Strategy in the Missile Age* (Princeton, NJ: Princeton University Press).

B. Brodie (1966) *Escalation and the Nuclear Option* (Princeton, NJ: Princeton University Press).

H. Bull (1966) 'International Theory: The Case for a Classical Approach', *World Politics*, 18 (3), 361–377.

M. Bundy (1969) 'To Cap the Volcano', *Foreign Affairs: An American Quarterly Review*, 48 (1), 1.

M. Bundy (1988) *Danger and Survival: Choices about the Bomb in the First Fifty Years* (New York, NY: Random House).

R.D. Burns (ed.) (1993) 'Encyclopedia of Arms Control and Disarmament' (New York, NY: Scribner Book Company), Vol. 1.

W. Burr (2012) Secret Notes by Deputy Secretary Roswell Gilpatric Show Early Interest in Trade of U.S. Jupiter Missiles for Soviet Missile in Cuba. National Security Archive Electronic Briefing Book No. 398, The National Security Archive, George Washington University, Washington, DC, http://www.gwu.edu/~nsarchiv/NSAEBB/NSAEBB398/, date accessed October 20, 2012.

G.H.W. Bush (1991) 'Address to the Nation on the Invasion of Iraq', January 16, 1991, http://millercenter.org/president/speeches/detail/3428, date accessed October 2, 2012.

G.H.W. Bush (1992a) 'Address before a Joint Session of the Congress on the State of the Union', January 28, 1992, http://www.presidency.ucsb.edu/ws/print.php?pid=20544, date accessed October 2, 2012.

G.H.W. Bush (1992b) 'Debate with Bill Clinton and Ross Perot', October 15, 1992, http://www.debates.org/index.php?page=october-15–1992-first-half-debate-transcript; http://www.debates.org/index.php?page=october-15–1992-second-half-debate-transcript, date accessed October 20, 2012.

G.W. Bush (2002) 'Address before a Joint Session of the Congress on the State of the Union', January 29, 2002, http://www.presidency.ucsb.edu/ws/print.php?pid=29644, date accessed September 28, 2012.

G.W. Bush (2003) 'Address before a Joint Session of the Congress on the State of the Union', January 28, 2003, http://www.presidency.ucsb.edu/ws/print.php?pid=29645, date accessed September 28, 2012.

G.W. Bush (2004a) 'Address before a Joint Session of the Congress on the State of the Union', January 20, 2004, http://www.presidency.ucsb.edu/ws/print.php?pid=29646, date accessed September 28, 2012.

G.W. Bush (2004b) 'Debate with John Kerry', September 30, 2004, http://www.debates.org/index.php?page=september-30-2004-debate-transcript, date accessed October 2, 2012.

L. Butler (2006) 'At the End of the Journey: The Risks of Cold War Thinking in a New Era', *International Affairs*, 82 (4), 763–769.

D. Campbell (1992) *Writing Security: United States Foreign Policy and the Politics of Identity* (Minneapolis, MN: University of Minnesota Press).

E.H. Carr (2001 [1939]) *The Twenty Years' Crisis 1919–1939. An Introduction to the Study of International Relations*, Reprint of the 2nd edition (Houndmills: Palgrave).

J. Carter (1977) 'Inaugural Address', January 20, 1977, http://millercenter.org/president/speeches/detail/3286, date accessed October 2, 2012.

J. Carter (1978) 'The State of the Union Address Delivered before a Joint Session of the Congress', January 19, 1978, http://www.presidency.ucsb.edu/ws/print.php?pid=30856, date accessed October 2, 2012.

J. Carter (1979) 'The State of the Union Address Delivered before a Joint Session of the Congress', January 23, 1979, http://www.presidency.ucsb.edu/ws/print.php?pid=32657, date accessed October 2, 2012.

J. Carter (1980) 'Debate with Ronald Reagan', October 28, 1980, http://millercenter.org/president/speeches/detail/5535, date accessed October 2, 2012

J. Carter (1981) 'Farewell Speech', January 14, 1981, http://millercenter.org/president/speeches/detail/5536, date accessed October 2, 2012.

W.J. Clinton (1994) 'Address before a Joint Session of the Congress on the State of the Union', January 25, 1994, http://www.presidency.ucsb.edu/ws/print.php?pid=50409, date accessed October 2, 2012.

W.J. Clinton (1995) 'Address before a Joint Session of the Congress on the State of the Union', January 24, 1995, http://www.presidency.ucsb.edu/ws/print.php?pid=51634, date accessed October 2, 2012.

W.J. Clinton (1996a) 'Address before a Joint Session of the Congress on the State of the Union', January 23, 1996, http://www.presidency.ucsb.edu/ws/print.php?pid=53091, date accessed October 2, 2012.

W.J. Clinton (1996b) 'Debate with Bob Dole', October 6, 1996, http://millercenter.org/president/speeches/detail/4598, date accessed October 2, 2012.

W.J. Clinton (1997) 'Second Inaugural Address', January 20, 1997, http://millercenter.org/president/speeches/detail/3443, date accessed October 2, 2012.

A. Coffey and P. Atkinson (1996) 'Concepts and Coding' in A. Coffey and P. Atkinson (eds.) *Making Sense of Qualitative Data* (Thousand Oaks: Sage), 26–53.

M.D. Cohen (2013) 'How Nuclear South Asia Is Like Cold War Europe', *The Nonproliferation Review*, 20 (3), 433–451.

C. Cohn (1987) 'Sex and Death in the Rational World of Defense Intellectuals', *Signs*, 12 (4), 687–718.

E.U. Condon (2007 [1946]) 'The New Technique of Private War' in D. Masters and K. Way (eds.) *One World or None* (New York, NY: The Federation of American Scientists), 107–115.

R. Cox (1981) 'Social Forces, States and World Orders: Beyond International Relations Theory', *Millennium – Journal of International Studies*, 10 (2), 126–155.

C. Craig (2012) 'Testing Organisation Man: The Cuban Missile Crisis and the Limits of Safety', *International Relations*, 26 (3), 291–303.

N.C. Crawford (2000) 'The Passion of World Politics: Propositions on Emotion and Emotional Relationships', *International Security*, 24 (4), 116–156.

N.C. Crawford (2014) 'Institutionalizing Passion in World Politics: Fear and Empathy', *International Theory*, 6 (3), 535–557.

A.W. Daum (2008) *Kennedy in Berlin* (Cambridge, MA: Cambridge University Press).

J.W. Davis (2005) *Terms of Inquiry: On the Theory and Practice of Political Science* (Baltimore, MD: Johns Hopkins University Press).

J. Derrida (1984) 'No Apocalypse, Not Now (full speed ahead, seven missiles, seven missives)', *Diacritics*, 14 (2), 20–31.

D.H. Deudney (1995) 'Political Fission: State Structure, Civil Society, and Nuclear Security Policies in the United States' in R.D. Lipschutz (ed.) *On Security* (New York, NY: Columbia University Press), 87–123.

D.H. Deudney (2007) *Bounding Power: Republican Security Theory from the Polis to the Global Village* (Princeton, NJ: Princeton University Press).

K.W. Deutsch (1963) *The Nerves of Government: Models of Political Communication and Action* (London: Collier-Macmillan).

M. Dobbs (2008) *One Minute to Midnight: Kennedy, Khrushchev and Castro on the Brink of Nuclear War* (New York, NY: Alfred A. Knopf).

Department of Defense (1961) *Fallout Protection: What to Know and Do about Nuclear Attack* (Washington, DC: U.S. Department of Defense).

J. Donnelly (2000) *Realism and International Relations* (Cambridge: Cambridge University Press).

F.S. Dunn (1946) 'The Common Problem' in B. Brodie (ed.) *The Absolute Weapon: Atomic Power and World Order* (New York, NY: Harcourt, Brace & Co.), 3–20.

L. Eden (2004) *Whole World on Fire: Organizations, Knowledge, and Nuclear Weapons Devastation* (Ithaca, NY: Cornell University Press).

L. Eden (2010) 'The Contingent Taboo', *Review of International Studies*, 36 (4), 831–837.

D.D. Eisenhower (1953a) 'Annual Message to the Congress on the State of the Union', February 2, 1953, http://www.presidency.ucsb.edu/ws/print.php?pid=9829, date accessed September 28, 2012.

D.D. Eisenhower (1953b) 'Atoms for Peace', December 8, 1953, http://millercenter.org/president/speeches/detail/3358, date accessed September 4, 2012.

D.D. Eisenhower (1953c) 'Chance for Peace', April 16, 1953, http://millercenter.org/president/speeches/detail/3357, date accessed September 28, 2012.

D.D. Eisenhower (1953d) 'First Inaugural Address', January 20, 1953, http://millercenter.org/president/speeches/detail/3356, date accessed September 28, 2012.

D.D. Eisenhower (1954) 'Annual Message to the Congress on the State of the Union', January 7, 1954, http://www.presidency.ucsb.edu/ws/print.php?pid=10096, date accessed September 28, 2012.

D.D. Eisenhower (1955) 'Annual Message to the Congress on the State of the Union', January 6, 1955, http://www.presidency.ucsb.edu/ws/print.php?pid=10416, date accessed September 28, 2012.

D.D. Eisenhower (1957) 'Annual Message to the Congress on the State of the Union', January 10, 1957, http://www.presidency.ucsb.edu/ws/print.php?pid=11029, date accessed September 28, 2012.

D.D. Eisenhower (1958) 'Annual Message to the Congress on the State of the Union', January 9, 1958, http://www.presidency.ucsb.edu/ws/print.php?pid=11162, date accessed September 28, 2012.

P. Erickson and J.L. Klein and L. Daston et al. (2013) *How Reason Almost Lost Its Mind: The Strange Career of Cold War Rationality* (Chicago: The University of Chicago Press).

A. Etzioni (2010) 'Rational Actors: Neither Mad nor M.A.D.: The Meanings of Rationality, Rogue States and Terrorists', *Defense & Security Analysis*, 26 (4), 431–438.

M.A. Evangelista (1998) 'The "Soviet Threat": Intentions, Capabilities, and Context', *Diplomatic History*, 22 (3), 439–449.

T. Farrell (2010) 'Nuclear Non-Use: Constructing a Cold War History', *Review of International Studies*, 36 (4), 819–829.

T. Farrell and H. Lambert (2001) 'Courting Controversy: International Law, National Norms and American Nuclear Use', *Review of International Studies* 27 (3), 309–326.

K. Fattah and K.M. Fierke (2009) 'A Clash of Emotions: The Politics of Humiliation and Political Violence in the Middle East', *European Journal of International Relations*, 15 (1), 67–93.

J.D. Fearon (1991) 'Counterfactuals and Hypothesis Testing in Political Science', *World Politics*, 43 (2), 169–195.

J. Fearon and A. Wendt (2002) 'Rationalism v. Constructivism: A Skeptical View' in W. Carlsnaes and T. Risse and B.A. Simmons (eds.) *Handbook of International Relations* (London: Sage), 52–72.

K.M. Fierke (2009) 'Agents of Death: The Structural Logic of Suicide Terrorism and Martyrdom', *International Theory*, 1 (1), 155–184.

C.F. Fink (1965) 'More Calculations about Deterrence', *The Journal of Conflict Resolution*, 9 (1), 54–65.

M. Finnemore and K. Sikkink (1998) 'International Norm Dynamics and Political Change', *International Organization*, 52 (4), 887–917.

G.R. Ford (1975) 'Remarks in Helsinki', August 1, 1975, http://millercenter.org/president/speeches/detail/3393, date accessed September 13, 2012.

U. Franke and R. Weber (2012) 'At the Papini hotel: On pragmatism in the study of international relations', *European Journal of International Relations*, 18 (4), 669–691.

H.B. Franklin (2008 [1988]) *War Stars: The Superweapon and the American Imagination* (Amherst: University of Massachusetts Press).

L. Freedman (2000) *Kennedy's Wars: Berlin, Cuba, Laos, and Vietnam* (Oxford: Oxford University Press).

L. Freedman (2004) *Deterrence* (Cambridge: Polity).

L. Freedman (2005) 'Deterrence: A Reply', *The Journal of Strategic Studies*, 28 (5), 789–801.

L. Freedman (2009) 'A New Theory for Nuclear Disarmament', *Bulletin of the Atomic Scientists*, 65 (4), 14–30.

J. Friedrichs (2009) 'From Positivist Pretense to Pragamtic Practice: Varieties of Pragmatic Methodology in IR Scholarship (in: The Forum: Pragmatism and International Relations)', *International Studies Review*, 11 (3), 645–648.

J. Friedrichs and F. Kratochwil (2009) 'On Acting and Knowing: How Pragmatism Can Advance International Relations Research and Methodology', *International Organization*, 63 (4), 701–731.

J.L. Gaddis (1987) *The Long Peace: Inquiries into the History of the Cold War* (New York, NY: Oxford University Press).

F.J. Gavin (2009) 'Same As It Ever Was: Nuclear Alarmism, Proliferation, and the Cold War', *International Security*, 34 (3), 7–37.

F.J. Gavin (2012) *Nuclear Statecraft: History and Strategy in America's Atomic Age* (London: Cornell University Press).

A.L. George and R.Smoke (1974) *Deterrence in American Foreign Policy: Theory and Practice* (New York, NY: Columbia University Press).

A.L. George and R. Smoke (1989) 'Deterrence and Foreign Policy', *World Politics*, 41 (2), 170–182.

D.J. Gill (2009) 'Review Article: Nuclear Deterrence and the Tradition of Non-Use', *International Affairs*, 85 (4), 863–869.

P. Gizewski (1996) 'From Winning Weapon to Destroyer of Worlds: The Nuclear Taboo in International Politics', *International Journal*, 51 (3), 397–418.

J. Goldblat (2002) *Arms Control: The New Guide to Negotiations and Agreements* (London: Sage).

C.S. Gray (1974) 'The Urge to Compete: Rationales for Arms Racing', *World Politics*, 26 (2), 207–233.

C.S. Gray (1999a) *Modern Strategy* (Oxford: Oxford University Press).

C.S. Gray (1999b) *The Second Nuclear Age* (Boulder, CO: Lynne Rienner).

J.M. Grieco (1988) 'Anarchy and the Limits of Cooperation: A Realist Critique of the Newest Liberal Institutionalism', *International Organization*, 42 (3), 458–508.

H. Gusterson (1996) *Nuclear Rites: A Weapons Laboratory at the End of the Cold War* (Berkeley, CA: University of California Press).

H. Gusterson (2004) *People of the Bomb: Portraits of America's Nuclear Complex* (Minneapolis, MN: University of Minnesota Press).

H. Gusterson (2009) Hiroshima and the Power of Pictures. *Bulletin of the Atomic Scientists*, http://thebulletin.org/node/7653, date accessed August 12, 2008.

S. Guzzini (2004) 'The Enduring Dilemmas of Realism in International Relations', *European Journal of International Relations*, 10 (4), 533–568.

S. Guzzini and A. Leander (2006) 'Wendt's Constructivism: A Relentless Quest for Synthesis' in S. Guzzini and A. Leander (eds.) *Constructivism and International Relations: Alexander Wendt and his Critics* (Milton Park: Routledge), 73–92.

M.H. Halperin and B. Tertrais and K.B. Payne et al. (2009) 'Forum: The Case for No First Use: An Exchange', *Survival: Global Politics and Strategy*, 51 (5), 17–46.

L. Hansen (2006) *Security as Practice: Discourse Analysis and the Bosnian War* (London: Routledge).

A. Harrington de Santana (2009) 'Nuclear Weapons as the Currency of Power', *Nonproliferation Review*, 16 (3), 325–345.

G. Hawthorn (1993) *Plausible Worlds: Possibility and Understanding in History and the Social Sciences* (Cambridge: Cambridge University Press).

J. Hayes and P. James (2014) 'Theory as Thought: Britain and German Unification', *Security Studies*, 23 (2), 399–429.

G. Hellmann (2002) 'Creative Intelligence: Pragmatism as a Theory of Thought and Action.' Paper prepared for presentation at the "Millennium" Special Issue Conference on "Pragmatism in International Relations Theory", London.

G. Hellmann (2009) 'Beliefs as Rules for Action: Pragmatism as a Theory of Thought and Action (in: The Forum: Pragmatism and International Relations)', *International Studies Review*, 11 (3), 638–641.

G. Hellmann (2010) 'Pragmatismus' in C. Masala and F. Sauer and A. Wilhelm (eds.) *Handbuch der Internationalen Politik* (Wiesbaden: VS Verlag für Sozialwissenschaften), 148–181.

B. Herborth (2010) 'Rekonstruktive Forschungslogik' in C. Masala and F. Sauer and A. Wilhelm (eds.) *Handbuch der Internationalen Politik* (Wiesbaden: VS Verlag für Sozialwissenschaften), 265–284.

B. Herborth (2011) 'Methodenstreit – Methodenzwang – Methodenfetisch', *Zeitschrift für Internationale Beziehungen*, 18 (2), 137–151.

E. Herschinger (2011) *Constructing Global Enemies: Hegemony and Identity in International Discourses on Terrorism and Drug Prohibition* (London: Routledge).

D.E. Hoffman (2009) *The Dead Hand: The Untold Story of the Cold War Arms Race And its Dangerous Legacy* (New York, NY: Anchor).

M. Hollis and S. Smith (1991) *Explaining and Understanding International Relations* (Oxford: Oxford University Press).

J. Hunner (2004) 'Reinventing Los Alamos: Code Switching and Suburbia at America's Atomic City' in S.C. Zeman and M.A. Amundson (eds.) *Atomic Culture: How We Learned to Stop Worrying and Love the Bomb* (Boulder, CO: University Press of Colorado), 33–48.

E. Hutchison and R. Bleiker (2014) 'Theorizing Emotions in World Politics', *International Theory*, 6 (3), 491–514.

P. Huth and B. Russett (1984) 'What Makes Deterrence Work? Cases from 1900 to 1980', *World Politics*, 36 (4), 496–526.

P. Huth and B. Russett (1990) 'Testing Deterrence Theory: Rigor Makes a Difference', *World Politics*, 42 (4), 466–501.

P. Huth and C. Gelpi and D.S. Bennett (1993) 'The Escalation of Great Power Militarized Disputes: Testing Rational Deterrence Theory and Structural Realism', *The American Political Science Review*, 87 (3), 609–623.

International Court of Justice (ICJ) (1996) 'Legality of the Threat or Use of Nuclear Weapons: Advisory Opinion of 8 July 1996', International Court of Justice, http://www.icj-cij.org/docket/files/95/7495.pdf?PHPSESSID=1878c4df1904a4a8cfdb989daabd6c0c, date accessed April 30, 2010.

F.C. Iklé (1973) 'Can Nuclear Deterrence Last out the Century?', *Foreign Affairs*, 51 (2), 267–285.

P.T. Jackson (2006) 'Making Sense of Making Sense: Configurational Analysis and the Double Hermeneutic' in D. Yanow and P. Schwartz-Shea (eds.) *Interpretation and Method: Empirical Research Methods and the Interpretive Turn* (Armonk, NY: M.E. Sharpe), 264–281.

P.T. Jackson (2011) *The Conduct of Inquiry in International Relations: Philosophy of Science and its Implications for the Study of World Politics* (London: Routledge).

R. Jackson (2007) 'Constructing Enemies: 'Islamic Terrorism' in Political and Academic Discourse', *Government and Opposition*, 42 (3), 394–426.

R. Jervis (1970) *The Logic of Images in International Relations* (Princeton, NJ: Princeton University Press).

R. Jervis (1979) 'Deterrence Theory Revisited', *World Politics*, 31 (2), 289–324.

R. Jervis (1982) 'Deterrence and Perception', *International Security*, 7 (3), 3–30.

R. Jervis (1984) *The Illogic of American Nuclear Strategy* (Ithaca, NY: Cornell University Press).
R. Jervis (1985) 'Perceiving and Coping with Threat' in R. Jervis and R.N. Lebow (eds.) *Psychology & Deterrence* (Baltimore, MD: Johns Hopkins University Press), 13–34.
R. Jervis (1988) 'The Political Effects of Nuclear Weapons: A Comment', *International Security*, 13 (2), 80–90.
R. Jervis (1989) 'Rational Deterrence: Theory and Evidence', *World Politics*, 41 (2), 183–207.
R. Jervis (1991) 'The Future of World Politics: Will It Resemble the Past?', *International Security*, 16 (3), 39–73.
L.B. Johnson (1964) 'Acceptance Speech at the Democratic National Convention', August 27, 1964, http://millercenter.org/president/speeches/detail/5660, date accessed September 28, 2012.
L.B. Johnson (1965) 'Annual Message to the Congress on the State of the Union', January 4, 1965, http://www.presidency.ucsb.edu/ws/print.php?pid=26907, date accessed September 28, 2012.
L.B. Johnson (1967) 'Annual Message to the Congress on the State of the Union', January 10, 1967, http://www.presidency.ucsb.edu/ws/print.php?pid=28338, date accessed September 28, 2012.
L.B. Johnson (1968) 'Remarks on Signing the Nuclear Nonproliferation Treaty', July 1, 1968, http://millercenter.org/president/speeches/detail/4037, date accessed September 28, 2012.
H. Kahn (1960) *On Thermonuclear War* (Princeton, NJ: Princeton University Press).
H. Kahn (1962) *Thinking about the Unthinkable* (New York, NY: Pelican Books).
H. Kahn (1968 [1965]) *On Escalation* (New York, NY: Pelican).
F. Kaplan (1983) *The Wizards of Armageddon* (New York, NY: Simon and Schuster).
M.A. Kaplan (1966) 'The New Great Debate: Traditionalism vs. Science in International Relations', *World Politics*, 19 (1), 1–20.
P.A. Karber and J.A. Combs (1998) 'The United States, NATO, and the Soviet Threat to Western Europe: Military Estimates and Policy Options, 1945–1963', *Diplomatic History*, 22 (3), 399–429.
P.J. Katzenstein (1996) 'Introduction' in P.J. Katzenstein (ed.) *The Culture of National Security: Norms and Identity in World Politics* (New York, NY: Columbia University Press), 1–32.
P. Katzenstein and R. Sil (2008) 'Eclectic Theorizing in the Study and Practice of International Relations' in C. Reus-Smit and D. Snidal (eds.) *The Oxford Handbook of International Relations* (Oxford: Oxford University Press), 109–130.
W.M. Kaufmann (1956a) 'Force and Foreign Policy' in W.M. Kaufmann (ed.) *Military Policy and National Security* (Princeton, NJ: Princeton University Press), 233–267.
W.M. Kaufmann (1956b) 'Limited War' in W.M. Kaufmann (ed.) *Military Policy and National Security* (Princeton, NJ: Princeton University Press), 102–136.
W.M. Kaufmann (1956c) 'The Requirements of Deterrence' in W.M. Kaufmann (ed.) *Military Policy and National Security* (Princeton, NJ: Princeton University Press), 12–38.
J.F. Kennedy (1961a) 'Annual Message to the Congress on the State of the Union', January 30, 1961, http://www.presidency.ucsb.edu/ws/print.php?pid=8045, date accessed September 28, 2012.

J.F. Kennedy (1961b) 'Inaugural Address', January 20, 1961, http://millercenter.org/president/speeches/detail/3365, date accessed October 9, 2012.

J.F. Kennedy (1961c) Letter From President Kennedy to the Supreme Commander Allied Powers Europe (Norstad). National Security Archive Electronic Briefing Book No. 310, The National Security Archive, George Washington University, Washington, DC, http://www.gwu.edu/~nsarchiv/nukevault/ebb310/10–20–61.PDF, date accessed August 25, 2011.

J.F. Kennedy (1962a) 'Audio Recording of "Executive Committee Meeting of the NSC on the Cuban Missile Crisis continued"'. October 27, 1962. Presidential Recordings Program, University of Virginia – Miller Center, Tape 41A, mp3 (98:33), http://web2.millercenter.org/jfk/audiovisual/whrecordings/meetings/jfk_041a.mp3, date accessed September 18, 2011.

J.F. Kennedy (1962b) 'Audio Recording of "Kennedy Summarizes a Late-Night Meeting on the Cuban Missile Crisis"'. October 18, 1962. Presidential Recordings Program, University of Virginia – Miller Center, Tape 31.1, mp3 (04:34), http://web2.millercenter.org/jfk/audiovisual/whrecordings/meetings/jfk_031_1.mp3, date accessed August 30, 2011.

J.F. Kennedy (1962c) 'Audio Recording of "Meeting on the Cuban Missile Crisis continued"'. October 18, 1962. Presidential Recordings Program, University of Virginia – Miller Center, Tape 30A, mp3 (95:01), http://web2.millercenter.org/jfk/audiovisual/whrecordings/meetings/jfk_030a.mp3. date accessed September 12, 2011.

J.F. Kennedy (1962d) 'Audio Recording of "Meeting with Maxwell Taylor on His Far Eastern Trip"'. September 25, 1962. Presidential Recordings Program, University of Virginia – Miller Center, Tape 23, mp3 (58:38), http://web2.millercenter.org/jfk/audiovisual/whrecordings/meetings/jfk_023.mp3. date accessed August 30, 2011.

J.F. Kennedy (1963a) 'Address on the Nuclear Test Ban Treaty', July 26, 1963, http://millercenter.org/president/speeches/detail/3377, date accessed October 9, 2012.

J.F. Kennedy (1963b) 'American University Commencement', June 10, 1963, http://millercenter.org/president/speeches/detail/3374, date accessed October 5, 2012.

R.F. Kennedy (1968 [1999]) *Thirteen Days: A Memoir of the Cuban Missile Crisis* (New York, NY: W.W. Norton & Company).

G. King and R.O. Keohane and S. Verba (1994) *Designing Social Inquiry. Scientific Inference in Qualitative Research* (Princeton: Princeton University Presss).

H.A. Kissinger (1957) *Nuclear Weapons and Foreign Policy* (New York, NY: Harper & Brothers).

H.A. Kissinger (1962) 'The Unsolved Problems of European Defense', *Foreign Affairs*, 40 (4), 515–541.

B.S. Klein (1994) *Strategic Studies and World Order* (Cambridge: Cambridge University Press).

J.W. Knopf (2010) 'The Fourth Wave in Deterrence Research', *Contemporary Security Policy*, 31 (1), 1–33.

F. Kratochwil (2006) 'Constructing a New Orthodoxy? Wendt's Social Theory of International Politics and the Constructivist Challenge' in S. Guzzini and A. Leander (eds.) *Constructivism and International Relations: Alexander Wendt and his Critics* (Milton Park: Routledge), 21–47.

F. Kratochwil and J.G. Ruggie (1986) 'International Organization: A State of the Art on an Art of The State', *International Organization*, 40 (4), 753–775.

S. Kull (1988) *Minds at War. Nuclear Reality and the Inner Conflicts of Defense Policymakers* (New York, NY: Basic Books).

M. Kurki (2006) 'Causes of a Divided Discipline: Rethinking the Concept of Cause in International Relations Theory', *Review of International Studies*, 32 (2), 189–216.

D.A. Lake (2011) 'Why "isms" Are Evil: Theory, Epistemology, and Academic Sects as Impediments to Understanding and Progress', *International Studies Quarterly*, 55 (2), 465–480.

J.H. Lebovic (1990) *Deadly Dilemmas: Deterrence in U.S. Nuclear Strategy* (New York, NY: Columbia University Press).

R.N. Lebow (2005) 'Reason, Emotion and Cooperation', *International Politics*, 42 (3), 283–313.

R.N. Lebow (2007) 'Thucydides and Deterrence', *Security Studies*, 16 (2), 163–188.

R.N. Lebow (2010a) 'Deterrence' in M.D. Cavelty and V. Mauer (eds.) *The Routledge Handbook of Security Studies* (New York, NY: Routledge), 393–403.

R.N. Lebow (2010b) *Forbidden Fruit: Counterfactuals and International Relations* (Princeton, NJ: Princeton University Press).

R.N. Lebow and J. Gross Stein (1989) 'Rational Deterrence Theory: I Think Therefore I Deter', *World Politics*, 41 (2), 208–224.

R.N. Lebow and J. Gross Stein (1994) *We All Lost the Cold War* (Princeton, NJ: Princeton University Press).

S.P. Lee (1996) *Morality, Prudence and Nuclear Weapons* (Cambridge: Cambridge University Press).

J.W. Legro and A. Moravcsik (1999) 'Is Anybody Still a Realist?', *International Security*, 24 (2), 5–55.

J. Lewis (2007) *The Minimum Means of Reprisal: China's Search for Security in the Nuclear Age* (Cambridge, MA: The MIT Press).

J. Lewis (2008) 'Minimum Deterrence', *Bulletin of the Atomic Scientists*, 64 (3), 38–41.

J. Lewis (2009) Minimum Means of Something, Blog Post, http://lewis.armscontrolwonk.com/archive/2230/minimum-means-of-something, date accessed November 4, 2010.

Life (1945) 'War's Ending', Editorial, *Life Magazine*, 19 (8): 25–38D, August 20, 1945, http://books.google.com/books?id=hkgEAAAAMBAJ&lpg=PA17&pg=PA17#v=onepage&q&f=false, date accessed May 27, 2010.

D. Lindley (2001) 'What I Learned Since I Stopped Worrying and Studied the Movie: A Teaching Guide to Stanley Kubrick's Dr. Strangelove', *PS: Political Science and Politics*, 34 (3), 663–667.

S. Lumet (1964) 'Fail-Safe' (DVD), 107 minutes, Sony Pictures Home Entertainment.

A. Lupovici (2010) 'The Emerging Fourth Wave of Deterrence Theory – Toward a New Research Agenda', *International Studies Quarterly*, 54 (3), 705–732.

J. Mahoney and G. Goertz (2004) 'The Possibility Principle: Choosing Negative Cases in Comparative Research', *American Political Science Review*, 98 (4), 653–669.

B.G. Marfleet (2000) 'The Operational Code of John F. Kennedy during the Cuban Missile Crisis: A Comparison of Public and Private Rhetoric', *Political Psychology*, 21 (3), 545–558.

J. Masco (2008) 'Survival is Our Business: Engineering Ruins and Affect in Nuclear America', *Cultural Anthropology*, 23 (2), 361–398.

J. Mason (2002) 'Organizing and Indexing Qualitative Data' in J. Mason (ed.) *Qualitative Researching* 2nd (London: Sage), 147–172.

D. Masters and K. Way (eds.) (2007 [1946]) 'One World or None' (New York, NY: The Federation of American Scientists).

J.B. Mattern (2014) 'On Being Convinced: An Emotional Epistemology of International Relations', *International Theory*, 6 (3), 589–594.

M. McCanles (1984) 'Machiavelli and the Paradoxes of Deterrence', *Diacritics*, 14 (2), 12–19.

R. McDermott (2004) 'The Feeling of Rationality: The Meaning of Neuroscientific Advances for Political Science', *Perspectives on Politics*, 2 (4), 691–706.

R. McKeown (2009) 'Norm Regress: US Revisionism and the Slow Death of the Torture Norm', *International Relations*, 23 (5), 5–25.

R.S. McNamara and J.G. Blight (2002): The Miracle of October: Lessons from the Cuban Missile Crisis. Unpublished article quoted with permission of James G. Blight, http://www.watsoninstitute.org/cuba/OctMiracle.pdf, date accessed July 18, 2008.

J.J. Mearsheimer (1995) 'The False Promise of International Institutions', *International Security*, 19 (3), 5–49.

J.J. Mearsheimer (2001) *The Tragedy of Great Power Politics* (New York, London: W.W. Norton).

J.J. Mearsheimer and S.M. Walt (2013) 'Leaving Theory behind: Why Simplistic Hypothesis Testing Is Bad for International Relations', *European Journal of International Relations*, 19 (3), 427–457.

J. Mercer (2005) 'Rationality and Psychology in International Politics', *International Organization*, 59 (1), 77–106.

J. Mercer (2010) 'Emotional Beliefs', *International Organization*, 64 (1), 1–31.

J. Mercer (2014) 'Feeling Like a State: Social Emotion and Identity', *International Theory*, 6 (3), 515–535.

J. Milliken (1999) 'The Study of Discourse in International Relations: A Critique of Research and Methods', *European Journal of International Relations*, 5 (2), 225–254.

P. Morgan (1977) *Deterrence: A Conceptual Analysis* (Beverly Hills, CA: Sage).

P. Morgan (2003) *Deterrence Now* (Cambridge: Cambridge University Press).

P. Morgan (2011) 'The Practice of Deterrence' in E. Adler and V. Pouliot (eds.) *International Practices* (Cambridge: Cambridge University Press), 139–173.

P.M. Morgan (2005) 'Taking the Long View of Deterrence', *Journal of Strategic Studies*, 28 (5), 751–763.

P.M. Morgan (2012) 'The State of Deterrence in International Politics Today', *Contemporary Security Policy*, 33 (1), 85–107.

H.J. Morgenthau (1964) 'The Four Paradoxes of Nuclear Strategy', *The American Political Science Review*, 58 (1), 23–35.

H.J. Morgenthau (1977) 'The Fallacy of Thinking Conventionally About Nuclear Weapons' in D. Carlton and C. Schaerf (eds.) *Arms Control and Technological Innovation* (London: Croom Helm), 255–264.

H.J. Morgenthau (2005 [1948]) *Politics among Nations. The Struggle for Power and Peace* 7th edition (Boston, MA: McGraw Hill).

J. Mueller (2010) *Atomic Obsession: Nuclear Alarmism from Hiroshima to Al-Qaeda* (New York, NY: Oxford University Press).

H. Müller (2013) 'Icons Off the Mark', *The Nonproliferation Review*, 20 (3), 545–565.

D. Munton (2012) 'Hits and Myths: The Essence, the Puzzles and the Missile Crisis', *International Relations*, 26 (3), 305–325.

V. Narang (2013) 'What Does It Take to Deter? Regional Power Nuclear Postures and International Conflict', Journal of Conflict Resolution, 57 (3), 478–508.

R.M. Nixon (1972) 'Address on the State of the Union Delivered before a Joint Session of the Congress', January 20, 1972, http://www.presidency.ucsb.edu/ws/print.php?pid=3396, date accessed September 13, 2012.

NSC-30 (1948) 'United States Policy on Atomic Warfare', Foreign Relations of the United States (FRUS), General; The United Nations: Vol. 1, Part 2, Government Printing Office, Washington, DC, http://images.library.wisc.edu/FRUS/EFacs/1948v01p2/reference/frus.frus1948v01p2.i0007.pdf, date accessed October 16, 2011.

G. Oakes (1994) *The Imaginary War: Civil Defense and American Cold War Culture* (Oxford: Oxford University Press).

B. Obama (2008) 'Debate with John McCain', September 26, 2008, http://www.debates.org/index.php?page=2008-debate-transcript, date accessed October 1, 2012.

B. Obama (2009) 'Remarks by President Obama at Hradcany Square, Prague', April 5, 2009, http://www.whitehouse.gov/the_press_office/Remarks-By-President-Barack-Obama-In-Prague-As-Delivered, date accessed September 28, 2012.

B. Obama (2010) 'Address before a Joint Session of the Congress on the State of the Union', January 27, 2010, http://www.presidency.ucsb.edu/ws/print.php?pid=87433, date accessed September 28, 2012.

B. Obama (2012) 'Debate with Mitt Romney', October 22, 2012, http://www.debates.org/index.php?page=october-22–2012-the-third-obama-romney-presidential-debate, date accessed October 27, 2012.

I. Oren (2009) 'The Unrealism of Contemporary Realism: The Tension between Realist Theory and Realists' Practice', *Perspectives on Politics*, 7 (2), 283–301.

R.E. Osgood (1979) *Limited War Revisited* (Boulder, CO: Westview Press).

R.E. Osgood and R.W. Tucker (1971) *Force, Order, and Justice* (Baltimore, MD: Johns Hopkins Press).

D. Panke and U. Petersohn (2012) 'Why International Norms Disappear Sometimes', *European Journal of International Relations*, 18 (4), 719–742.

H. Patomäki and C. Wight (2000) 'After Postpositivism? The Promises of Critical Realism', *International Studies Quarterly*, 44 (2), 213–237.

T.V. Paul (2009) *The Tradition of Non-Use of Nuclear Weapons* (Stanford, CA: Stanford University Press).

T.V. Paul (2010) 'Taboo or Tradition? The Non-Use of Nuclear Weapons in World Politics', *Review of International Studies*, 36 (4), 853–863.

G. Perkovich (2009) 'Extended Deterrence on the Way to a Nuclear-Free World', International Commission on Nuclear Non-proliferation and Disarmament, icnnd.org/Documents/Perkovich_Deterrence.pdf, date accessed 16/03/2015.

C. Perrow (1984) *Normal Accidents: Living with High-Risk Technologies* (New York, NY: Basic Books).

V. Pouliot (2010) 'The Materials of Practice: Nuclear Warheads, Rhetorical Commonplaces and Committee Meetings In Russian-Atlantic Relations', *Cooperation and Conflict*, 45 (3), 294–311.

R. Powell (1985) 'The Theoretical Foundations of Strategic Nuclear Deterrence', *Political Science Quarterly*, 100 (1), 75–96.

D.G. Press and S.D. Sagan and B.A. Valentino (2013) 'Atomic Aversion: Experimental Evidence on Taboos, Traditions, and the Non-Use of Nuclear Weapons', *American Political Science Review*, 107 (1), 188–206.

G.H. Quester (1988) 'Crises and the Unexpected' in R.I. Rotberg and T.K. Rabb (eds.) *The Origin and Prevention of Major Wars* (Cambridge: Cambridge University Press), 127–145.

G.H. Quester (2005) 'If the Nuclear Taboo Gets Broken', *Naval War College Review* 58 (2), 71–91.

G.H. Quester (2006) *Nuclear First Strike: Consequences of a Broken Taboo* (Baltimore, MA: The Johns Hopkins University Press).

M. Quinlan (2008) *Thinking about Nuclear Weapons: Principles, Problems, Prospects* (Oxford: Oxford University Press).

R.W. Reagan (1983) 'Address to the Nation on National Security', March 23, 1983, http://millercenter.org/president/speeches/detail/5454, date accessed October 2, 2012.

R.W. Reagan (1984) 'Debate with Walter Mondale', October 21, 1984, http://millercenter.org/president/speeches/detail/5463, date accessed October 2, 2012.

R.W. Reagan (1985) 'Second Inaugural Address', January 21, 1985, http://millercenter.org/president/speeches/detail/3923, date accessed October 2, 2012.

R. Rhodes (2005) *Dark Sun: The Making of The Hydrogen Bomb* (New York, NY: Simon & Schuster).

R. Rhodes (2008) *Arsenals of Folly: The Making of the Nuclear Arms Race* (New York, NY: Vintage Books).

N.M. Ripsman and J.S. Levy (2007) 'The Preventive War that Never Happened: Britain, France, and the Rise of Germany in the 1930s', *Security Studies*, 16 (1), 32–67.

T. Risse and K. Sikkink (1999) 'The Socialization of International Human Rights Norms into Domestic Practices: Introduction' in T. Risse and K. Sikkink and S.C. Ropp (eds.) *The Power of Human Rights: International Norms and Domestic Change* (Cambridge: Cambridge University Press), 1–38.

C. Robin (2004) *Fear: The History of a Political Idea* (New York, NY: Oxford University Press).

R. Rorty (1979) *Philosophy and the Mirror of Nature* (Princeton, NJ: Princeton University Press).

R. Rorty (1989) *Contingency, Irony, and Solidarity* (New York, NY: Cambridge University Press).

K.D. Rose (2001) *One Nation Underground: The Fallout Shelter in American Culture* (New York, NY: New York University Press).

D.M. Rosenbaum (1977) 'Nuclear Terror', *International Security*, 1 (3), 140–161.

R. Rosenbaum (2007) The Return of the Doomsday Machine? Please Don't Count on Me to Save The World Again, http://www.slate.com/id/2173108 date accessed May 25, 2009.

R. Rosenbaum (2011) *How the End Begins: The Road to Nuclear World War III* (London: Simon&Schuster).

D.A. Rosenberg (1983) 'The Origins of Overkill: Nuclear Weapons and American Strategy, 1945–1960', *International Security*, 7 (4), 3–71.

D.A. Rosenberg and W.B. Moore (1981) '"Smoking Radiating Ruin at the End of Two Hours": Documents on American Plans for Nuclear War with the Soviet Union, 1954–55', *International Security*, 6 (3), 3–38.

P. Rosenthal (1991) 'The Nuclear Mushroom Cloud as Cultural Image', *American Literary History*, 3 (1), 63–92.

A.A.G.Ross (2006) 'Coming in from the Cold: Constructivism and Emotions', *European Journal of International Relations*, 12 (2), 197–222.

A.A.G. Ross (2010) 'Why They Don't Hate Us: Emotion, Agency and the Politics of "Anti-Americanism"', *Millennium – Journal of International Studies*, 39 (1), 109–125.

A.A.G. Ross (2014) *Mixed Emotions: Beyond Fear and Hatred in International Conflict* (Chicago, IL.: The University of Chicago Press).

R.L. Rothstein (1972) 'On the Costs of Realism', *Political Science Quarterly* 87 (3), 347–362.

M. Rühle (2009) 'NATO and Extended Deterrence in a Multinuclear World', *Comparative Strategy*, 28, 10–16.

H. Rytövuori-Apunen (2009) 'Abstractive Observation as the Key to the "Primacy of Practice" (in: The Forum: Pragmatism and International Relations)', *International Studies Review*, 11 (3), 641–645.

S. Sagan and K. Waltz and R.K. Betts (2007) 'Live Debate: A Nuclear Iran: Promoting Stability or Courting Disaster?', *Journal of International Affairs*, 7 (2), 135–150.

S.D. Sagan (1993) *The Limits of Safety: Organizations, Accidents and Nuclear Weapons* (Princeton, NJ: Princeton University Press).

T.C. Schelling (1966) *Arms and Influence* (New Haven, CT: Yale University Press).

T.C. Schelling (1979 [1960]) *The Strategy of Conflict,* Sixth printing (Cambridge, MA.: Harvard University Press).

T.C. Schelling (1982) 'Thinking about Nuclear Terrorism', *International Security*, 6 (4), 61–77.

T.C. Schelling and M.H. Halperin (1975 [1961]) *Strategy and Arms Control* (Millwood, NY: Kraus Reprint Co.).

E. Schlosser (2013) *Command and Control* (London: Penguin Books).

B.C. Schmidt (2002) 'On the History and Historiography of International Relations' in W. Carlsnaes and T. Risse and B.A. Simmons (eds.) *Handbook of International Relations* (London: Sage), 3–22.

L. Scott (2012) 'Should We Stop Studying the Cuban Missile Crisis?', *International Relations*, 26 (3), 255–266.

O.J. Sending (2002) 'Constitution, Choice and Change: Problems with the 'Logic of Appropriateness' and its Use in Constructivist Theory', *European Journal of International Relations*, 8 (4), 443–470.

H. Shelton (2010) *Without Hesitation* (New York, NY: St. Martin's Press).

C.S. Signorino and A. Tarar (2006) 'A Unified Theory and Test of Extended Immediate Deterrence', *American Journal of Political Science*, 50 (3), 586–605.

R. Sil and P.J. Katzenstein (2010) 'Analytic Eclecticism in the Study of World Politics: Reconfiguring Problems and Mechanisms across Research Traditions', *Perspectives on Politics*, 8 (2), 411–431.

G.H. Snyder (1960) 'Deterrence and Power', *The Journal of Conflict Resolution*, 4 (2), 163–178.

J. Steinbruner (1975) 'Beyond Rational Deterrence: The Struggle For New Conceptions', *World Politics*, 28 (1), 223–245.

F.M. Szasz (2012) *Atomic Comics: Cartoonists Confront the Nuclear World* (Reno, NV: University of Nevada Press).

N. Tannenwald (1999) 'The Nuclear Taboo: The United States and the Normative Basis of Nuclear Non-Use', *International Organization*, 53 (3), 433–468.

N. Tannenwald (2005a) 'Ideas and Explanation: Advancing the Theoretical Agenda', *Journal of Cold War Studies*, 7 (2), 13–42.

N. Tannenwald (2005b) 'Stigmatizing the Bomb: Origins of the Nuclear Taboo', *International Security*, 29 (4), 5–49.

N. Tannenwald (2007) *The Nuclear Taboo: The United States and the Non-Use of Nuclear Weapons Since 1945* (Cambridge: Cambridge University Press).

B. Tertrais (2011) 'In Defense of Deterrence: The Relevance, Morality and Cost-Effectiveness of Nuclear Weapons', Proliferation Papers: 39, Institut Francais des Relations Internationales (Ifri), Paris, www.ifri.org/downloads/pp39tertrais.pdf, date accessed October 7, 2011.

C.A. Titus (2004) 'The Mushroom Cloud as Kitsch' in S.C. Zeman and M.A. Amundson (eds.) *Atomic Culture: How We Learned to Stop Worrying and Love the Bomb* (Boulder, CO: University Press of Colorado), 101–123.

R.F. Trager and D.P. Zagorcheva (2005/06) 'Deterring Terrorism: It can be done', *International Security*, 30 (3), 87–123.

H.S. Truman (1945a) 'Announcing the Surrender of Japan', September 1, 1945, http://millercenter.org/president/speeches/detail/3341, date accessed October 2, 2012.

H.S. Truman (1945b) 'Message to Congress on the Atomic Bomb', October 3, 1945, http://www.atomicarchive.com/Docs/Deterrence/Truman.shtml, date accessed October 5, 2012.

H.S. Truman (1945c) 'Statement by the President Announcing the Use of the A-Bomb at Hiroshima', August 6, 1945, http://millercenter.org/president/speeches/detail/3820, date accessed October 2, 2012.

H.S. Truman (1946) 'Message to the Congress on the State of the Union and on the Budget for 1947', January 21, 1946, http://www.presidency.ucsb.edu/ws/print.php?pid=12467, date accessed October 5, 2012.

H.S. Truman (1947) 'Annual Message to the Congress on the State of the Union', January 6, 1947, http://www.presidency.ucsb.edu/ws/print.php?pid=12762, date accessed October 5, 2012.

H.S. Truman (1948) 'Annual Message to the Congress on the State of the Union', January 7, 1948, http://www.presidency.ucsb.edu/ws/print.php?pid=13005, date accessed October 5, 2012.

H.S. Truman (1949) 'Annual Message to the Congress on the State of the Union', January 5, 1949, http://www.presidency.ucsb.edu/ws/print.php?pid=13293, date accessed October 5, 2012.

H.S. Truman (1950) 'Annual Message to the Congress on the State of the Union', January 4, 1950, http://www.presidency.ucsb.edu/ws/print.php?pid=13567, date accessed October 5, 2012.

H.S. Truman (1951) 'Annual Message to the Congress on the State of the Union', January 8, 1951, http://www.presidency.ucsb.edu/ws/print.php?pid=14017, date accessed October 5, 2012.

H.S. Truman (1952) 'Annual Message to the Congress on the State of the Union', January 9, 1952, http://www.presidency.ucsb.edu/ws/print.php?pid=14418, date accessed October 5, 2012.

H.S. Truman (1953a) 'Annual Message to the Congress on the State of the Union', January 7, 1953, http://www.presidency.ucsb.edu/ws/print.php?pid=14379, date accessed October 5, 2012.

H.S. Truman (1953b) 'Farewell Address', January 15, 1953, http://millercenter.org/president/speeches/detail/3355, date accessed August 30, 2012.

R.W. Tucker (1984) 'The Nuclear Debate', *Foreign Affairs*, 63 (1), 1–32.

S. Van Evera (1984) *Causes of War* (Berkely, CA: Dissertation Manuscript).

S. Van Evera (1997) *Guide to the Methods for Students of Political Science* (Ithaca, NY: Cornell University Press).

J.A. Vuori (2010) 'A Timely Prophet? The Doomsday Clock as a Visualization of Securitization Moves with a Global Referent Object', *Security Dialogue*, 41 (3), 255–277.

O. Wæver (2002) 'Identity, Communities and Foreign Policy: Discourse Analysis as Foreign Policy Theory' in L. Hansen and O. Wæver (eds.) *European Integration and National Identity* (London: Routledge), 20–49.

O. Wæver (2009) 'Waltz's Theory of Theory', *International Relations*, 23 (2), 201–222.

W. Walker (2004) 'Weapons of Mass Destruction and International Order', *Adelphi Paper No. 370.*

W. Walker (2010) 'The Absence of a Taboo on the Possession of Nuclear Weapons', *Review of International Studies*, 36 (4), 865–876.

W. Walker (2012) *A Perpetual Menace: Nuclear Weapons and International Order* (New York, NY: Routledge).

K. Waltz (2011) Interview. Theory Talk #40, http://www.theory-talks.org/2011/06/theory-talk-40.html, date accessed June 20, 2011.

K.N. Waltz (1979) *Theory of International Politics* (Reading, MA: Addison Wesley).

K.N. Waltz (1981) 'The Spread of Nuclear Weapons: More May Be Better', *Adelphi Paper No. 171.*

K.N. Waltz (1986) 'Reflections on Theory of International Politics: A Response to My Critics' in R. O. Keohane (ed.) *Neorealism and Its Critics* (New York: Columbia University Press), 322–345.

K.N. Waltz (1988) 'The Origins of War in Neorealist Theory' in R.I. Rotberg and T.K. Rabb (eds.) *The Origin and Prevention of Major Wars* (Cambridge: Cambridge University Press), 39–52.

K.N. Waltz (1990) 'Nuclear Myths and Political Realities', *The American Political Science Review*, 84 (3), 731–745.

K.N. Waltz (1993) 'The Emerging Structure of International Politics', *International Security*, 18 (2), 44–79.

K.N. Waltz (2003a) 'More May Be Better' in S.D. Sagan and K.N. Waltz (eds.) *The Spread of Nuclear Weapons. A Debate Renewed*, 2nd Edition (New York, NY: W.W. Norton), 3–45.

K.N. Waltz (2003b) 'Waltz Responds to Sagan' in S.D. Sagan and K.N. Waltz (eds.) *The Spread of Nuclear Weapons. A Debate Renewed*, 2nd Edition (New York, NY: W.W. Norton), 125–155.

K.N. Waltz (2012) 'Why Iran Should Get the Bomb', *Foreign Affairs*, 91 (4), 2–5.

S.R. Weart (1988) *Nuclear Fear: A History of Images* (Cambridge, MA: Harvard University Press).

S.R. Weart (2008) 'Interview', *Bulletin of the Atomic Scientists*, 64 (2), 9–12.

E.A. Weitzmann (2000) 'Software and Qualitative Research' in N.K. Denzin and Y.S. Lincoln (eds.) *Handbook of Qualitative Research* (Thousand Oaks: Sage), 803–820.

A. Wendt (1992) 'Anarchy Is What States Make of It: The Social Construction of Power Politics', *International Organization*, 46 (2), 391–425.

A. Wendt (1995) 'Constructing International Politics', *International Security*, 20 (1), 71–81.

A. Wendt (1999) *Social Theory of International Politics* (Cambridge, MA: Cambridge University Press).

N.J. Wheeler (2009) 'Beyond Waltz's Nuclear World: More Trust May be Better', *International Relations*, 23 (3), 428–445.

WHT (2001a) *The Presidential Recordings: John F. Kennedy – The Great Crises* Volume One (New York, NY: W.W. Norton & Company).

WHT (2001b) *The Presidential Recordings: John F. Kennedy – The Great Crises* Volume Three (New York, NY: W.W. Norton & Company).

WHT (2001c) *The Presidential Recordings: John F. Kennedy – The Great Crises* Volume Two (New York, NY: W.W. Norton & Company).

C. Wight (1996) 'Incommensurability and Cross-Paradigm Communication in International Relations Theory: 'What's the Frequency Kenneth?', *Millennium – Journal of International Studies*, 25 (2), 291–319.

C. Wight (2002) 'Philosophy of Social Science and International Relations' in W. Carlsnaes and T. Risse and B.A. Simmons (eds.) *Handbook of International Relations* (London: Sage), 23–51.

M.C. Williams (1992) 'Rethinking the "Logic" of Deterrence', *Alternatives*, 17, 67–93.

A.M. Winkler (1993) *Life Under a Cloud: American Anxiety about the Atom* (Oxford: Oxford University Press).

A. Wolfers (1946) 'The Atomic Bomb in Soviet-American Relations' in B. Brodie (ed.) *The Absolute Weapon: Atomic Power and World Order* (New York, NY: Harcourt, Brace & Co.), 111–147.

D. Yanow (2006a) 'Neither Rigorous Nor Objective? Interrogating Critieria for Knowledge Claims in Interpretive Science' in D. Yanow and P. Schwartz-Shea (eds.) *Interpretation and Method: Empirical Research Methods and the Interpretive Turn* (Armonk, NY: M.E. Sharpe), 67–88.

D. Yanow (2006b) 'Thinking Interpretively: Philosophical Presuppositions and the Human Sciences' in D. Yanow and P. Schwartz-Shea (eds.) *Interpretation and Method: Empirical Research Methods and the Interpretive Turn* (Armonk, NY: M.E. Sharpe), 5–26.

S.C. Zeman and M.A. Amundson (2004) *Atomic Culture: How We Learned to Stop Worrying and Love the Bomb* (Boulder, CO: University Press of Colorado).

Index

9781137533739